BLACK BASS AND THE FLY ROD

Black Bass and the Fly Rod

Charles F. Waterman

Stackpole Books

3 1336 03198 0866

Copyright © 1993 by Charles F. Waterman

Published by
STACKPOLE BOOKS
Cameron and Kelker Streets
P.O. Box 1831
Harrisburg, PA 17105

All rights reserved, including the right to reproduce this book or portions thereof in any form or by any means, electronic or mechanical, including photocopying, recording, or by any information storage and retrieval system, without permission in writing from the publisher. All inquiries should be addressed to Stackpole Books, Cameron and Kelker Streets, P.O. Box 1831, Harrisburg, Pennsylvania 17105.

Printed in the United States of America

10 9 8 7 6 5 4 3 2 1

Interior line drawings by Ernest W. Lussier

First Edition

Library of Congress Cataloging-in-Publication Data

Waterman, Charles F.
Black bass and the fly rod / Charles F. Waterman.
p. cm.
Includes index.
ISBN 0-8117-1630-9
1. Black bass fishing. 2. Fly fishing. I. Title.
SH681.W37 1993
799.1'758—dc20 92-28802
CIP

CONTENTS

FOREWORD

YOU JUST NEVER know how it's going to start, do you?

Fifteen years ago a family vacation took me to Florida. Scratching a day out of the middle of it, I called Charley Waterman to suggest we get together, and he said, "Sure. Want to go fishing?"

Ten days later I was in a boat out of Moore Haven, fly fishing for bass with Charley on Lake Okeechobee. Think of it as being led to the Mother Lode by the Master and you'll have a sense of why today I own as many bass bugs as I do trout flies, and why I still "waste" most August evenings casting poppers toward lily pads, working shallow water while the bigger fish are surely hunkered into deep water, sneering at count-down crankbaits.

Why? Well, you'll have to come up with your own answer, but you can start here: Fly fishing puts less equipment between you and your quarry than any other method, and a bass puts less caution between his appetite and your hook than most any fish that swims in fresh water. There's a purity here that every angler should reach for, and no one knows it better than Charley Waterman. Let him show you.

"Is this, then, the Mother Lode?" you ask. Well, no. This is a book, and because of it you'll know what to do when you get there, when you're on Mother's bass water with a fly rod in your hand. "Okay then," you say, "it's not the Lode itself, but is this book really by the Master?"

Yes.

Ed Gray
April 1992

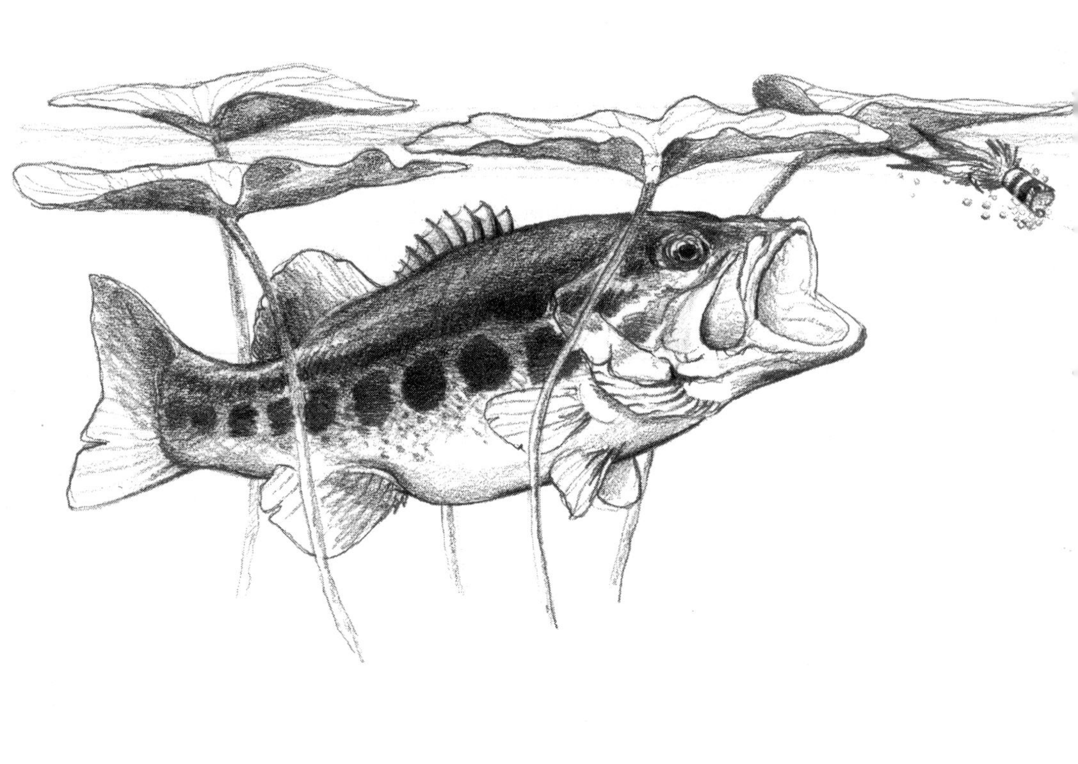

HE WILL RISE to the artificial fly as readily as the salmon or the brook trout, under the same conditions. . . . I consider him, *inch for inch and pound for pound, the gamest fish that swims.* The royal salmon and the lordly trout must yield the palm to a black bass of *equal weight.*

That he will eventually become the leading game-fish of America is my oft-expressed opinion and firm belief. This result, I think, is inevitable; if for no other reasons, from a force of circumstances occasioned by climatic conditions and the operation of immutable natural laws, such as the gradual drying up and dwindling away of the small trout streams, and the consequent decrease in brook trout, both in quality and quantity; and by the introduction of predatory fish in waters where the trout still exists. . . .

Cast a straight line; keep it taut; strike upon sight, or touch; kill your fish on the rod; take your time. It is better to cast a short line well, than a long one bunglingly.

Dr. James A. Henshall
Book of the Black Bass

Fly Rod for Bass

AMERICA'S MOST POPULAR game fish needs no press agent. It is method we're going to deal with.

Before they had a name for the new fish, the first Europeans in bass country probably caught them on trout or salmon flies—long before baitcasting and certainly long before modern spin fishing. We heard more about fly fishing for bass after the bass bug appeared early in this century, but the fly rod is still considered a trout tool by most observers.

A few years back I was having a pretty good day with bass and a fly rod on a California lake, when I overheard some bait fishermen in another boat.

"Look at that poor guy," one of them said. "Should we go over and tell him there are no trout in here?"

Sound travels well across water, especially when speakers are talking over the mutter of idling outboard motors. In the South, where nearly all panfish are called "bream," I have heard one remark many times in almost exactly the same words.

"Lookit that brim fisherman over there. I wonder what he'd do if an ole bass grabbed that thing!"

It invariably gets a laugh.

The general public's knowledge of fly fishing for bass is very skimpy, however well they may be versed in other methods as shown on television programs. I have observed that most of them overlook it in outdoor magazines. One angler brought his boat a good three hundred yards to straighten me out.

"Every time you throw that bait," he said, "your pole bends way over in back. You'd better learn to use it before it breaks."

And at one dock another fisherman examined the big belly section of my bug-tapered fly line without noticing the 9-pound leader.

"I thought fly fishermen were sports," he said. "That line must test a hundred pounds!"

Fishing for trout and salmon with flies has become a highly technical and well-documented sport, partly because much of it requires delicacy and appropriate tackle and partly because it involves entomology, an almost endless science. Modern bass fishing with plugging and spinning tackle has become equally technical in an entirely different way, especially in the field of electronics.

Fly fishing for bass, frankly, has been considered much cruder than trout fishing and much less technical than modern plugging, spin fishing, and flipping. We must admit that most bass fishing with flies is less complex, however much skill it requires. Nevertheless, even though fly fishing is essentially a shallow-water game, there are some highly delicate procedures that have worked well below the surface.

I have said that bass fishing is a good beginning for fly rod use, but some of the eerily successful fly users have preferred the bass to other targets. And it is really two games: smallmouth and largemouth bass.

Just when I announce that all bass fishing with flies is simple, a strange phenomenon appears—a fly fisherman who catches more bass than anybody else in his particular area and does it year after year. Often this paragon makes no secret of his methods, and perhaps he does not recognize his own magic touch. Sometimes he uses the same equipment and flies as those who are happy to catch a third as many fish as he does. But sometimes his methods are a little weird.

All of this adds up to a pretty good excuse for writing a book about fly fishing for bass.

OF ALL THE fish that inhabit our fresh waters bass have defeated me more times than any other and they probably will continue to do so. They are the most capricious fish of our inland waters and by far the least understood. No matter how poor the trout fishing is, one with any degree of skill can usually make a showing of a fish or two after some hours of concentrated effort. But when bass fishing is "off" it is bad indeed, for both expert and novice; whether one works like a trojan or fishes with indifference. You see, I recognize and admit my limitations as a bass angler. . . .

Because sometimes one may take bass on a hand line and exceedingly coarse terminal tackle does not mean that the method is the best to use or that one will be able to do so under every condition. . . .

. . . these very pockets yielded many fine bass who rose to a bass bug as if it were the most desired morsel in the world. The minnow and frog fishermen dredging the weeds did practically nothing and the plug fishermen fared no better. The day after that feather minnows did the trick and the bass did not seem to be interested in anything else. It only goes to show how quickly the bass change in their moods and likes.

Ray Bergman
Just Fishing

ONE

To Begin With

WHEN THE EUROPEANS first came to America they were pretty busy for a while, and fly fishing for bass was definitely not top priority. The fish didn't even have a name and certainly no press agents.

The Spaniards surely encountered the largemouth in the South, where the Florida subspecies grew the largest of all, and there were largemouth black bass in Mexico. There were both largemouth and smallmouth black bass in the Northeast and much of the Midwest, but compared with more recent times, the range was very limited.

There were largemouth in southeastern Canada, through the Great Lakes, and throughout most of the Mississippi Valley and along the Atlantic coast south of Maryland. Smallmouth had an original range confined to the Great Lakes; the St. Lawrence drainage; and the upper Mississippi, Ohio, and Tennessee river drainages. The fish didn't migrate much on their own, but man scattered them so successfully they're now recognized in every one of the United States except Alaska. And although it gets cold in Alaska, I have never been convinced there aren't some bass somewhere in the southern parts.

The black bass isn't a bass at all—it's a sunfish—but when the earliest fly fishermen found it pugnacious, scrappy, and hard-fighting, they associated it with the true basses, which had a better sporting reputation than the sunfishes had.

But the black basses collected a great many local names, names in the dozens, because they were late in getting classified at all. In about 1840, when someone finally got around to checking on them, it was logical to send specimens to France, where ichthyology was the most advanced. The French had a rough time of it, because evidently the specimens sent were deformed. I saw a drawing of one of them, and it looked as if it had been stepped on.

Maybe "growler," one of the first local names, was as good as any, although its origin is a little vague. And they all came to be known as black bass except where the largemouths were called "linesides" or "green trout" or something else and the smallmouths were called "brownies" or "blacks" or something else. There are, of course, some subspecies, but *largemouth* and *smallmouth* cover things in general.

The first sports fishermen for bass undoubtedly used flies, bringing their rods from European trout and salmon waters. The flies they used were those tied for salmon or simply enlarged trout flies. Dry flies were in use late in the nineteenth century, probably for both trout and bass.

It was the railroads that truly spread black bass across the continent. With the speed of steam trains, cans or buckets of bass fingerlings could

The first bass flies were enlarged trout and salmon patterns that were fished wet. Those shown here are with an early automatic reel (left) and a single-action built before 1900.

travel considerable distances without even a change of water. The bass is a pretty tough customer. So millions of shining fingerlings showered down from hundreds of railroad trestles across the land in a continuation of man's irrepressible passion for distributing wildlife to anywhere it can live, for better or worse. In the case of bass, it has generally been for the better despite the disapproval of some who have felt it has displaced more highly valued trouts. In most cases, however, the bass has moved in where trout could no longer prosper—in slowed and warmed rivers and creeks.

Much of the bass distribution, of course, was handled by individuals who simply wanted a new fish in a particular stream or lake, but the railroad companies did their own planting. By the introduction of bass, they made their own sporting resorts more attractive and carried more fishermen as paying passengers. Anyway, it is impossible to set definite dates for the arrival of bass in particular areas. They're still coming and going, appearing as surprises in a thousand creeks or ponds.

I didn't get in on the first introductions, but it was the railroad that really gave me a start in fly fishing for bass. Although I tried it in little prairie creeks, it was the "tank pond" that made me an addict.

Feeling like some sort of prairie patriarch, I should explain "tank ponds" to younger anglers, many of whom are not even familiar with the term "tank town."

When the railroads came through the prairie country, the steam locomotives needed water at regular intervals, and one way of getting it was to dam up a stream that naturally crossed the new right-of-way. The dam itself would be the railroad grade, and the elevated tank that held water for the engines made it a tank pond. (It is similar in construction to the artificial impoundments called "stock tanks" in ranch country, but it is completely different.)

Somebody tended the water tank, and he and his family were the beginning of a "tank town," which might later have a good country store and could even become a city. The largemouth bass that lived in the tank ponds received little publicity, and by the time I fished there in southeastern Kansas, no one remembered how they had gotten their start.

I got sentimental about tank ponds in a book I wrote years ago, and I promise this will be the only time I quote from myself, but I can't say it any better today.

> "The huffing wood and coal burners had to have water for their steam boilers, and as broad-backed immigrants pushed the ringing steel into prairie sunsets, they left tanks and "railroad ponds" in their wake. Railroad ponds were among the first impoundments built in the name of power. Only the waterwheel dams of the eastern mills preceded them." (from *Fishing in America*)

There was romance to the tank pond for a country kid who heard the steam whistle just before he went to sleep in a farmhouse at night, the engine with the whistle headed clear to Kansas City and no telling how far from there. When I first fished with worms at Farlington Pond, bass were almost unattainable prizes, and when I later threw South Bend Bass Orenos and Heddon Game Fishers at them with a steel baitcasting rod, I hadn't dreamed there would be a day in 1933 when I would watch one slash at my popping bug.

By the late 1920s the tank ponds were already very old. Most of them were beginning to fill in at the upper end where the little creeks came in, and many of them were partly covered with mossy surface growth that we tended to call scum, feeling it made a pond somehow impure.

It was the early thirties before I really got started with fly rods at Farlington Pond. Earlier, I had hauled an old cypress rowboat up there on a trailer improvised from a buggy chassis, but we generally waded in late summer evenings with split bamboo rods. Mine would be a Number Eight today, and I still have it. The leader was gut, and the most popular attraction was the Dragon Fly, miserable to cast but even now a fine bass bug. It whooshed in the air, its hair wings at right angles to its body, and it twisted the leader so that it hopped convulsively on the surface after it hit the water. An ominous swirling refusal was almost as exciting as a splashy strike.

For readers used to poetic descriptions of tinkling trout streams crossed by ancient bridges, or of great Atlantic salmon rivers, the railroad lake or the farm pond is a little short on romance. But angling sentiment is in the soul of the angler, and the Kansas tank pond had summer evenings with enormous thunderheads and unheard lightning flashes in their huge folds. There were the roost-bound crows in ragged, undulat-

Bass fishing with the fly rod has changed in many ways, but basically it remains a winner for relatively shallow water. A large share of fly fishermen for bass are waders, their equipment appearing much the same as that of trout and salmon anglers. This is typical largemouth bass bug water with vegetation as cover.

ing lines and the faraway mutter of a Fordson tractor as some tired farmer worked late in his busy season. At no time or place would a coyote's evening song sound quite so good.

In my first tank pond, we waded wet with old tennis shoes and bib overalls, and our spare bugs were in our hats, for we went deep, partly because of the building vegetative sludge on the bottom. We waded in from the shallow end, our cars parked off the highway that was getting what we thought was considerable traffic by the 1930s. Now and then we'd get in a little too deep and have to swim a little, awkward in clinging water weeds. In much of the water we fished, the vegetation would have grown to within a few inches of the surface, and sometimes there would be only target gaps in the emergent growth. A good-sized hooked bass under such circumstances presented a difficult problem, which was part of the game. If you waded really deep, you did your casting with your wrist, pretty tiring if your rod carried heavy line and a big lure.

My second railroad pond was prettier than the first, and it had more prestige. It was a membership situation, and we had little wooden skiffs for our chosen few. I don't remember just what the annual fee was, but it was certainly less than five dollars. The club had been operating long before I joined up, and I am a little vague about how it was started. We really needed the boats, for there was more deep water than at Farlington, a simple matter of more of the lake being bound by the railroad grade. That's the way the land was shaped.

I'd been using that lake for a couple of years when I saw what appeared to be the tallest man in the world casting rhythmically over near the grade one summer dusk. It developed he was aboard an improvised harness in a truck inner tube, the first "belly boat" or "floater bubble" I'd ever seen.

A part of the shoreline was timbered but very shallow, and there were bluegills along it, but I never caught bass there. For the bluegills, I used my bass rod with some wet trout flies—Black Gnats and Yellow Sallys. I'd try to catch some bluegills early in the evening and be into the bass business somewhat before dusk. By that time I was using a variety of bass bugs, and after a year or two I felt I knew the lake perfectly. My confidence received severe jolts on two separate occasions, though, both as a result of entertaining guests from outside the club.

My first guest was a well-known angler I'd heard about for a long time, and I was glad to paddle the skiff in hopes of learning something. The man had a high-grade split bamboo rod and one of the first tapered silk lines I'd seen. He preferred very large popping bugs that overmatched his rather light rod. At that time (and occasionally now) an ultralight rod was a sign of proficiency in many circles. He wore a clean vest with more than the usual number of pockets. He was one of the worst casters I have ever seen. He was a big man, and as I gradually crouched lower and lower in the boat, he slashed violently in all directions. His line ripped on the pickup, and when his backcast struck the water behind us, he accepted that as part of the game. He used both hands on his little rod to yank loose from sundry hangups in the weeds, and I felt the whole thing was some sort of joke. Who had introduced me to this angling simian?

It was a rather unpleasant evening, made more so by the fact that the club-fisted maladroit caught bass—large bass, small bass, and medium-sized bass—all evening. He seemed not at all surprised, complimented me on the beauty of the lake and its plenitude of fish, thanked me profusely, and presented me with one of his wretched bugs when we left the boat. The bug was nameless and deserved it. Long afterward I learned that on rare occasions, in some areas, the unpredictable largemouth black bass is attracted to any surface commotion, ranging from dropped oars to gunfire.

All of my fishing life I have repeatedly cast to the same logical bits of bass cover, generally with pretty good results. On our club lake, though, there was a large tree that had died and fallen in a fairly deep spot along the shore, and no matter how carefully I cast to it or how sneakily I approached it, I had never had more than a tentative bluegill *plip* there. My explanation was that it was such a standout target no fisherman could pass it by, and any bass that moved in there would be caught before it could get comfortably established.

My old friend, the late Jack Gowdy, went with me to the lake one evening. It was his first time there, and I don't recall why he'd never been there before. Jack was a top bass fisherman with a rod I'd long admired, and he threw his Dragon Fly bug expertly, raking the edges of weed beds and missing nothing that looked like fish cover. He caught a couple of small bass, and on the way in to the dock I paddled him past the old tree.

I'd caught him watching it for some time as we'd fished nearby. I didn't tell him that approximately five hundred casts at it during the past two years had gained me nothing. He slid the bug neatly near a fork in the white and broken branches, left it lie for a few seconds, and twitched it gently while I stared off toward what appeared to be a circling pair of teal. It was getting along toward fall.

Of course you know what happened next, but the bass was bigger than you expected. It banged the bug hard—one of those splashing strikes that frequently knock the bug away so it isn't even grabbed, but this time the fish had it and Jack had the fish. I remember it jumping with the dead limbs in the background, and it was just like one of those bass on the covers of the outdoor magazines. Jack leaned pretty hard on it and got it into the open, where he slid his net under it. I believe it was the biggest bass I ever saw caught in that lake.

"I thought that old tree looked pretty good," Jack said.

I didn't tell him it had looked pretty good to me for a couple of years. This is not just a gimmicky fishing story. Big bass habitually live in one chosen area, with sometimes predictable movements in early morning or late evening. I had checked that old tree at all times of day. There aren't many fish that big in a single little lake. Had he changed living quarters from somewhere else, or had he been lying there watching those hundreds of casts I had made to him? I lean toward the latter, but there's no proof.

From then on I never passed the old tree without at least three or four casts, and although Jack had released the big one, I never had a strike. I tried the same type of bug Jack had used, and I also tried several other bug patterns and some streamers. Was the grumpy old bass still there and keeping the smaller fish away?

When I was a member in the tank pond club, I worked for the Pittsburg, Kansas, *Headlight* newspaper, and once a week I drove past the area of the pond to check news sources in nearby towns. With considerable wangling I once got permission to leave two hours early in the newspaper car so I could fish the pond at daylight. That big bass struck near a bed of lily pads just as the sun came up, and I can remember how green and iridescent he looked as I held him up in the first sun rays. There was no one there to take my picture, and I slid him back into the water.

A hooked bass is more of a digger and tugger than a runner. This angler isn't worried about getting the fish on the reel but hopes to keep its head up amid an assortment of obstacles.

Maybe it's better that there was no photographer present, for I probably remember those fish as larger than they were.

Many years later I went back but I couldn't find the pond. I located the railroad grade, but the rails were gone and I guess the pond had been drained. Anyway, it was no longer there if I had found the right place. But the newspaper I had worked for was gone too. I wonder if there's a yellow file anywhere that holds my story of the sunrise bass. Probably not, because they tend to preserve such things electronically these days. I would rather see it on brittle, yellow newsprint. Some of the old railroad ponds have been improved into miniature resorts, and some have been superseded by bigger impoundments, intended primarily for recreation. Somehow it is hard for me to visualize an outboard motor or a plush bass boat over those old weed beds.

Some of the best fly fishing for bass today is in small impoundments, although most of the original railroad ponds have tended to become silted in. The simple impoundment that involves damming a small creek or a depression that runs water only in really wet weather is still a good target for fly fishing, especially with a lure that works on the surface. One of the best features of the simple impoundment is that it has a shallow end, giving fish a choice of depth. Of course, most of the vegetation is in the shallow end. The most modern of livestock impoundments (called "tanks" in some ranch country) may have a somewhat different construction with less "shallow end," but within a short time most of them will have enough vegetative cover to accommodate largemouth bass and some of the panfish they feed on.

I go into detail on this because there's undoubtedly considerable good bass water across the country that simply is not fished, often because it looks too weedy. Fishing it is hard work, but many anglers are missing a good bet. Still, the environmental balance can be delicate, even for a ruffian like the largemouth bass, and state fish managers constantly meet puzzles. For example, bass feed upon small bluegills, but bluegills eat bass eggs and are likely to become stunted through overcrowding. When a puzzled pond owner asks why the bass don't keep the bluegills down, he's into a complex subject, hard to explain even if the fish biologist knows the answer—and he doesn't always.

In fertile water bass often bring a bundle of wet greenery with them—an argument against ultra-light tackle.

I didn't start my "fly fishing" for bass with bugs on weedy lakes. I began with spinners, miserable to cast but effective on bass and green perch in slow-moving creeks. For many years later I was a little ashamed of such beginnings, but now I find famous trout fishermen who wouldn't touch a spinner but throw nymphs with a variety of sinker lashups—just as hard to cast as a spinner-fly combination.

My favorite whirligig rig was the Pflueger Luminous Tandem Twin Spinner. This original was much imitated at lower cost but was a good job of engineering, and the airplane-type spinners turned with the slightest movement in water. I don't know how much help the luminous paint was on the spinners. On the fly-rod size, the spinners were easily clogged by debris in the water, and the lure wasn't intended for weedy water. It was called a "spinner-fly combination," but the "fly" was just a treble hook of the appropriate size with some short feathers on it, red, white, and speckled.

It was much easier to cast a simple little spoon-shaped spinner, but it was not so reliable after it hit the water and was more easily clogged than the tandem. Generally, when using the spoon-shaped spinners, we cast true single-hooked flies and sometimes a shred of fly rod pork rind. I have always assumed a spoon wobbles, while a spoon-shaped spinner actually spins around a shaft, but if a spinner is big many fishermen call it a spoon.

And here we may as well get the fly rod ethics business over with. I know fishermen who will not cast any lure that is basically made of anything other than hair or feathers, grudgingly accepting a few shreds of mylar for glitter. They say if you use anything else it isn't fly fishing. There are other good fishermen who will use a live minnow on a fly rod if they feel it's necessary. I'm somewhere in between, being perfectly willing to use lures containing balsa wood or cork. I don't use any kind of natural bait and haven't used fly rod plugs or spoons for years, but I don't feel the sun shines any brighter on me than it does on the wretches who do.

In telling of most of the things that have been used for bass on fly rods, I list some that I don't really consider fly fishing. I think they belong in here, though, whether a reader uses them or not. I do not intend to degrade the game—and if you scorn hardware or bait, remember that it's possible some other reader might have even more persnickety views than yours. For example, there is the topnotcher who will use no fly he has not tied himself—and the other fellow who uses a Number Five trout rod for bass, no matter how much of a handicap it proves to be in many cases.

Most of the strange and heavy lures used on fly rods got their start before spinning came along to fill the gap between flies and baitcasting. A few of them are at their best on fly rods, and others are still used because the user feels there's prestige in saying he's fly fishing.

Anyone choosing to use a spinner-fly combination can simplify things by careful choices. For one thing, a rather bulky streamer may actually work a little better than a skimpy one—a simple matter of its planing through the air better without falling into the caster's ear. Of course, the spinner should be as light as possible and should turn freely, often requiring a little doctoring. When we first started using spinner-fly combinations, I noticed the spinner wasn't working about half the time, either because it was clogged by trash from the water or because it simply didn't turn easily around the shaft. You could catch bass sometimes with the spinner hung up, but the rig looked a lot better when it turned. Sometimes "gold" spinners work better than "silver," I suppose, but I have no startling revelation on that subject.

Some very tiny spinners are attached to the fly hook itself and cause little wind resistance, providing just a little extra glint. Some of them may offer a little attraction if the fly is twitched as it sinks after the cast. I've never found that any of the larger spinners did much as the fly sank unless you yanked them pretty hard, somewhat defeating the effect generally supposed to imitate a dying creature of some kind. It's the wobbling spoon that looks especially good as it sinks, whether it's on a baitcasting rig or a fly line.

As with other lures, most of the spoons we used for bass and panfish were simply miniatures of baitcasting lures. The Dardevle, for example, was produced in very small sizes, and dozens of less expensive imitations could be thrown with fly rods. Most of them were pretty small for bass, but they have worked as combinations in a thousand places where bass and panfish lived together. It was many years later that I used the Cather spoon, which is almost as much fly as hardware. A tuft of hair is tied to the rigid hook.

I ran into the Cather spoon when trying to find something that would take Florida shad consistently on a fly rod. Joe Cather, who invented it, trolled it from a fly rod on monofilament line when after shad, but then cast it at schooling bass taking very small minnows near the surface. At other times I considered it too small for bass. When trying to work out shad flies, however, I cast it instead of trolling. I accepted it as a standard for schooling bass, sometimes working better than fur or feathers. Remember that it has the typical wobble and glisten of a sinking spoon.

Before spinning arrived, almost every popular bass lure was made in a fly rod size, and the Shannon Twin Spinner was an obvious ancestor of the modern spinner bait. Fly rod pork strips, pork chunks, and pork frogs have been a staple for a long time. A pork frog is handled in about the same way as a good-sized popping bug. Pork rind strips are easy to cast in the proper size.

Trolling with fly rods deserves special mention. It's been done for many kinds of fish for several reasons. Before spinning tackle took over most light trolling, fly rods were often used because their action could give lures special movements at the slow trolling speeds generally used for black bass. Where light lines or leaders are used, the fly rod is more forgiving than something shorter and stiffer.

A great many of the split bamboo rods made in the early 1900s were extremely soft. Even the best bass rod that I used in the thirties would be considered unusually soft by modern standards and would be said to have very slow action. At the same time, there were rods that would compare favorably with those produced today—and some of those from famous makers have become valuable to collectors. For that matter, some of them are still in use, throwing modern lines in modern situations. I don't find many of them being used for bass fishing, however, bass fishing generally calling for pretty rough treatment. An exception would be the big Atlantic salmon rods, but generally they are too long and heavy for black bass.

Extremely soft rods had an advantage in fishing natural baits and can cast a delicate thing pretty gently for short distances, be it minnow, worm, grasshopper, or cricket. I think some of the makers had that in mind but simply didn't mention it. In the sixties one well-known maker showed a rod that was "good for garden hackle" as well as flies.

Split bamboo was considered the finest construction for fly rods for about a hundred years, but the casting characteristics of these rods have varied greatly. At one time, late in the last century, there were many efforts at making them stronger, including steel linings. Modern experts have scoffed at most of those gimmicks, but there have been some all-steel fly rods that actually worked pretty well. There was a lightweight, hollow-steel True Temper rod, quite a few of which are still around, although I don't know of any being used today. Lightweight steel rods were fairly easily damaged. This is pretty thin material.

There were numerous telescopic steel rods that made no attempt to compete with fine bamboo. Actually, most of them were used as bait rods, although many carried the reel below the handle in true flyrod style, and they weren't expensive. As a kid I slammed some flies and streamers around with one but, frankly, I didn't know how real fly casting worked and it was just a fishing pole with a fifty-cent reel. I had one split bamboo fly rod that cost something like two dollars, and although it didn't cast much better than a willow pole, I still wonder how they could stick it together for that price, complete with bright silk wrappings that looked pretty to me until they began to come off. I don't know how long the outfit lasted, but I distinctly remember cornfielding green sunfish with it. Even at two dollars there was a sort of cork grip. I guess there was a little varnish.

When I got my first "good" split bamboo for bass, glue was still a problem, and some of the most expensive rods had wrappings very close together. My rod was nameless but was sold to me by an expert. He handled a considerably more costly model that had innumerable wrappings, but assured me that mine would hold together since glues no longer gave way. He said his more expensive model had copious wrappings simply because that was accepted as a sign of quality and that the extra silk wasn't really needed. Twenty-some years later when I had it refinished at the Winston Rod Company shop in San Francisco, they told me it was a good glue job. I haven't used it much lately, but it looks like new. It has three sections, which was typical when it was made. At about that time some of the owners of rods with a great deal of silk concluded that it actually hampered the rod's action. For years, glue was a common subject, and I knew a tournament caster who won trophies with homemade rods with gaping sections where the glue had given up between strips. He said it was no beauty contest and challenged any critic to outcast him. No takers.

Wire snake guides were used on most of those good rods, although the stripping guides were agate. I knew a fine bass fisherman who insisted that he wanted agate all the way to the tip, and the resultant custom job was extremely heavy with a greatly altered action. It was slow, all right, and he said that was what he wanted.

By the thirties the bass bug was well developed, and some of those we used in the tank ponds would sell in today's tackle shops. I suppose there had been dry flies used for bass, especially smallmouths, for a long time, but even the trout fishermen hadn't reached advanced dry-fly fishing until late in the nineteenth century. The bass bug is believed by many to have developed from the "bob," a surface gadget used by Southern bass fishermen employing stiff poles.

The "bobbing" technique is still used in the South, especially at night. It's generally run from a boat with oars, paddle, or electric motor. The boat goes along the shoreline, and the fisherman keeps a big lure, generally with feathers, dancing along on the surface. It makes a splashy fuss and is seldom lifted into the air. The idea is that the end of the pole, the line, the fisherman, and probably the boat are obscured by the constant splashing. Some early descriptions indicate the "bob" was actually carried in the air much of the time, but I never saw it done that way. In quite recent years a detailed scheme for this kind of angling was advertised and sold as a package, together with equipment. It works. Modern names for the method include "jiggerbobbing" and "doodlesocking."

Once a fish is hooked with the typical bobbing outfit, he is worked in hand over hand, the heavy line being only inches long. Experts find little use for a reel of any kind and simply don't let the bass run.

We'll get to the history of the bass bug later and steal some information from Paul Schullery and others. Schullery knows an awesome amount of fly-fishing history and put much of it into his book, *American Fly Fishing.* Anyway, the "modern" bass bug must have come into being around 1910, getting its start almost simultaneously in several localities. And, of course, there may have been unrecorded moves toward the true "bugs" before that.

When I got into fly fishing for both largemouth and smallmouth bass, we already had excellent surface bugs, but the people I fished with hadn't gone into the deep streamer and nymph fishing very far. If we wanted our silk lines to sink, we simply didn't dress them. I used a level silk line for years before getting a forward taper.

I won't go into the horrors of fishing with silk lines. They took a lot of care but lasted well if you dried them carefully and doped them thoroughly. To dry them, you simply stretched them out and wiped them clean with a cloth. We used Mucilin as dressing, and it works on modern lines as well. We used gut leaders, keeping them between damp pads. None of this was as much of a handicap as it sounds, and we didn't need extremely fine leader tippets for bass. Automatic fly reels were more popular then than they are now, but I always used a single-action. Some of the good automatic-reel users preached that they could keep their running line out of the way and make it last longer. Can't argue with that.

Some of the prairie creeks I waded wet would be passed by many bass fishermen because they appeared too small to hold bass. Some might call them "wet-weather creeks," but I want to make an important distinction. If there is no water in a streambed during dry weather, I call it a wet-weather creek. If it simply stops running but holds water, however, we have a different situation. There are creeks where I caught bass for years that probably actually ran only a third of the time. It was simply a matter of a streambed that was divided into a series of ponds with little or no current.

Some sectors that contained bass were pretty small, and my streamer-fly combinations or ordinary wet flies didn't work very well there. I found the ideal lure was a rather small bass bug (around Size Six), and I did best with deer-hair models, fishing them very slowly and crouching as low as the most cautious trout fisherman. In that particular area the green sunfish were good sized and would take a Number Six bug with earnest pops. That was murky water, and a rain would make fly fishing a waste of time.

Such streams are highly vulnerable to all sorts of chemical runoffs or extreme drought. I do not know if any of the ones I fished in those days would have bass now, but if not, there are others of similar makeup that would. I do know that when I was fishing them I was almost entirely alone and they weren't considered large enough to be worthwhile. Small-time bass fishing is not advertised.

Along with the tank ponds and the prairie streams came the Ozark rivers where I had camped as a kid, when I should have been working on the farm. I was barely into fly fishing at first, years before I had a really good outfit, and I slept under a tarpaulin, cooking over a rotten stump I regularly doused with kerosene. More-aesthetic wilderness life didn't interest me. My goal was to survive where the fishing was good.

The great power dams have changed most of the good Ozark rivers now, and although the impoundments entertain more bass fishermen and many more bass than the rivers did, I moodily reflect that the eddies and "shoals" where I fished are now at the bottom of deep lakes and visible only on the electronic instruments of a later model of bass fisherman. Drift fishing (the "float trip") was the most effective sports angling of the Ozark rivers, vacationing sportsmen coming for great distances to pay mountain men to paddle them downstream in big johnboats. A float trip could run from half a day to weeks, the boats returned to their starting places by rail at first and later by truck.

The bronzebacks (they called them simply "black bass") were found in some pretty heavy currents, especially below the boat-thumping rapids the natives called "shoals." They took bugs, streamers, or streamer-fly combinations, although most of the "floaters" were plugcasters. There were some special tactics with flies.

River bass are river bass, whether in 1930 or 1992. Most of the time it was best to work the shorelines, especially those with willows or heavy boulders. It was best to cast well ahead of the boat, especially when you hugged the shore and the day was bright. On the long, slow pools filled with small boulders (what we called "chunk rock"), it was especially important to keep the bug or fly well away from the boat, and it still is. Any division of current should be worked, especially where the water forms what we now call a "braid." Selecting spots is especially important in drift fishing, as you can't cover it all. Many a strike is heard or felt when a fisherman is eyeing a new target.

Anywhere a feeder stream came into the float river, you found a change of current and often a feeding spot. When a feeder stream was a little muddy from a rain that hadn't affected the main river, there was likely to be a hot spot where the currents mingled. A rain washed in food. And when the main river was a little dirty, the smallmouths tended to gather where a clearer creek entered. With a sweating paddle man trying to hold the boat back, you sometimes had only a single cast at a likely area. Side channels were often passed up by guides who didn't want to dodge rocks and shallow water. Really ambitious fishermen sometimes beached their boats and did a bit of wading in such spots, but from a boat, targets must be chosen while a previous cast is still in the water. I guess you could call it speed reading.

I have often said good smallmouth water that moves is the same as trout water, except generally slower, but there are times when smallmouths feed where rapids swirl and foam—not really against the main current but holding very close to it. In wading the float rivers, especially the old James River near Galena, Missouri, I found the fish were likely to be found in such swift current that only an expert could get in a cast when banging downstream in a johnboat. As they cleared the rapids, the guide would generally have to run a considerable distance to find a beaching spot, and most of them didn't bother. The sports would rather stick to their canvas camp chairs anyway. I'd generally wade at the bottom of the fast water where there were braids, whirlpools, and often willows. I caught fish in such places when guideboats were having poor days. It was youthful energy rather than knowledge. Well, maybe a little thinking.

But I learned that local experience is irreplaceable, and I met a barefoot mountain boy with a big stringer of bass he'd caught on a giant plug with spinners and five treble hooks. I checked my bugs and streamers carefully. I still don't know his secret, but he was wading a little side channel where the water barely reached his knees—the same kind of channel I'd been wading all day. He simply knew where to throw his giant plug, and no one had told him it was completely unsuitable for such waters.

Some of the best fly fishing along the Ozark rivers was in the weedy sloughs that bordered sections of moving water. Call them "backwaters." Although there were largemouth bass in the moving rivers, they were confined mainly to the slower pools and were generally greatly outnumbered by the smallmouths. Some of the more thoughtful float clients encouraged their guides to set up camp near sloughs where the bug fishing would be good in late evening. Sometimes the "linesides" furnished more action than the "blacks" in the main rivers.

When the power dams began to still the roars and ripples of Ozark mountain rivers, there were brief periods of excellent bass fishing. It's an old story now, but when the newly flooded fields, forests, and villages yielded fine bass fishing, we thought it would last. Fisheries biologists knew the boom in bass was simply a matter of plentiful food derived from newly flooded areas, and within a few years they could estimate just how long the "new" fishing would last on a given impoundment. We thought the super fishing would be forever, ignoring the forecasts and the past experiences of older lakes. The first big impoundment I caught early in its career was Lake of the Ozarks—really farther north than the streams I had fished for years. I got there without a boat, hoping to rent something to get me away from one of the new resorts. In a burst of extravagance I hired a guide to take me out for a couple of hours in late evening.

He headed his outboard boat toward a cove not far from the dock and began rowing at the mouth of it—a typical new-lake cove with skimpy water plants getting a start at the edges and a few dead trees left from the drowned forest. Timber grew to the shoreline.

The guide had never seen a fly rod. He said fishing had been poor but it was a nice evening. He could not decide if I was a showoff or simply a dude who knew no better. I wasn't sure myself, but the nameless old bamboo worked smoothly and the level silk line had been doped to do its snaky best. The yellow and white Dragon Fly spatted at the shoreline and waited the usual period before I twitched it. The guide stared at it, a little hypnotized, I guess. It was then that I saw the bass, two of them, suspended several feet from the weedy edge. That hasn't happened to me often on impoundments. I was sure they saw us, but I threw the bug that way anyhow, and one of them swam slowly toward it as if attempting classification. He took it in a lazy swirl and turn, and shortly afterward I caught what I think was the other bass.

I was a hero at the landing, and the guide's story was just the way I wished it had happened: a cast of exquisite delicacy, a masterful play of the fish, and a calm appraisal of the second victim. But I guess I ate it up. There have been too many times when I have been fishless while plugcasters or bait fishermen filled stringers.

I remember the following evening just as well, when I was back at the cove with a doctor from St. Louis. His name was Tremaine, and he sought suitable coves with an outboard motor on a skiff, towing a canoe. He was a beginning fly fisherman with a mismatched outfit, but we swapped mine back and forth. When he was casting, he stood with one foot on each gunwale of the canoe for added height, wearing the craft as if it were his shoes. I remained nervous but he never slipped.

The highlight of that evening was the chugging strike I had when I laid a hair bug well out from shore, either through ineptitude or in straightening my line. That fish went down and down with no attempt at shoreline vegetation and was unbelievably hard for me to handle some twenty feet deep, but there was nothing for it to hang up in and it was, of course, a good smallmouth. The fish no longer had a river to run in, but it had the cool impoundment depths where big smallmouths are found today. It was the first time I had yearned for the good old days, and I wished he had come from a gliding current in White River, or the James, or some other moving Ozark stream where I could hear an unseen axe in late evening and often a single hound's greeting of sundown. There are still smallmouth bass rivers, but many of the best ones are now lakes—more fish than ever, but the deep-water smallmouth is a poor target for surface fly rod lures.

Years and a war later I hurried about new Shasta Lake in northern California, sleeping on islands and eating while I ran an outboard motor on an aluminum dinghy, still with the enthusiasm of exploring youth. The bass came from newly drowned treetops, still green in the depths, and there were game trails that ended where the new waters had risen, puzzled mule deer a little uncertain about their new and abbreviated world. I recall the bass that hung up my fly somewhere down deep, and the water was clear enough that I located him in the top of a drowning pine. I was alone, so I anchored my boat and dove to get him, but he got away.

There is a powerful feeling when I drive a modern boat over a submerged river with its drowned villages. And there was the time in Nevada when I felt a little lost in a brand new lake and worked a deep shoreline with rocky precipices above it. I couldn't seem to catch a bass against the rocks, and I finally drifted off to make a few casts over submerged cactus in four feet of water—and there were the bass. I told it to a local angler, feeling I had discovered something new.

"Yeah," he said, "I catch almost all my fish in those cactus patches."

Of course, the cactus patches were simply the crowns of flooded desert hills and are gone now. The impoundments are tough for fly rods, but there are ways.

SOME OF THE techniques in my style of casting border on heresy. For instance, I advocate the full use of the body and the wrist at one point in the cast and very little use of force during any of the cast. I urge the caster to make his back cast as low as conditions will permit and to drop his arm and hand far to the rear on longer casts. I also recommend the full use of the wrist on the power stroke for all types of casts. . . .

No power should be applied to the rod during any stage of the dropback. If you carry the power stroke into this phase of the cast, you will find that the loop will open and the cast will deteriorate. . . .

Because the rod has dipped very low on the dropback, the line and fly will travel low behind you. Therefore, if you must throw a high back cast because of specific conditions, you may find the dropback difficult to use. However, whenever possible, incorporate the drop-back into your cast, as it will allow you to cast farther with more ease. . . .

[Accompanied by illustrations showing the rod tip carried back until the rod shaft is nearly level with the ground.]

Lefty Kreh
Fly Casting with Lefty Kreh

TWO

Making It Work

BLACK BASS CAN be caught with flies waved from ordinary cane poles, but fly rods work better. Bass fishermen are not noted for artistic casting, and some of them don't try very hard.

Sloppy casting misses a lot of fish, and sloppy casters miss a lot of fun. Here I get a little corny with the feeling that efficient fly casting of any kind is pleasure, both for the caster and for observers. And I have a feeling that if there are no fish to be caught, I'd rather not catch them with a fly rod than any other way.

One of the finest fly casters I know is eighty-two years old, and she invariably does her fishing with a smile. When a fish comes unbuttoned she laughs; when she lands one she laughs, and I am not sure which pleases her more. Is she on the fish's side? If there are no strikes, she throws picture casts with small, tight loops and reminds me of a concert pianist playing for her own amusement. She smiles as she does this.

There is no such thing as perfection in fly casting, whether the subject is bass, tarpon, trout, or a tournament target, and veterans learn continually from each other. After a long lifetime of fly casting, many an expert will travel great distances to watch another expert—and the true master is never satisfied. That's why he *is* a master.

Fly-casting instruction is pretty important business for anyone starting, and the way he begins may decide his fly-fishing future. Instruction procedures are important for veterans, too, for hardly any fly fisherman will fish very long without finding himself teaching someone else how to do it. His students may be youngsters or adults. They can be athletes or folks who have misplaced their reflexes. They can be family members, good friends, or nearly total strangers. If a fly caster wants to do a good job at teaching, he should be a careful observer of everything his pupil does or tries to do with a fly rod. And he should teach only people who are willing to take his instruction gracefully.

For psychological reasons, husbands and wives frequently have difficulties in teaching each other. Long before a teaching session degenerates into rage or tears, those involved should realize when an outside teacher is necessary. This problem isn't in fly fishing only. It's not always like that, though, and often a spouse can do a good job. And starting with his or her own tackle boosts morale.

Anyone reading this will probably be a student or teacher of fly fishing, and the simple facts are the same for both. It's easy for a teacher to get carried away by his own importance and be unable to understand why seemingly bright students make hard work out of what he considers simple and elemental.

My wife and I struck out miserably many years ago when we got into some sort of casting seminar at the University of Florida. We were to have an hour or so to teach elemental casting, and the school came up with a bundle of matched outfits for us to use. I'd never had a chance to work with so many people at once, so I issued the outfits with enthusiasm, gathered the victims into a large circle, and persuaded my long-suffering wife to circulate among the students and to correct specific problems. Feeling very important, I got into the center of the ring and demonstrated the basic casting motions, showing what the loops should look like.

I told my class that each one should take his issued rod and follow my lead. After ten minutes or so they were all flailing away, with my wife scurrying about trying to help.

"And now," I announced, "we have about half an hour left. Just do as I do and learn to throw that loop. Keep those lines in the air."

I stupidly ignored the fact that anyone with the wrong timing would probably wear down completely with half an hour of jerky casting. My wife was shaking her head at me.

As I collected the rods and received faint thanks from my students, I overheard someone say that if fly fishing was that much work, he'd stick to weight lifting and handball. An athletic-appearing young woman said it was obviously a game for men in good shape. An experienced fly caster can throw flies all day, wading or from a boat, and his feet or seat will get tired before his arm does. A beginner, who is fighting the gear, needs a rest after a few minutes.

The point I am making is not merely my own stupidity, but that a great many fly-fishing dropouts quit after they have already learned to cast well—*but have not perfected their timing to the point that it becomes easy.* It's still a lot of work. Maybe added experience will make it easy, but the victim may be doing something wrong that someone else can see quickly. This is no place for ego to overcome good judgment. Believe me, if it is hard work throwing thirty-five feet of fly line with a matched outfit on a calm day, the caster is in very poor physical condition or is doing something wrong. In most cases he simply has not caught the "feel" of casting.

I am guessing that more than 50 percent of those who try fly casting either give it up completely after a few trips or prefer some other kind of fishing. We can draw diagrams, we can give demonstrations, and we can hold forth with terms like "rod loading" and "line speed," but if a beginner doesn't feel things working, he's not there yet.

This business of feeling what's happening with a rod and line is what makes it possible for an experienced caster to pick up almost any rig and cast passably with it. There is nothing supernatural about this, but for some otherwise well-coordinated people, the "feel" is a little elusive. They're probably looking for something else. Anyway, a beginner generally knows when he begins to get it, and a good instructor should be able to tell when the light begins to dawn, whether it happens in the first fifteen minutes or after hours of frustration. Few other pursuits employ the same kind of coordination, but I have had some surprises.

Hugh Peltz was a rancher who had at various times guided elk and deer hunters. He was a competition roper and felt conspicuous without his hat and high-heeled boots. He had never cast a fly until he was middle-aged and then took up fly fishing to please an eastern friend who had come West for the trout fishing. To everyone's amazement, Hugh was almost immediately able to throw a very long line with near-perfect timing—and although he liked powerful rods, it didn't make much difference what combination you handed him. I had this figured out almost instantly—I thought. Throwing a lasso required much the same moves as fly casting—I thought. So I cornered him and revealed that I knew his secret, not that Hugh had been showing off—he'd simply done the casting in a matter-of-fact way. I got a jolt.

"Naw," Peltz said. "For years I ran pack strings through the mountains, and throwing a fly line is the same move as dusting a mule with a whip."

Okay, I can see that. Bullwhip, blacksnake whip, or cow whip—whatever you call it—requires the same type of timing you get with a fly line. I ran into the same thing many years later when Joe Kenner, a Florida Parks Service naturalist, decided to do a little fly fishing and adapted to the casting business almost instantly. He'd been a bass guide but said he'd never used a fly rod. Some time later pretty Mrs. Kenner laughingly mentioned that when they were quite young, they'd had an act in which Joe would crack an object from her lips with a cow whip. I confronted Joe with this information, and he said yes, the whip and the rod used the same motions. He said teaching someone to use a whip required the same routine as showing someone how to use a fly rod—and added that the common mistakes were just the same in each case.

I don't recommend that all fly-casting instructors carry bullwhips, but spectacular progress in the early stages of fly casting often indicate something in the student's past that has similar moves, although he or she may not realize it. Mr. and Mrs. Lee Wulff (as Joan Salvato, Mrs. Wulff was a national casting champion) used a soft, whiplike gadget to demonstrate the basic moves. It wouldn't make you a world-beater, but it sure emphasized the principles.

Anyone with normal arm movement can learn fly casting, although there are some common blocks. A competitive male athlete is almost invariably able to go through the moves very quickly but frequently has a characteristic problem: After elementary instruction, he gets a line to working through sheer power and feels that's all there is to it, sometimes condemning himself to a lot of hard work. Strength has been substituted for timing.

Now and then you'll find a youngster or woman who has watched a good caster, seen that little effort is needed, and doesn't want to use the few crisp movements needed to make things smooth. Golfers are good students, not because they use the same movements in their game, but because they have been drilled as to timing and can quickly accept a new series of moves.

I suppose that if I had to choose the ideal students to start with from scratch, they would be youngsters of high school age or female athletes. The female athletes know about coordination and timing, but they are less likely to force things than a professional linebacker. I never had a chance to teach one, but I'll bet a ballet dancer, male or female, would be a quick study where fly rods are concerned. I am not nitpicking. The sharper instructors have learned that fly fishing must be fun to keep people interested. Showing someone how isn't a complete success unless he is intrigued enough to continue doing it. The basics must become easy.

Some of the best fly casters in the world are entirely self-taught. It may take a little longer, but the thoughtful fisherman can make it. His chief obstacle is satisfaction that comes too early in the game. He catches fish and he decides that's as far as he needs to go. This is especially tricky in bass fishing, because there are conditions under which simple "flop casting" will catch fish. When he needs a little longer line or must fish under some kind of weather or terrain handicap, he's out of business and gets discouraged. Good casters have more fun.

Self-teachers sometimes don't even read a pamphlet on fly casting. I once used binoculars to watch a man using unusual methods on a small lake, fishing from shore. He would work out considerable line, lay his fly on the water, and then reel it all the way to the rod tip before laboriously working out line for another cast. I have seen pretty good self-taught casters who did their casting with the rod in an orthodox position, and then turned the reel to the upper side of the rod before cranking it. Nothing wrong about learning to fly cast on your own, but it's profitable to at least check some fly-fishing literature.

There are thousands of pictures of casting techniques by both artists and photographers. One problem has been solved by the number of dealers handling fly tackle today. I have seen some terribly mismatched gear used by people who have simply mail-ordered what they thought they needed. That isn't necessary at all.

Necessity can sometimes produce expert casting from so-so performers. This happened with my wife, Debie, who used flies for a long time before she learned to throw long casts. I hesitate to tell the story, because it's falsely assumed that all husbands are better casters than their wives. In our case at present that isn't true except for extremely long throws with heavy rods. In delicate operations she is somewhat more efficient than I am. Okay?

I had fished before my wife got started, and she had a little difficulty with hauling and "double hauling" for distance. Strangely, although most of her fishing had been for other fish, it was on a big trout river that she began to throw the long ones. She was too light to wade into the heavy water, and that's where I had to fish from. I was catching fish and she wasn't, on the first day. On the second day I was surprised to find her streamers striking very near mine in midstream. She was throwing most of her fly line and catching trout. She explained that she hadn't really taken an interest in long casts until she needed them. It had seemed like just extra work to her.

Go ahead and learn the long casts (or teach them if you're an instructor). It's more fun, comes in handy occasionally, and is best learned as soon as you're ready to assimilate the procedures and before you get too set in your ways. Some users of small water have developed procedures that don't work well when the casts are more than sixty feet.

If I could pick the outfit for every caster to start with, I'd prefer a slightly overloaded rod, even though it might not be what he wanted after he got started. The heavily loaded rod gives more "feel" than a perfectly matched outfit, especially when we start with very short casts. The more line there is out of the rod tip, the heavier it will feel and the more likely the caster is to get the timing. But to begin with it's going to be a short line anyway. I wouldn't want beginners to go around buying extra heavy lines just for that purpose, but if a heavy-line outfit is available, it's a good starter.

We won't go into grain weights here, but the number of the rod or line is larger as they get heavier. That is, a Number Seven rod should work with a Number Seven line, and a Number Eight rod and line would be heavier. Line and rod sizes go clear down to One for very delicate fishing on small water with little flies. Until this classification was accepted some years back by the manufacturers, there were a variety of systems, usually with letters, a B line being lighter than an A line. Since the bass fisherman is likely to use something around a Seven or Eight weight,

In very heavy cover a powerful rod is needed, not only for handling fish but for working lures through the growth. The rig used here is the same as used for light salt water angling and includes a Number Nine rod.

one of those is a good starter, with an Eight, for example, giving more "feel" with a Nine line *to start with.* As he progresses, his style may favor an overloaded rod—or one with a light line. Quality doesn't help if the weights are wrong for the caster.

Beginning casters will probably get their start over grass. I'd put some kind of a leader on the line and use something with a little wind resistance as the "fly." A little piece of cloth will serve and will probably be snapped to shreds in the early going. Without the leader and fly, the feel won't be quite right and the line tip will be damaged.

The standard grip is with the thumb on top. With light rods, some casters keep the forefinger on top of the grip, thus restricting wrist motion and allowing them to point naturally at a target. I can point about as well with my thumb as with my forefinger. For close-range accuracy, however, the forefinger on top might be a help to some.

At one time it was believed only the wrist should be used in casting, proper form making it possible to hold a book between the elbow and the body. Now there are gadgets built to hold the wrist perfectly straight so that all of the motion will be in the forearm. I believe in the forearm for beginning, but once timing is developed a caster may use wrist, forearm, upper arm, and back in a long throw. Having watched a lot of fine casters using very different methods, I believe in few hard and fast rules after the basics are conquered. Using the entire body in a very long cast doesn't necessarily mean you're fighting the rod. It can be smooth and graceful. Changing the motions can be restful on a long day, but when extreme accuracy is necessary, most of us find that the forearm is best.

A beginner should start with enough line to make the rod work, even if it ends up around his neck on the first try or two. With about twenty feet of line laid out on the grass and with the rod pointed straight ahead, he should start lifting the rod tip slowly and accelerate until it throws the line into the air and back past his head. To begin with, he should stop the rod at about twelve o'clock (straight up) or slightly back toward one o'clock. The line should go back a little above the rod tip, should roll into a loop in back of him, and should be started forward again as the loop is forming. The rod should be swept forward until it is about parallel with the ground and stopped there while the line rolls out and drops the leader and fly on the grass.

The thing to remember is that what goes up is what comes down, and there is no rule against the caster watching his backcast form. That's the important part, and he should be able to see his mistakes without help. In fact, no matter how good the instructor, it's good for the caster to see his backcast; then when there's no teacher around, he can catch his own mistakes. The most common error is to let the backcast sag to the ground with so much pause that it will crack when the rod is whipped forward too fast. The exact opposite gets a similar result when the rod is pushed forward fast before the backcast loop is formed. With a good backcast, the fishing, or forward, cast comes pretty naturally. The rod is stopped about horizontal to the grass, but the angle isn't critical.

The twelve o'clock or one o'clock position of the rod tip in making the backcast is the way to start. After a caster has established timing, he can carry the tip back much farther and undoubtedly will on most casts. In very long throws, the rod can be pointed nearly straight back for the backcast, but doing this in the beginning makes it difficult to get the timing.

After a grass workout or two, the caster should operate over water, as the water pickup will feel different. Except in the case of children who need extra incentive, it's actually better to practice where you don't expect fish. Even a bluegill can destroy concentration. I'm a perfect example of someone who was too eager to get to the fish part. When I had the bare principles, I began to use a heavy spinner-fly combination because I was catching fish with it. It was almost "strip casting" and probably set me back considerably.

Twenty or thirty feet of high-floating line comes off water pretty easily, the pickup starting slow and accelerating until it is almost a flick as it goes over the shoulder. Too fast or too slow a pickup causes slack and ends the cast. Once you feel the rod work, the proper speed soon comes naturally. The bending rod forgives some errors. I used to believe a very slow rod was best to begin with, but I changed my mind when I found young beginning casters choosing a crisp action if given a choice.

Here we can mention the actual attitude of the rod as the line is picked up and thrown over the shoulder. For casting accuracy, it is best to have the rod come straight up so that it is a clean vertical as it reaches the top of the pickup, and it should be kept in that plane as the forward, or fishing, cast is begun. Now a large share of experienced casters work their rods at a slight tilt away from their heads (tipped a little to the right for a right-handed caster), and this seems a little easier for most of them, but when they have to deliver a fly with extreme accuracy, they'll work the rod in a vertical plane and keep it pretty well in front of the face.

So now we come to the line hand (left hand for the right-hander), which retrieves line when necessary, feeds line on casts, and does the hauling necessary for distance casting or casting on windy days. There is quite a bit to line handling in any throw longer than thirty or forty feet. Most experienced casters can change rod hands, and one who is strongly right-handed can quickly learn to throw fairly good loops with his left—but the line handling is a different problem. I know a good caster who changed from right to left because of a shoulder injury; he got the rod part quickly but gave up on the line handling several times before he finally became proficient enough to actually go fishing.

After a little practice, the line hand aids in picking up line, simply pulling line away from the stripping guide as the rod tip begins to go up. It's more important the more line is picked up. So you pull in some line as the rod tip is elevated. Then when the rod tip is brought back forward toward the water and has some momentum, you release what you've held in your hand, and you have done the most elemental haul to gain line speed and, consequently, casting distance.

Most of your lure retrieving is done by pulling line over the first and second fingers of the rod hand. Some anglers use the first finger only, but I've found that the two work better, the middle finger being long enough to make catching the line easy. A short, quick pull with the line hand serves for hook setting, the rod tip being pulled up or to the side at the same time.

A great many fine fly fishermen have grown old without ever using the double haul, but those seeking maximum distance are badly handi-

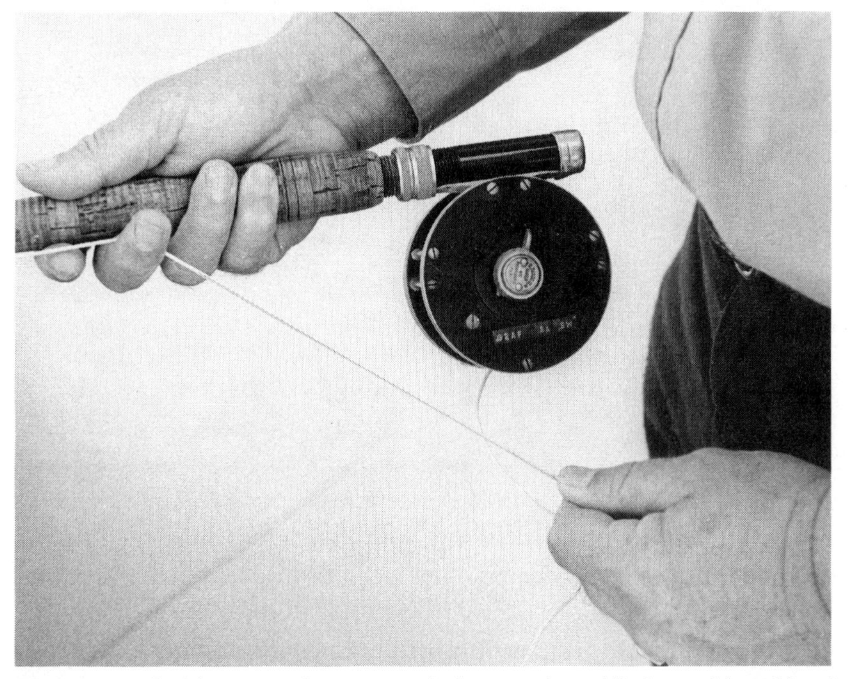

Many veteran fly fishermen prefer to retrieve the line over the middle finger of the rod hand because it is more easily extended than the forefinger while grasping the rod handle.

When going for extreme distance, the double-haul can be made with a very long pull, similar to that used by tournament casters.

capped without it. It's best to leave the double haul until a pupil has mastered the other casting operations. A description of it is simple, but the actual operation is a little like patting your head and rubbing your stomach at the same time. It is simply a matter of hauling on the running line to gain speed on the pickup, feeding extra line through the guides as the false-casting loop forms—and then pulling hard with the line hand as the rod goes forward. It's a big help in high wind with big lures.

The line hand can carry considerable extra line in loops, although they should be of different sizes to avoid tangling. Most of us can't handle more than four loops without minor tangles, though there are some specialists who do considerable fishing from tall grass and weeds and make a special effort at learning to "store" line in their hands. For short lengths it is possible to learn to wrap line snugly around the fingers. Generally, the extra line is dropped to the ground, water, or boat deck, and when the caster shoots, the line is picked up and pulled through the guides. Nothing beats an automatic fly reel for line storage if you're walking a brushy bank—but the automatic is not favored by master anglers.

Automatic reels have not been made to store large quantities of line and then release it with an even drag. It is possible that an auto reel could be made to handle more capacity, but the spring wind is a limiting factor so far. Frankly, an automatic holds enough line for most bass fishing, but it won't handle long-running fish, and most bass fishermen hope someday to hook something that runs to the horizon. Automatic reels don't seem to be nearly as popular as they once were, even though running line can be a problem and a hazard. If a fisherman will spend an hour or two learning to store loops on his hand, he'll be far ahead of most of us. I've learned to do it pretty well a dozen times but have then gotten sloppy and have forgotten how I did it.

There are several specialty casts that can be developed quickly after the basics are learned. Most of them have names, but different authorities often use their own. I like the name "wind cheater."

Wind has been a curse of fly casters since before the rods were made of solid greenheart instead of graphite. Some fine fishermen simply quit when there are high winds, but there's no reason why you can't fish comfortably if it's no more than thirty miles per hour. I've been surprised to see some fine bass bug fishermen simply reel in and go home in a wind like that, and often in something not nearly so strong. Many casters simply resort to a sideswipe in a high wind—no matter where it comes from. Keeping the line close to the surface is a help, but the true wind-cheater cast takes advantage of the wind instead of simply ducking it.

The rule is simply to keep the loop high and wide when you want it to go in the direction the wind is blowing, and low and tight when it is being driven into the wind. That goes for either the fishing cast or the backcast. If you are fishing into the wind, place your backcast high and

In dealing with difficult winds, it is possible for a right-handed caster to simply tilt the rod tip over his head and do all of his line work on his left side.

rather soft, and let the wind carry it back for you. Then, when you make your fishing cast, drop your rod into a sideswiping pattern and push hard with a very small loop the wind can't affect much. The bigger the loop, the more effect the wind has on it. Even if you don't want to sideswipe, you can adopt the method in part by pushing very hard on a high fishing cast.

The worst wind for a right-handed caster is one that comes all or partly from the right. If it isn't too strong, he can simply sideswipe to keep the hook out of his ear. If that doesn't work, he can use what I'll call the "crossover" cast, in which the right-handed caster simply picks up the line with his rod pointed to the left, backcasts over his left shoulder, and makes the fishing cast from that side. In doing this, some casters put the right hand well past the center of the body, and others simply tilt the rod to bring it into the desired plane, leaving the casting arm on the right

Backhanded sideswipe doesn't get a caster much distance, but it works in many situations. Few casters bother to learn it.

side. In the latter method, it's necessary to lift the right hand high so the rod will clear the head.

This gets pretty close to the true backhand cast, often used to get under bushes when there's no room to the right. In that, the rod is held in the usual way, but the casting arm is put nearly across the body so that the entire cast works on the left side of a right-hander. Usually, that cast is kept low, because it comes more naturally to most of us.

In all of these casts the grip is the same, with the thumb in the same spot with relation to the reel, but in the sideswipe cast some keep the reel hanging down and others turn the wrist so that the flat side of the reel is parallel to the ground, water, or deck, ahead of the rod. I can't see any advantage one way or the other and catch myself splitting the difference—with the reel at an angle. But here we come to "splining," seldom mentioned anymore.

Splining is not as important as it once was, but it can have a bearing on accuracy—often unnoticed by a rod user. It means simply that a rod blank bends most naturally in a given way, and in building a rod, the maker will install the guides so that the rod bends most easily toward the guides or away from them. If the guides are installed otherwise, the rod will not throw the line quite in the direction the caster's arm works. Generally, a custom rod maker simply puts the tip of a blank on the floor with the large end held rather high. As the blank bends, it shows which way it works most naturally, and he knows where to put the guides. Now and then there are some really poorly built blanks that have such erratic construction it's hard to tell how they'll work best. Good rod makers would probably keep their names off such pieces and might sell them as seconds. Not all inexpensive rods are poor buys, but it doesn't hurt to check how they bend. Inaccuracy due to splining is seldom noticed.

On order, one custom maker built rods especially for sideswiping. His theory was that in many kinds of fishing it was undesirable to show the rod tip high in the air, and he built rods that would bend naturally with the usual hand hold when extended straight out from the body and about parallel to the water. But if a rod is splined in the usual way and you cast in a sideswipe, you will get the best accuracy by tipping the reel until its flat side is parallel to the ground, boat, or water.

Most of the "trick" casts used by fishermen come along naturally. An angler needs to throw under some brush, and he finds himself side-swiping—or he meets a wind that rattles the tules and slaps his line into his face, and he improvises without knowing a name for what he does. But one cast, the roll cast, doesn't come very naturally and requires a little practice. Its purpose is to throw a line where there is no room for a back-cast, and most of us do it with all the grace of a backward ape, satisfied to simply get the fly a few feet in front of us instead of in a tree behind us. You can do better than that.

With some line in the water in front of the caster, he simply lifts the rod tip and moves it somewhat back of vertical over his shoulder. While the line on the water is still coming toward him and forming a little curve below the rod tip, he drives the tip hard forward, the line rolling to the front. He uses up hardly any space to the rear, and with a little practice he can shoot line as the cast goes forward and get fifty feet pretty easily. There are some steelhead fishermen, using a "shooting head" and monofilament running line, who can get in the neighborhood of one hundred feet. In fact, bass fishermen must acknowledge that many of the best casting tricks have come from steelheaders, who have thrown long lines and caught big fish on big water under very difficult conditions.

A given dry-fly line, even when it fits the rod perfectly, can go from excellent to terrible in an hour or so. Dressing a line is a nuisance once you've started fishing, but there are few bass waters where it won't need cleaning after a couple of hours. Bass water, especially largemouth water, generally has a great deal of suspended material, and "floating" doesn't completely describe a line. It can sit up high and dry and seem barely to touch the water, but it can gradually take on dirt and soak up moisture until two-thirds of it is actually below the surface, and a lot of bass fishing is done with line barely floating. The pickup becomes hard and slow, and the rod seems to lose its life.

The only remedy is to clean line regularly, and most of the line cleaners also act as floatants. True, the modern floating lines are waterproof, but the junk they attract on the surface carries water into your backcast. Oldsters who began with silk lines are used to regular cleaning, and if you didn't dope those lines they'd simply sink.

Line stiffness is a delicate and important factor. New lines are generally constructed so they are stiff enough that they won't sag much between the rod's guides and thus should shoot easily, but this is a rather delicate matter, since too much stiffness would slow their progress from the line hand to the first guide. The makers are walking a pretty fine line here. It's easy to examine the way the line runs through the guides, and too much sagging is obvious. It kills distance.

Although the line hand can carry several loops, the chances are a caster will let his running line fall to the deck of a boat or into the water if he's wading, and about half of the longer casts are cramped by the way the running line feeds into the stripping guide. In boats, I've used two special methods of handling running line. I have used what I call a "doily," simply a piece of minnow seine spread over anything in the boat that will catch errant loops. My other gadget is a plastic garbage can into which the line can be fed on a retrieve, and it picks up smoothly when I cast. Generally, bass fishing doesn't require long casts, but there are exceptions.

The minnow seine isn't too obvious, but I've had some problems with the garbage can, various companions feeling it lacks class when we dock our boat or pass other fishermen. I have been thinking of getting a garbage can painted either in a scenic nautical view or in camouflage that will fade into the boat's interior, but the fact is I don't use the garbage can much anymore. My friends say it implies that we are using live bait or keeping everything we catch.

In one case the minnow seine caused trouble when a fish and game warden wanted to know what it was used for. I explained, but I don't think he knew about fly fishing and he wasn't convinced. My case was complicated by a very funny companion who told the officer I used the net to catch baby ducks.

When it comes to playing fish, the line hand is pretty busy, and the results can be low comedy. There is a long-standing rule that when a fish is hooked, the angler should get it "on the reel" with all loose line spooled as soon as possible. This is excellent advice for any fish that is likely to take off for considerable distance but doesn't work so well with bass, which are likely to run about very close to the rod.

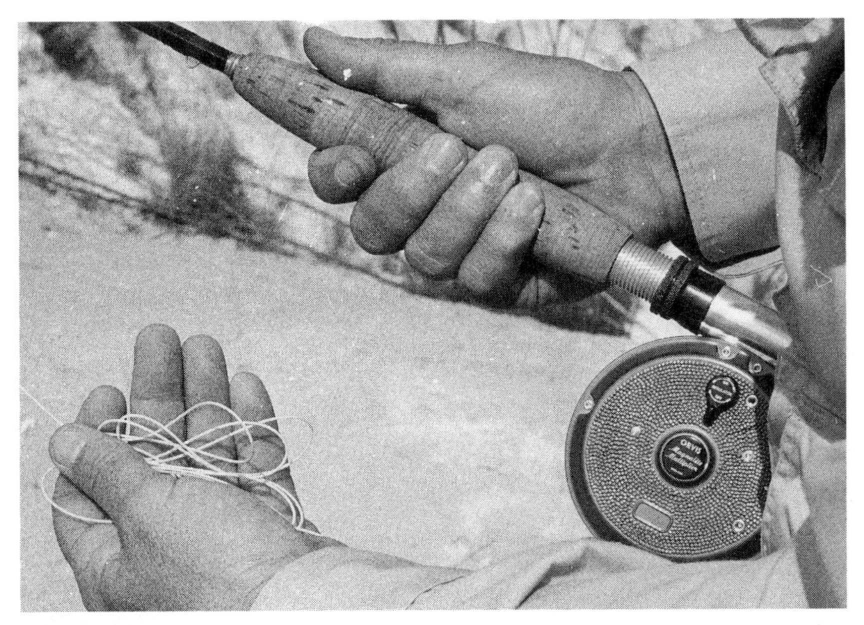

Slow-worked lures can be handled with the "hand-twist retrieve," which keeps extra line away from decks, ground, and feet.

If a fish won't leave, it is almost impossible to crank in all of the running line without giving slack. I'd say that the first rule is to keep the line taut—and any way you can get line on the reel without slack is fine.

I recently did a clown act with an appreciative audience. I was wading through weedy water near a pair of plugcasters in a boat, when I hooked a pretty good bass that made one jump and then came toward me. Instead of pulling in slack as fast as possible with my line hand, I decided to get him on the reel, but that was too slow. He made good use of the slack, swimming around me three or four times, and the resultant tangle brought appreciative laughter from the audience. The bass got tired and came to the surface somewhere behind me while I sorted things out, provoking more laughter that I considered unnecessarily boisterous. My excuse is that since he was very near deeper water, I thought the bass would head for it and make me look good.

It's a good rule to play the fish with your line hand until he takes out the slack himself. Keep a bend in the rod and continue to slide your running line under the fingers of your rod hand. Bass don't really run very fast and generally not very far. I don't recall one ever taking line down to my backing (using all of the fly line), but it has occasionally happened to acquaintances—a matter of a heavy fish deciding to change locations. Be prepared for it but don't count on it.

You can set your reel drag quite loose, with just enough resistance to keep the spool from overrunning from a quick jerk. Bass are seldom broken off while running in open water. The breakoffs generally occur at the strike when the hook is set or when the angler tries to hold the fish out of cover. Hook setting is simple—but so is lifting an anvil. It's the execution that causes trouble.

Regardless of the kind of lure used, the ideal position for the rod is nearly parallel to the water and pointing nearly toward the fly. Being right-handed, I like the tip to be pointed a little to the right of the fly so I get a good start on a quick pull in setting the hook, taking the rod a little sideways. Hook setting with streamers or nymphs is very simple. In using bugs it can get complicated, however simple it looks. The normal use of surface bugs nearly always produces some slack in the leader, and a jerky pickup of slack can produce surprising strains.

With nearly all subsurface lures, there's a little tension on the leader during normal fishing. With popping bugs, especially those that are worked pretty hard, there is generally slack line while the bug is at rest. Bass have countless ways of taking bugs, and some of the more explosive strikes are impossible to hook, simply because the fish never really does get the bug into his mouth. You see, a large surface bug, propelled by the fisherman, makes more fuss than anything living of the same weight could possibly cause.

So the bug pops loudly from a hard yank and the fish strikes at it, assuming it has enough weight that it won't hop out of the way. This little problem of hooking can be demonstrated by floating a good-size bass bug in a wash basin and trying to catch it in your hand by grabbing it from underneath. It simply floats away, and the same thing happens when a fish strikes hard at it—part of the time.

Of course, the fish can come down on top of it, but it's hard to tell what has happened when you hear a loud strike. You're apt to yank very hard in setting the hook, and as the slack leader comes taut, there's more strain than you'd expect. But the job of the line hand is to pull quickly just as the rod tip moves to one side or up. It takes judgment. You probably can't break a 6-pound leader in a steady lift on the rod with one hand, but a jerk does it easily. If you strike with the line hand fast enough, the rod won't have bent much, and it will be almost a straight pull on the fish.

Now the single-action fly reel can be operated with either hand, many of them built so they can be altered easily for right- or left-hand operation. For many years I operated the reel with my left hand. It seemed logical, because I never had to switch the rod from one hand to the other. Then I encountered saltwater fish that ran very far and fast, and speed of retrieve was essential in picking up slack. Being strongly right-handed, I could crank twice as fast with my right hand as with my left. Anyway, I switched the reels and have been cranking right-handed ever since.

The decision about left- or right-handed cranking is not earthshaking, but it has to be made as it's best to have all your reels cranking from the same side. The main advantage of the left-hand drive for right-handed fishermen is that there is no necessity for changing hands in a hurry. Some don't like it because they say it's good to rest your hand now and then, and shifting the rod is an easy way to do it.

Most of us have done some cranking with other reels, of course, and those who have used spinning reels a great deal have probably acquired extra skill with their left hands. If you're used to baitcasting and winding from the right side, it's some argument for the right-hand drive. The more nearly ambidextrous you are, the less important that decision—but you might as well standardize.

ADMITTING THAT ONE gets more feel from the play of a fish on a fly rod, I can't see that it is any more sporting than plug fishing. As a user of both methods, but preferring the fly rod, I contend that plug fishing matches fly fishing in every way, especially in the degree of skill required both in the using of the lure and the playing of the fish.

Indeed, playing a fish with a fly rod is more simple than playing one on a bait casting rod. A fish can't get away from the ever present pull of the bending arch of a fly rod, nor can it get a direct pull against it and so exert the pressure against the lure which might cause a break or pull-out. . . .

. . . losing fish has a particular charm all of its own. One never waxes sentimental over large fish landed and killed except in those rare instances when one is mounted and placed in an honorable place on the wall and so becomes a symbol of all the fish, past and present, that are caught and released.

Personally I find it very easy in this last home stretch of my life to call inclement weather bad fishing weather despite the fact that my records of past years prove that I've had some wonderful fishing when the weather was anything but pleasant. I'm getting old enough to shun the physical discomforts incidental to bad weather angling.

Ray Bergman
Freshwater Bass

THREE

The Tools

IT'S GETTING BETTER, but fly fishing has long been surrounded by a haze of misunderstanding. During the brief period in which I learned I was not cut out to be a black bass guide, I met some people with some strange ideas about the game, some of whom felt anything would work if it cost enough.

There was the early morning when I met a new client at a dock and was impressed by the beautiful bamboo rod he pulled from its case. He confessed he was an angler of long experience and that he figured you might as well go first class. He said he was primarily interested in the larger bass and that he had pretty well been through the program with steelhead, salmon, and the larger trout.

"I have always felt," he explained, "that the object of the game is to catch bragging fish. Once you have learned the game well, catching ordinary fish becomes boring. It has been that way with other kinds, and I assume it's the same way with bass."

After explaining his attitude toward fly fishing, the man reached into a new tackle box and brought forth a Pflueger Supreme baitcasting reel (at that time, the Supreme and its reliable level wind was pretty well top drawer in the plugcasting business). The Supreme had been well filled with brand new silk casting line. I had nothing to say, so he next brought out a wobbling spoon weighing about ¾ ounce and asked if I thought that was what the local bigmouths would like.

At this point I rose to the occasion and said the spoon might work well with some pork rind attached. We trolled. Fishing wasn't too bad, although I winced occasionally at the strain the big spoon put on the fine trout rod. It was a harder day than usual, since at that time electric motors were in something of an experimental stage so I rowed. Anyway, after an hour or so I lacked the nerve to explain fly fishing to the man, and for all I know, he's still using a fly rod and a plugging reel. Of course, you can troll with a fly rod, and they've used that method on landlocked salmon for generations. Maybe he planned to do that all along.

Mismatched tackle can be a nuisance with any kind of gear. With fly equipment it makes casting nearly impossible. No matter how high the quality, a Number Nine fly rod doesn't work well with a Number Two fly line. All of this makes it desirable for a tackle dealer to have a place to cast somewhere around the store, whether there's water or not.

The rod, of course, is the most important fly-fishing tool, and veterans tend to collect them, most of which they'll never use much. Rods have been constantly improved since before Izaak Walton, largely because of better materials, and there is a popular opinion that bamboo rods are completely out of date. But there are a few split cane rods worth many times their original cost after half a century. (Bamboo is a species of cane, and "cane" is the currently stylish term for these rods.)

Here we have a combination of distinctive action along with an antique status. Don't sneer at the users of those old rods, because some of the old-timers really do throw a line in a special way. Not every fly caster can appreciate their feel, and there are no two exactly alike. In my case, I'm conscious of exceptional qualities in some light bamboos, whether built years ago or of current manufacture. Frankly, although I began bass fishing with bamboos built more than half a century ago, when we get into bass-weight rods (generally Number Six or larger), I nearly always prefer glass or "carbon" (graphite or boron).

Bass fishermen can use fine rods to advantage as well as can salmon or permit fishermen. Somehow, many of them haven't learned that. They are missing part of the game—and some of them change attitude when they enter the complexities of trout fishing. Why? Black bass do strike some coarse lures and baits, but big trout are often caught on sucker meat.

Modern rods of boron and graphite can be so nearly duplicated that even a veteran caster cannot distinguish between individuals of a given model. It wasn't so with bamboo and most glass. I have two Number Six graphite rods that are perfect duplicates as nearly as I can tell, and that's after using them for ten years. Of course, there are instruments that could find differences in the way they cast, but I doubt if any caster can. I can switch butt and tip sections with impunity. They are a well-known make, and their manufacturer has produced an almost endless series of actions, weights, and lengths, evidently probing constantly for winners. I doubt if the builder still makes these particular Number Sixes at all anymore. He probably has something the public likes better.

But I'll bet his plant has old specifications to duplicate them if he wanted to do it. Probably the best gimmick of all in this business is the fact that the two were made at the same time to match a much older rod, and as far as I could tell they did it perfectly. I guess the old stick had softened a little, but I hadn't noticed it. I have worn out glass and bamboo rods. Number Six is the lightest rod I regularly use for bass.

Craftsmen who make bamboo rods confess that no two are exactly alike, and the differences are plain to them when they do test casting with

Given open water, even very light gear is usable for bass. This smallmouth took a hair bug, and the rod was a Number Six. The fish came from a northern lake.

nearly finished ones. And even the two tip sections in the same tube are not exactly the same.

Very few bass are caught on bamboo these days, and hardly any bamboos are made specifically for that. Most are light models for trout, with a few heavy ones for salmon and steelhead. For bass rods I use Number Sixes to Number Nines almost exclusively, and the most common bass weights are Seven and Eight. (The larger the number the heavier the action. Manufacturers decided on a universal classification some years back.)

Now and then there is a special need for special rods. In a few cases when operating in very weedy water, I have used a Number Twelve tarpon rod, knowing I'd have to yank loose from frequent hangups. It isn't very aesthetic and takes some of the fun out of the game, but it's better than not fly fishing for bass at all.

Most of us are poor judges of rods in tackle shops, whatever they're made of, and some of the testing wiggles, waving, and whipping is pretty dramatic, whether they reveal anything or not. One dealer said most of the customer's testing indicates nothing about how the rod will fish but certainly proves how tough it is. When I check a rod, I just go through a brisk casting motion with it to see how it bends, and I don't learn very much except that its action is faster, slower, lighter, or heavier than whatever I've been fishing with lately and whether it "recovers" from a bend quickly rather than continuing to wave. A dealer needs a place to demonstrate rods, whether on water or grass.

A very few people have handled so much tackle and have so much feel for it that they can judge rods almost instantly, knowing what a blank will do even before the handle and guides are attached. I suppose I have waggled a couple of thousand rods, and I can come fairly close, but I need the line on one before I can be sure. At one time I was making a big deal out of finding cheap rods that were just as good as expensive ones, and I did find a few, but I went home with some dogs, too.

I fished with a fellow who made up rods as a hobby, and he took me along to "buy a couple of sticks." We went to a maker of glass rods he knew, and I was a mite surprised when my friend was led to a pile of culled blanks. He went through them and selected a couple, which he bought for lunch money. He said they would be as good or better than the "good" blanks to be made up for regular distribution with the maker's name on them. Was he just a kooky fisherman pretending to know it all? Well, hardly. He had won several national casting championships. I can't judge rods that well, and maybe you can't.

It's hard to describe a rod's action, and the accepted terms don't tell the whole story. It goes like this: If a rod bends about equally through its full length, it's said to have a slow action. If the lower part (near the butt) remains straight while the tip bends, it's said to have a fast action. Wups! Let's watch this all-knowing description.

The bitter truth is that you can have an overly soft tip, which gives you a rather unusual effect. Some years back a manufacturer of glass rods employed a very light tip section that seemed to perform separately from the rest of the rod, the idea being that if you had a heavy line or made a very long cast, you'd work down into the beefy part of the stick. If you had a very light line, you'd cast with only the tip area. That one has long since disappeared from the market. I didn't like it but am not prepared to analyze its faults.

When the rod becomes gradually stiffer toward the butt, we call it a parabolic action, and nearly all of the good rods of today have this conformation in varying degrees. One manufacturer was persuaded by a sales representative to build "slow, powerful" rods that bent in circular arcs—that is, the bent rod would be part of a perfect circle. They didn't sell, for they came along too late. Many years ago such actions were used considerably, but the "new" slow actions seemed to be a step forward.

Some of those very slow *old* rods worked pretty well. My first true bass rod (circa 1930) was quite slow and bent very nearly in a circular conformation. Some of the old-timers will explain that many of those old sticks were used for bait fishing and had to move very gently or the fragile worms, minnows, frogs, or whatever would be thrown away.

There is such a thing as a "combination" rod, intended for spinning as well as fly casting. The ones I've tried weren't very good for flies, and most of them have been discontinued. These weren't necessarily cheapies, and there was one fairly expensive one made of split bamboo, but it has long since disappeared.

The standard construction of today is two sections of equal length.

That works for graphite and boron as well as cane and glass. For many years, ferrules were a curse, but they have that pretty well whipped now. They're still a bit delicate in bamboo construction and require a little attention. A stuck ferrule is likely to end up in something worse, and a little corrosion coupled with haste in assembling a rod can cause breakage in extreme cases. The overly tight ferrule on a bamboo rod tempts the user to leave it only partly engaged, and that's asking for trouble with undue strain on the coupling.

I have a number of horror stories about ferrules. My wife, Debie, had a top-notch bamboo rod with rather tight ferrules, but she was able to separate them without help. Then she was crushed to find the base part of the tip had actually split. The ferrule was fine, but after checking her procedure, we found she had been bending the tip badly in pulling it apart. People damage more rods than fish do. There's not much ferrule trouble in top-notch graphite rods, however.

Most rods today are two-piece, regardless of the material used. The travel and pack rods come in four to six sections, and wonder of wonders, the high-grade ones cast almost as well as two-piecers. Most of these are graphite.

Rod length for bass fishing (usually about Number Eight) generally runs between 8 and 9 feet, although there is no magic figure. In very light bass rods used with small lures, 7 or 7½ feet is fine. A few years back there was an epidemic of very long graphite rods, up to 10½ feet. They worked very well, but they were awkward in a boat, and so much length was hard to handle when a fly was hung up. Very few such rods are sold today.

Car doors and windows break a great many more rods than fish do—and often it's just the tip that gets cracked. Any time more than two or three inches is broken from the tip of a rod, the action will probably change drastically; even an inch will make a detectable difference, for that's the part the action begins with. Having broken a great many rods myself, I feel I am something of an authority on the subject. I've broken numerous rods running boats in brushy creeks. My crowning achievement came when I rolled up an electric window on a station wagon with a bunch of expensive rod tips sticking out. Some of us were spot fishing a

Careful use of a light panfish rig worked for this bass in cluttered water, but something like a Number Eight outfit would have been a much better choice.

roadside canal, and my guests didn't know that regulars habitually put the rods into a wagon with the tips forward and the handles on the rear deck. The sound isn't very loud, but it is sickening.

There are some neat ways of breaking rod tips, although it's harder to do than it used to be. I've seen them broken when the fly was hung up in a tree and instead of making a series of quick individual pulls, the fisherman flipped the tip back and forward so rapidly that he caught it in a double bend. *Snap!*

I haven't had graphite or graphite-boron wear out on me, but when I was fishing a great deal, I did soften up a good glass rod in a single season. One fisherman I know regularly wore out two rods a year. Glass and bamboo would bend just so many times before softening up, and I suppose that's also true of graphite, although it takes a lot of bending and I've had none that wore out.

When a hard-used rod gets worn down until its action is softened, it's usually a matter of repeated bending while casting. Some have been softened by riding in a boat so that they flexed constantly. I knew of one good glass rod that was softened up on a single fish. My scheming friend hooked a heavy fish in cover and actually held its head out of water until it tired out. He saw it take the fly. The leader was 15-pound test, and I was in the boat with him. He had borrowed my wife's rod, and I forgot the bit of low comedy until several days later when she started to use it and said it had gone limp. It had softened up about two line weights, and all of the crispness was gone from the action.

In trying to learn something about treatment of high-grade glass rods, I inquired from a manufacturer, who explained that inferior resin and fibers would soften up through use but added that none of his would do so. So I collected several of his top-line numbers from friends and took them to show him. All of them were softened almost beyond usefulness. He said that no rods could be expected to withstand that much use.

If the walls of a hollow rod of any kind are uneven in thickness, there will be weak places you can't see from the outside. I've seen some that were paper thin in places, generally seconds that had been bought at very low prices, and most of which did not carry the maker's name. And

Rod length and stiffness is needed in handling bass from weedy water. This is a freshly flooded flat, and some of the weeds are stiff.

in the hurry to get a new design or material mix on the market, some makers have sold rods that would simply fly apart with hard use. The word "explode" isn't much too strong for some such sticks. It usually happens during a long cast and can be disconcerting. It wasn't unusual at all with the old hollow steel rods—even the expensive ones—but steel didn't crackle the way glass and graphite did. I haven't heard of this lately, but beware of old rods taken from dusty shelves. Many a manufacturer has been blamed for breakage when a rod is crushed by large feet, car doors, or outboard-motor gasoline cans. Bamboo is generally treated more carefully than the other materials, being expensive and having a reputation for fragility.

Even the finest bamboo rods can "take a set" through long use, simply being softened up in the direction they are bent most frequently. This happens to a lesser extent with other materials and is a part of the softening process. Bamboo rods can be refinished with addition of new varnish, wrappings, and guides, and in extreme cases a rebuilder tries to spline them anew to get back to an original action. Touchy and expensive business. Most high-quality cane rods come with two tips, and by alternating them you can avoid sets for a long time. Bass fishing is a tough business for a rod, especially where there's lots of cover to work over and through.

Now and then someone comes up with a real freak rod, sometimes touted as a breakthrough, but they seem to disappear after short lives. When most of us were using bamboo bass rods, I had a friend who was hooked on agate guides. That was before the modern metals that have taken the job. Not only did he want a true agate stripping guide, but he wanted agate for the entire length of his 9-footer, and that's the way he had it remodeled. The result was a very heavy rig with a truly slow action. He could cast with it, but for that matter an experienced angler can cast with a canoe paddle, however sloppily. And he got into the problem of rod balance. He needed a lot of weight at the butt to save his wrist, so he used a big automatic reel and a little lead. The business of counterbalance can get argument, even now.

Balance of the rod in the hand isn't too important unless the tackle is pretty heavy. In theory, it's ideal to have the weight of the working section of the rod completely offset by the weight of the reel and butt. To accomplish this, some reels (notably the long-popular Pflueger Medalist in larger sizes) have compartments that can hold lead shot added to offset the tip and line weight. It feels good on something like a Number Nine rod, but I don't think it's important on anything lighter. Some experienced casters insist on light reels, explaining they can't feel their line and rod work unless the outfit is a little top-heavy. I feel that way about very light outfits, but remember that once the rig is throwing line, there may be considerable weight out front—enough that a couple of ounces on the reel end is no longer felt. The working end will overbalance it anyway.

Automatic reels are usually quite heavy for bass-weight rods and generally offset the working part. At one time I used a heavy-duty saltwater reel on a bass rod—simply because I was using the same weight line and rod for both snook and bass. Then I viewed a picture of myself with that outfit, together with a bluegill, obviously outweighed by the reel. It looked silly enough that I confined the big winch to salt water only. Of course, reel size has nothing to do with playing a bluegill. It was a matter of appearance, and I have my pride. Reel weight within reason is a minor part of the equation.

The actual scale weight of a rod has lost much of its significance with modern materials. When nearly all rods were bamboo, you could get some idea of a rod's power by the number of ounces it weighed. It meant much less with glass and means still less with graphite. Nevertheless, an outdoor type who will carry an 8-pound shotgun all day without complaint will study specifications carefully to decide whether he wants a rod that weighs 2 ounces or one weighing half an ounce more. Most of this actually comes from the bragging rights you get with a light rod, and when you say you caught a big fish with a 3-ounce rig your public is impressed. The emphasis on actual rod weight is carried over from a time when it really meant something. Once it is wearing a reel on one end and a lot of fly line on the other, a fraction of an ounce doesn't mean much. But the manufacturers dutifully state the actual scale weight in their advertising—and frequently on the rod itself.

The combination of handle shape, casting style, and rod-line weight sometimes causes the rod handle to rock somewhat in the caster's hand. In extreme cases it causes blisters, most prevalent when the tackle is heavy. *Generally,* that can be corrected with a firmer grip. And there is the "fly fisherman's callus," formed at the heel of the palm just above the

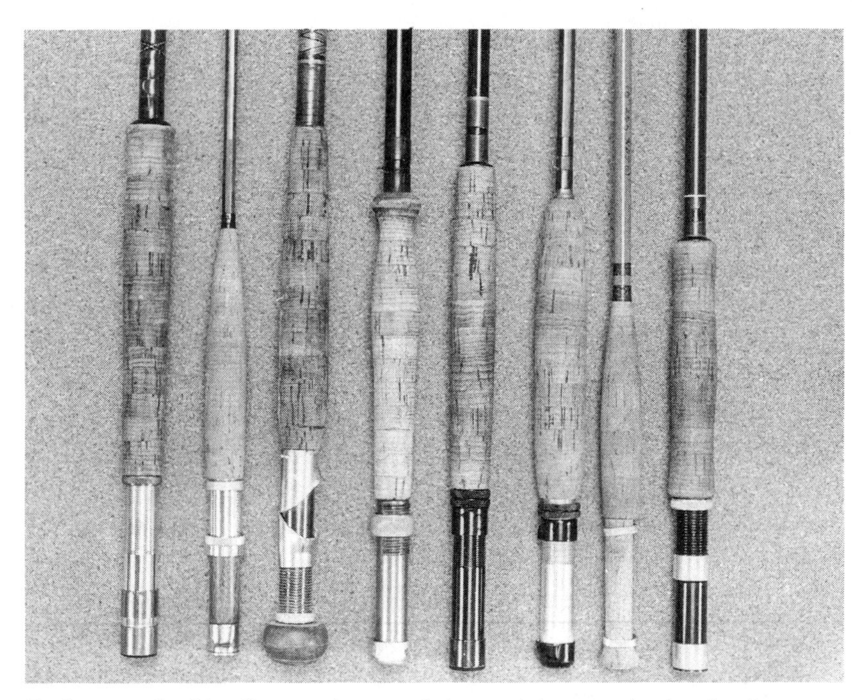

Reel seats and rod handles come in many designs and shapes, and rod makers have spent more than a hundred years trying to make a seat that will hold a variety of reel feet. There are names for many handle designs, but the main thing is comfort in use. Two of these handles are for rods generally too light for casting bass lures and are short on gripping surface.

wrist. Most casters acquire it if they fish a great deal. I had it for many years, but it nearly disappeared—for no known reason, since I didn't knowingly cast differently.

This hand-and-blister business gets around to casting method. If you cast with a completely stiff wrist, the rod handle may be less likely to rock back and forth, but the stiff-wrist format is questionable as a steady diet. I *do* find that a change of grip, however slight, can relax the hand and avoid soreness. Even veterans can get sore arms or hands with constant casting after a layoff.

A friend who had been fishing with a light trout rod almost daily spent several days with me bass fishing in some weedy waters. We used Number Nine rods, and after three days he had such severe blisters he needed a glove—and a bandage. Until then he hadn't realized he continually moved the rod handle in his fist. That's an old story with veterans and beginners alike who make extended fishing trips.

The sore palm business isn't really an argument for a carefully fitted rod handle, as the fitted rod handle actually allows for less shifting of position if your hand gets sore. The very small rod handle feels good at first but causes more wear and tear on your fist, being short on gripping surfaces. In fact, I once had a couple of rods made up with outsized grips (in circumference). I got them too big at first, but when I finally decided they were right, they were a little larger than most factory grips. Cork remains the most popular handle material, although there are some other things that work pretty well, usually used on heavy-duty rods.

You may not like to use a glove for most of your casting, but anytime you plan several days of constant fishing, it's good to have one with you. There are fishing gloves that leave the fingertips exposed, or you can get something like a weight lifter's type or the ones used by bicyclists. Baseball batting gloves feel awfully good, but anything that covers the fingertips can be a nuisance in handling lines and leaders. Gloves for casting aren't a sissy item, and I know a burly weight lifter who always uses one on his casting hand. And for cold weather there are some specially knitted numbers you can use on both hands, leaving the fingertips free.

Bass fishing with fairly heavy tackle in very weedy water requires more energy output than most other fly fishing. Trout fishing generally means light tackle. Sight fishing for saltwater species like bonefish and tarpon may require pretty husky stuff, but you generally have few casts per day. Most steelhead and salmon angling requires steady casting. These aren't rules, just some samples. Anyway, it's good to look ahead when planning a long trip.

Endurance? It's no athletic contest. Probably the best way to get in shape for fly casting is to cast flies. It may require use of some muscles not used much in your other activities. If you do it right, it generally isn't hard work, and I often brag that my seat or feet get tired before my hand or arm—but there are special cases such as high winds and waters that demand long casts.

I felt safe in putting the endurance business in with the rods, but some frustration quotients come in here, too, headed by some of the more imaginative reel seats. I have no idea how many types of reel seats, clamps, and rings have been designed. After we put a man on the moon, I thought fastening a reel to a rod would be pretty easy, but the designers simply used more imagination and cooperated with reel makers in making real challenges of the matter.

I believe I hold the world's record for dropping fly reels into deep, cold water with fish on the other end of the line. I have been aided in this by diabolical schemes of designers operating in secret chambers of rod factories. I seldom hear others complain of this, probably because they are (1) more mechanically minded, (2) ashamed to admit the reel seats have them whipped, or (3) long-suffering souls who simply feel that reel seats and taxes go with the territory.

I recently read an article by a veteran angler in which he extolled the merit of simple rings that hold the reel's foot against a simple cork handle with no threads or metal on the rod itself. When brand new, a cork handle will hold these rings fairly well. As the cork has worn, I have dropped reels into streams and lakes over much of the civilized world and in a few areas popularly known as backcountry. This usually happens when I have a fish on, and in most cases retrieving the reel is more sporting than landing the fish. It is a time when drag setting becomes of vital importance.

The simple double-ring setup appears only on the lighter rods, but I have had it on several that I used for bass, most of them Number Sixes. Remedies have included adhesive tape over the reel foot, building up the tattered cork area with glue and cork scraps, and throwing the whole grip setup away.

Now that I have been cute about the simple ring reel seat, I confess that if the foot of the reel is exactly right with a very slow taper where the rings fit over it, it may stand up for quite a while, but the reel makers and rod makers frequently have different ideas. The shape of the reel's foot is a big factor in the efficiency of any kind of reel mounting.

I bought a very expensive reel I couldn't afford, intending to use it for heavy saltwater operations, but liked it so well I took it off on a bass-fishing trip where I intended to use a Number Nine rod. Now ordinarily I wouldn't start off on such a pilgrimage without a pretty good idea that everything worked, but in this case I couldn't see how a new reel with the same old line and rod could sabotage my efforts.

Well, the accursed reel had a foot that couldn't be pushed, pulled, or hammered into the seat and screw clamps of the rod. As a result, I reshaped the gold-colored bar-stock aluminum foot with the only file I could find—a very coarse one—and the resulting eyesore is still with me. Another common mess is that a damned reel foot is simply too long to work.

A few words on rod history won't help you catch more bass, but some of the origins are nice to know. The first fly rods, as nearly as I can figure, couldn't cast flies the way the modern rod does. They were simply long poles with line, leader, and fly attached, and they were made from all sorts of woods. Material for solid-wood rods was often pretty exotic stuff and secured from hard-to-reach sources all over the world. Fairly early in the game, fly fishermen began to use tips made of something that worked with considerable spring and fastened them to butt sections that were virtually rigid.

I guess fly casting was really in business somewhere around 1800, the angler's skill simply waiting for a rod material that would come to life. There were all sorts of rods made by various methods of sawing and splicing sections for the tips, and just when we came to the split bamboo rod is a little hard to say. The most commonly accepted beginning of true split bamboo was a "rent-and-glued" rod made up by Samuel Phillippe of Easton, Pennsylvania, in 1848. Up until then, a material and type of construction hadn't really been settled on.

Dr. James A. Henshall, who copyrighted his *Book of the Black Bass* in 1881, said, "I consider the split-bamboo rod to be the greatest invention ever made pertaining to the art of angling, equaling the invention of the breech-loading rifle and shot-gun for field sports."

Henshall studied the subject pretty well and listed some of the woods that had been tried with varying success as rods. They included cane, ash, hickory, maple, basswood, ironwood, hornbeam, cedar, barberry, bamboo, memel, lancewood, mahoe, greenheart, bethabara, noib, snakewood, dagama, and service-berry. He said lancewood, ash, greenheart, bethabara, "cane or reed," and Calcutta bamboo made the best bass rods.

Some of those solid woods weren't as shabby as I used to think. An old-time angler once gave me a fly rod he'd inherited from a "real fisherman." It was made of some kind of solid wood, and by golly, you can cast pretty well with it. I'm sure a student of the matter could name the wood in an instant, but I don't see any of them standing around. Incidentally, the reel seat is better than some of the modern ones I've been victimized by.

Well, once they got into the split bamboo business ("rent and glued"), the manufacturers got pretty far out. They advertised widely concerning magic formulae for rod improvement, and there was at least one maker who developed metal support for cane rods, in the form of wire reinforcement. I guess it didn't hurt much. Incidentally, although the fly-fishing business came here mainly from Britain, the American rods of the late nineteenth century were proven to be better than what the British were making at that time. They held casting contests.

After these centuries of rod building, it's just possible that we've gone about as far as we can go in construction. For one thing, the modern carbon rods, and to a lesser extent the fiberglass and modern bamboo, are much more forgiving and much tougher than those of the past. I'm sure a Number Eight graphite rod will work for you with any make of Number Eight fly line, but if you prefer a heavier line, you won't hurt it if you use a Number Ten, and if you prefer a lighter one, you'll get by clear down to a Number Four. This destroys some of the magic of rod and line selection, but that's the way it is. I never said the Number Eight wouldn't be the best choice.

But with the great variety of rod actions, we find that one maker's Eight can be another maker's Six. I have a Number Six that does a beautiful job with an Eight—better for me than the line recommended for it. This is a little confusing, but they are all good rods, and with all this choice in lines for a given unit, there is more need for practice casts than ever before. Blessed is the dealer with room to throw a fly somewhere around the place.

For most bass fishing, the reel simply holds the line and backing, and although fine reels are fun, they come in well behind rods and lines in importance. You're not likely to encounter a sailfish when bass fishing, but there are some things to argue about.

The automatic isn't used much by experts anymore, but it has advantages in special cases. It's hard to beat when you're fishing canals or creeks from weedy banks, for it can keep stray line from underfoot and from tangled brush, taking up slack instantly. That's no place for throwing expensive fly line around, and feet, brush, and boat decks do more damage to line than fish and water do. But the automatic has little capacity and doesn't work well in playing fish that make runs. The tension on the fish is hard to regulate, and the mechanism is pretty complex. I have never heard of an automatic built to bring the kind of price that is asked for precision-made single-actions.

Of course, the most popular fly reel is the simple single-action, and an inexpensive one is satisfactory for most bass fishing, although a handmade and precise masterpiece can cost hundreds of dollars. A smooth and easily adjusted drag is the most important feature of the expensive reel. In some cases its precise tolerances are a disadvantage, and it might tie up with a little grit that an inexpensive reel wouldn't mind. Long ago I bought a fine British reel, dropped it on a rock, and went to a handyman to get it turning again.

"My God!" he commented. "I doubt if I ever can get that straightened. It's like a damned watch! Try a jeweler."

When in doubt, choose the larger size in reels. It gives you more room for line and backing, and a big spool takes up line much faster, a helpful feature when playing fish—or when casting, for that matter. Then, too, the big spool stores the line loosely enough that it has less tendency to kink.

Modern lines that have kinked up a bit on the reel can be straightened pretty easily by hand—but in an emergency they can greatly increase drag tension when yanked through the guides. They can cramp your style when you suddenly need a long cast and the kinks won't shoot through the stripping guide.

Not much is said about the dramatic increase in drag tension on the line as the supply dwindles on the reel. As the spool gets smaller, it comes off much harder, and a drag adjustment that was perfect to begin with starts to put a strain on things. You may never need a lot of backing to handle fish with, but it builds up your arbor so that the drag works more nearly the way you set it. Most reels in the middleweight class as used for bass fishing employ clicks that squall when the drag is letting line run, and there are fishermen who love to hear one sing when something eats the fly. These are fine for light and medium fishing, but if you should take your bass reel into really heavy fishing, the click causes a slight unevenness in drag tension, and some persnickety trophy hunters won't have it. They are proud of the fact that their big reels, generally bar stock aluminum, are whisper quiet.

Some of the bigger and most expensive reels have fairly wide spools, all the better to hold more line and backing. There were really wide spools on some of the old vom Hofes and Zwargs, for example. That made it possible to store a lot of line without a spool large in outside diameter, and it made the drag a little more constant from full to empty. But these things come with a price, as there's no built-in level wind and you have to spread the line manually. In fact, you must do a little of this with most reels, even those with fairly narrow spools. Most experienced fishermen do this without thinking, using the forefinger of the hand holding the rod. I have an ancient Zwarg meant for heavy fishing, and if you don't smooth the spooling you'll tie things up—or have the line cut down into its spool until the drag means nothing.

Again, this probably won't happen in bass fishing, but you may as well get reels that can be used for heavier stuff on demand. If you ever need to use your backing (probably about 20-pound-test Dacron), this cutting-in business becomes really important, and such fine stuff demands level winding.

It's been a long time since I've seen a regular multiplying baitcasting reel used with a fly rod, but it used to be pretty common. A level wind looks good but doesn't shine with large-diameter fly line, and the small diameter of the loaded spool would produce artistic kinks that wouldn't find their way through the level winder. Forget it. Even if there was some dramatic breakthrough for fly reels, tradition wouldn't stand for it.

We've been through the business of right-hand or left-hand reel operation, and whichever you want, you'll need all of your reels turned from the same side. Some of the finest reels are built so that whipping lines can get between the handle and the reel body, which can be either a nuisance or a tragedy. The most unobtrusive reel handle, and the most common, is simply fastened to the outer rim of the spool, and is counterbalanced on the more expensive models. For bass fishing, this business of

Almost all fly reels require a little line guidance, but the wide-spool types demand careful use of rod-hand fingers.

delicate balance isn't very important, but it helps make an even drag for long-running fish.

Except for really big game, the drag works best when set pretty light—just enough that it won't overrun when there's a quick jerk in casting or playing a fish. Most of us then add extra tension as needed by cupping a hand around the spool, running the line through our fingers, or actually pressing a finger against the spooled line as it goes out.

A really helpful design leaves the outer rim of the spool completely open so that you can play your finger or hand on it in restricting line as it goes out. With such a reel it's usually quite easy to change spools. The main thing to watch for here is that since the spool isn't entirely enclosed by the reel's frame, it's easier to knock it out of line when dropping it on an anchor or boat dock or when sitting on it in a relaxed moment.

I have long felt that many drag-and-click arrangements are designed in a chimpanzee retirement home, and it is scary even to look at them. There are some good and rugged ones, however, even though the drags aren't especially smooth on most light reels. Big game fly reels are another story, and I have often used them on a bass rod simply because they go so smoothly, but they look a bit out of place. Lately some of the better builders have been making truly precision reels in "trout" sizes, and they're joys to use although some of the spools are a bit small.

Multiplying fly reels have never caught on very well, although I've used a double multiplier without complaint. It's handy when fishing from a brushy bank along canals, since you can retrieve loose line from the clutches of various flora. Being naturally sloppy, I tend to stroll along a bank, feel a tug, and note that my running line is attached to a thorn bush of some kind twenty feet in the direction I came from. Then I jerk on it, and no telling what happens to it.

Most heavy-duty reels have easily adjusted drags, and anyone who knows his reel can pretty well tell how much drag he's adding or subtracting in a hurry. Lighter gear may have good drags, but hurried adjustment is likely to be pretty sketchy. With what seems to be demand for very high quality in fly reels, there are more and more medium reels with accurate and smooth drags lately. Anyway, unless you've tested the results with your particular outfit, you'd better not get too free with the drag adjustment when a fish is on. With bass, you can generally handle increased

Many modern reels can be controlled by rim pressure when playing fish, affording a supplement to the built-in drag when extra pressure is needed.

drag with your fingers. Many otherwise excellent reels have been made with Tinkertoy drag mechanisms. They aren't being thrown away, but their owners are wise to remember their faults.

The biggest decision with heavy-duty reels is whether one should be freespool or not. With the freespool feature, you can let the built-in drag take care of tension on the line, and the handle doesn't turn as a fish runs. This can save excited fumbles that sometimes lose fish. But there are many fishermen who want to overpower the drag and take up line at certain points, as when a fish has tired and is not likely to make a quick run. When a fish is fresh, they prefer to stick with their predetermined drag setting. This isn't generally important with bass, but you should have a fish-playing routine in mind. Rod angle and bend and the amount of line left on the spool can multiply and divide drag pressure. Study reels, but in bass fishing, lines and rods come first.

I have never known anyone who collected fly lines as a hobby, and they really don't have the appeal of fine rods or reels, but from a practical standpoint they're a good investment. With a suitable variety of lines, an angler can promptly adjust the depth of his lures, can make short or long casts more easily, and can get the most from any fly or bug. He can keep his bug easy to pick off the surface, he can cause a streamer to sink fast or slow, and he can cast for great distances.

Lines tapered for special purposes have been available for a very long time, the tapered silk ones of half a century ago being no novelty at all, and other materials having been laboriously fashioned into tapers before that. Tapers of one kind or another make distance casting easier, deliver flies more delicately, and drive them into the wind. A single rod can use half a dozen different types of line for that many different fishing situations.

Most of us don't use much of an assortment of lines for bass fishing. We tend to get a "bug taper," a sinking tip, and possibly a complete sinking line and let it go at that. I think more than half the bass fishermen in the world use only one line, generally a bug taper floater. Good fly lines are expensive, and it's more fun to buy other things. Prices change greatly through the years, but as of now a first-class tapered fly line costs about a tenth of the price of a top-grade graphite rod or a little more.

Line and rod matches are not quite as pat as they sound. For example, a rod being used for very short casts will work better with a line heavier than usually sold for it. That is, a Number Seven rod used for fishing a shoreline from a close-in boat would work a little more easily with an Eight—or possibly a Nine—line. The same rod used by a wader reaching for distant cover will go better with its "fitted" Seven line or possibly a Six. The rod works because of the weight of the line it is throwing—and the longer the line, the heavier it gets. So as we get into advanced fly casting, things become just a little more complicated. The man or woman who has gotten into the "advanced" classification, however, can adapt to minor mismatches—and often to extreme ones. Without nitpicking, I think I can say more than half the world's casters could do better with a combination other than what they're using most of the time. But most of them have adapted to their equipment and the "right" rig wouldn't work well for a while.

The most frequently used line by serious bass fishermen is the floating weight-forward bug taper, or something very much like it. The bug taper is almost exactly the same as the "saltwater" taper. It has a short tapered front section, a short heavy section, and a long section of running or shooting line. It throws farther than a level line or a double taper, but it is not the distance line many fishermen believe. A "torpedo" taper with a longer heavy section casts farther.

There are somewhat different names for the various line profiles. For example, "torpedo" and "rocket" tapers are similar, but those names are used by different manufacturers. We sure won't go far into the feet and inches measurements, but a Number Eight bass bug taper could well have about 5 feet of taper from the leader connection to the "belly," or heavy part. Then the belly would be about 26 feet long and have a 10-foot taper down into the running line, with the whole works about 100 feet long. A "regular" weight forward would have a front taper of something like 10 feet, and the belly, or body, would be more than 30 feet long with a back taper of 6 feet or so.

Double-tapered lines (tapered at each end with a very long body between) were popular for a long while for delicate fishing but have lost ground lately. They aren't good for long casts, because there's no small running line to shoot with. They have the advantage of duplicate ends, so they can be reversed, giving a "new" line when one end wears badly.

Often called "traditional" for light fishing, they simply don't sell very well anymore according to people in the line business. Even the delicate trout and panfish anglers like to have some small running line for an occasional long throw. Old-timers who used nothing else worked long false casts and didn't shoot much. I wouldn't say they have much application for bass fishing.

Most fly fishing for bass could be done pretty well with floating level lines, although distance casting is difficult. The level line is inexpensive, usually listed as a sort of afterthought in a tackle catalog, but for short-range casting it works fine. Fact is, most long-time fly fishermen haven't used a level line for so long they don't know how one performs with a modern rod. I use one for canal and ditch fishing where the treatment is rough and the distances short. I absentmindedly picked up a reel with a level line on it a few months ago and fished a shoreline from a boat for half a day. I vaguely noticed that something wasn't quite normal when I made a slightly longer cast, but I never even realized what I was using for quite a while. A level line is nice to have somewhere in your vest or box for emergencies.

But if you go forth to buy a level line, remember that it could well have been on the shelf for quite a while, and since it's an economy item, it may not have all of the latest features of construction. Frankly, none of the tackle folks are going to get rich from level line sales, and maybe some of them wish the whole idea would be forgotten. I have here a fat catalog that doesn't even mention this poor relation of the industry.

Let's not go into the details of line construction, which I don't understand anyway. Having watched the various tapers come out of the machines like colorful spaghetti, I am awed by the know-how and science of the whole business. But we can touch on some of the features of top-grade lines that weren't considered until recent years.

Most bass lines are floaters, and this term covers a lot of things. The higher it floats, the easier it is to pick up for the next cast. Those brought up with silk lines recall how those lines gradually rode lower in the water until lifting one sounded like a horse's foot in sticky mud. They required regular doping or they wouldn't float at all: That's not just cleaning but waterproofing to keep them on top. Modern lines will float naturally, but they need frequent cleaning to keep them high on the water. On some waters the cleaning should be done every hour or so, as all sorts of foreign things bog the line down. It's not a lot of work; you can just run the most-used section through a pad or cloth with the recommended cleaner in it. Just a quick dry rub helps, and clean water does too.

Lines with a poor grade of coating may actually soak up water you can't rub out, but that's not much of a problem with the later designs. To complicate things, note there are some surface lures that actually work better when the line doesn't ride too high. But there are otherwise good bugs that will "hook" on the pickup if the line bogs down a little.

One of the touchiest parts of floating fly line construction is the matter of stiffness. If the material is too limp, it will hang down between the guides and hamper the cast. If it is too stiff, it will come off the reel in kinks and refuse to shoot properly. The touchy compromise is one that stays almost straight between the rod guides but is flexible enough to feed smoothly through the stripping guide as it shoots. Extremes of air temperatures are likely to have some effect. The objectives of the makers are an ideal stiffness, a hard coating for shooting and for resistance to surface dirt, and durability in use.

The part that generally wears out is the running line, which is most frequently handled in fishing. If it doesn't get stepped on, it is at least crushed, wadded, jerked out of accidental kinks, and subjected to insect dope, sunscreen, and dirty guides.

When some expensive lines came apart on me some years back, I got scientific, put various insect dopes in saucers, and dunked various types of line in them. One combination of insect dope and line resulted in the coating's simply coming off within a couple of minutes. Most late-model lines will stand up to most accidental treatments, but there are a great variety of chemicals in insect repellents. So watch it, and unless you're sure of the results, keep the repellent off the palms of your hands and off the line when you push the spray-can button.

The sinking-tip line is capable of a great deal of manipulation, getting unusual effects from all sorts of flies and bugs. It's generally used to get a fly down a certain distance to where it is twitched, retrieved, or drifted, but a sinking tip used with a floating bug can cause it to dive, hurry back to the surface or nearly to the surface, or simply perform as a wiggling subsurface lure. The sinking tip can be a fast sinker or a slow sinker, and it can be cropped to various lengths, of course. It's possible to buy the tips separately from the lines so they can be attached to regular floaters. This is pretty advanced stuff and should be handled along with fishing tactics.

The sinking line, generally called a "whole sinking line" for clarification, is simply heavier than water and sinks when it strikes the surface. The makers have gone far enough to classify the various sinkers as to the number of inches they sink per second, and their choice depends on fishing tactics.

The shooting head, or shooting taper, is simply a section of fly line (generally around 30 feet long) that can be attached to monofilament running line or very light fly line for distance casting. It's usually a sinker, although some anglers (notably the late Ted Trueblood) have used floating heads with excellent results. The shooting head is easily cropped to fit situations we can take up later. These things are seldom used for bass, but they sure work.

Leaders are important tools, but their lengths and construction vary with the kind of fishing you're doing. Many bass fishermen never use tapered leaders at all, but you can get a variety of effects with them. After long study I have concluded that I don't know much about leaders, but when we get into the various flies and tactics, I sure won't hold anything back. I do know that they're more important than most bass fishermen give them credit for.

Owning fishing tackle in itself can be fun, and there are a few collectors who don't fish at all. And there are some highly productive bass fishermen (generally operating in a limited area) who use one rod, one line, one reel, and one bug pattern and have done it for years. Somewhere between the extremes would be a very competent and fully equipped bass angler with about three rods of different weights, about four reels, and about half a dozen different lines. He could fish bass anywhere in the world and would be prepared for other fish besides bass. The longer he fished, the more flies and bugs he'd have, but I can't see him with less than a hundred. Could he get by with less? Of course he could. Would he have more fun with more? Maybe.

YELLOW SEEMS TO be one of the best colors to use for bass but robin's egg blue is also good, especially for smallmouth. And black is greatly overlooked. Black has always brought me plenty of strikes and yet there are probably fewer professionally made poppers in black than in any other color. Combination colors that pay off are the bugs with head of red on a yellow body, red on white, and blue on white. . . .

An excellent strike getter is the all-black popper with yellow dots all over it, and another one is all white with black dots on side and back. . . .

"There's such a thing as casting too far," I have said. "For efficient fly or bug play and for a quick strike, and for line work in general, I'd say that 55 to 70 feet would be the best distance to cast. Over 80 feet the strike impulse takes too long to get to the fish and he may spit out the fly before he's hooked. And the greater distance away, the harder it is to see the flash of a fish as he goes for the lure, and so you may strike too late." . . .

Often on rivers I creep close enough to get off casts of only 40 feet. And if I were to choose one over-all perfect casting distance, I would take 50 feet. At that distance you have control, it's hard for the fish to see you but fairly easy for you to see him.

[Brooks's prophetic remarks about popping bug colors were made in 1958.]

Joe Brooks
Fly Fishing

FOUR

Bass Almost Everywhere

WE WENT TO Maine to fly fish for bass, a journey that seemed rather strange to some of the native trout fishermen. Until a few years back, many Maine folks resented black bass. The bass had taken over from the brown trout in waters that no longer could support browns—and the browns, for heaven's sake, had taken over in waters that would no longer support native brook trout.

I suspect there is still a little resentment of the bass in some parts of Maine, but the truly bitter generations of fly fishermen are gone. For a time the bass was not recognized as a savior of warmed or polluted trout waters, but as an immigrant indication that things weren't going well. The smallmouth bass was accepted more readily than the largemouth, of course, the smallmouth generally found in clearer, cooler water. In many Maine waters, however, the two live together, the water being a bit chilly for largemouths and maybe a bit warm for smallmouths, but bass adapt.

There is something special about smallmouth bass where I am concerned—so special that I didn't like the description by the tournament fisherman who wrote of "them old brown fish." My wife, Debie, is a smallmouth addict—and when the fish are quite small in a smallmouth creek, she downscales her tackle, uses a Six rod and small flies, and treats a ½-pound fish as a golden treasure, even though it's a little dark to be real gold.

We followed our road map, which took us a little off the tourist paths. We admired the big Maine farmhouses, and as we approached the resort, we drove down a winding gravel road, catching shiny glimpses of what we'd already begun to call "our lake." I don't remember its name because it has been a long time.

There wasn't much doing at the resort. We didn't even see boats in the water. This was the beginning of June and the bass season, and summer folks hadn't showed up yet. The man who ran the place seemed just a little surprised that we had come from goodness-knows-where just to fish for bass. He said, though, that there were lots of people who liked bass. He said there was a man in Portland who ate the things. He said there were big bass in the lake and that he and his wife had caught them on live bait. They spent the winters in Florida, he said, and he wanted to talk about the fishing there when he saw we had a Florida license tag. The cabins weren't really open for business but he'd fix one up for us.

They got the cottage ready, and then they put a wooden skiff in the water. It was one of those old boats that show a lot of handwork, and like a lot of rental boats in New England in those days, it was a sort of grudging compromise between rowboat and outboard. And it leaked. It leaked a lot. It takes some time for one of those boats to get soaked tight after it's been laid up all winter.

The proprietor of the place said he was sure sorry he didn't have a boat really ready for us, but he hoped we wouldn't get our feet wet. Debie hardly glanced at the boat. She was assessing the lake—the great boulders that showed above the surface here and there, and the weedbed in a shallow cove.

We wrestled the ten-horse motor from the car trunk and screwed it to the transom.

"Better not open that thing up," I said. "That's a pretty old boat."

"Yeah," said Debie, staring off toward a steep, rocky shore.

It was early morning when we bailed the boat and started out toward the weed line in the distant cove. The water was clear enough that all of the boulders seemed prepared to break propellers. I was running the boat, and I went very cautiously. We reached the weed line, and Debie was more ready with her rod than I was ready with the oars. She had the Number Six rod, a 9-foot leader, and a Number Six hair bug.

I cut the motor well out, and we drifted in a little closer with Debie already reaching for the weeds, the purposely ragged little hair bug coming through the quiet morning air with a very soft swish and landing with a tiny *spat* at the edge. It rode high because the upper part of it had been doped with line dressing, and even the leader tippet was floating. She twitched it gently, and the wavelets receeded slowly. She twitched it hard, and it came as near a *pop* as it was capable of. She made it swim a little, leaving a distinct V. Then she cast again, and it went well back past the edge, where she worked it gently to avoid a hangup—no weed guard.

The strike was a satisfying *plop,* and the fish jumped almost immediately, but I wasn't quite sure what I saw until Debie lifted her fish up for inspection.

"Doggoned bigmouth!" she grumbled. "I didn't think it acted quite right."

Up to then we hadn't realized there were largemouth bass as well as smallmouth in our lake. A little later, though, I caught a smallmouth along the weed line. We decided to try the boulders—and then we caught no more largemouths. The fish would come up from the deep, just dark spots at first, coming up fast from the dark boulder shadows, and they would sometimes hit the hair bug without pausing. They wouldn't go clear into the air, but you could often see their heads as they took.

It had been a nearly dead calm with only little patches of tiny wavelets showing here and there as patches of breeze seemed to be searching for direction. But the wind began around midmorning, enough to make a few inches of chop, and our hair bugs danced a little. We twitched them harder, and the bigger fish began to show up, no longer able to study our equipment so plainly from below. The best one came from far down, I am sure, but the deep granite boulders no longer showed except as lighter and darker areas. He struck with a *chug,* a fish large enough that he would make no wild leap in taking something so small. A short run, and he made a jump to fit a wildlife calendar, but then he dug as deep-water smallmouths are likely to do, and I took up enough running line to get him on the reel, pumping to keep him out of the caverns somewhere down there. We netted him and went back to the cottage. By then the wind was a little too brisk for the best of bug fishing.

The folks who ran the resort diplomatically noted that the bigger fish were caught on bait, and we were careful not to mention weights, happy enough that we were not prepared for sympathy, having caught no 10-pounders. I do not remember the name of the lake or in what part of Maine it is located, but from time to time Debie brings up the subject.

"If you ever want to go back to that Maine place," she'll say, "I've got that map stashed under *Smallmouth.*"

It took me a long time to get to Maine, some fifty years after I first read of it as the fishing and hunting paradise of the outdoor writers I worshiped as a kid on a Kansas farm. In those days, it seemed, all of the outdoor writers lived and worked in New York and did their research in Maine, wearing battered felt hats and often high-laced boots. They caught their bass largely with fly rods from canoes, smoked pipes, and slept in stained-wall tents.

Even in the twenties there were no buffalo on the outskirts of Cleveland, but West Coast steelhead fishing was a sort of super fly rod sport recounted as if it were a split bamboo adventure into the unknown. I see now that Maine was easily reached by rail or automobile and was a sort of mainstay for those who covered the outdoor scene. A magazine or newspaper writer could go there for a long weekend, even then. It has always been a wonderful place, but not even Maine merited the space it got in the writings of the twenties.

When Debie and I first fished "our" lake, it was not my first trip to Maine. I had gone there pretending to research a book, and when my host launched his Grumman aluminum canoe, he apologized that it wasn't traditional wood and fabric. The smallmouth bass came from the cities of granite boulders in deep, clear water, the loons cried on cue in the evenings, and what I thought were mosquitoes late one day turned out to be black flies. I thought they had killed me but I survived.

Almost every bass fisherman has a home river or a home lake where he feels comfortable, knowing, or at least thinking he knows, how the bass perform there. Our home lake is in the Florida big bass belt, but I have never caught a really big bass there. There are times when bait fishermen or plastic worm casters catch big ones, but although it's a pretty fair bass bug spot, I get hardly anything but small ones. I have no explanation for this, and with the eternal hope of the puzzled angler, I have dis-

A smallmouth that came up from the granite boulders in a Maine lake to take a hair bug on a Number Five rod.

cussed the place with fisheries biologists. I fish the shoreline where weeds and a few lily pads come out fifteen feet from the true bank, and where the water varies from two to eight or ten feet deep.

"Unless you dredge the bottom with something big, I don't think you can count on any whoppers," the fly-fishing biologist said. "There are saucer lakes like that all over Florida—always a few fish around the edges, but nothing really big."

He had no fishing advice and no surefire management suggestions. A professional guide did introduce some threadfin shad, and after that there was spasmodic top-water schooling, but no revolution. So I was happy with the two or three small bass I'd get each evening along the shoreline. It took only three hours to get out there, launch the aluminum johnboat, watch the wading birds come to roost, and possibly see a streaking pair of wood ducks heading for wherever they spent the night.

I guess nothing special had ever happened at the home lake. Two or three times we had sighted some fish striking minnow schools on top and had scored a little extra, but the routine was to slide lazily along for two or three hours, pick up the two or three small bass (and some really big bluegills if the time was right), and then pull the johnboat out and get home, just a little late for dinner.

I always preach careful observation of conditions and attention to detail but tend to gawk at passing herons and try to make out alligator eyes and noses along the shore rather than figuring why the bass are working or why they're not. I like to think I played it very smart on that one particular evening, but it was probably just luck.

The lake had been very low for years, drought and irrigation taking an ongoing toll, and the waterline had been at the very edge of the shoreline vegetation. Then came heavy rains, and the level came back to average within a few days. Two of us were puttering around with the johnboat, working a shoreline and looking for spots where there were run-ins from higher ground. We found some run-ins but fishing was even slower than usual, and although one bass bulged under a popping bug, I felt he might be yawning rather than preparing to strike. Then I saw a splash about two hundred yards away where I happened to be staring at the moment. It was in a tiny cove decorated by a small island. Could have been a bass strike, or a playful alligator—or my imagination.

After I noted the splash, I made a few more casts at the shoreline. Then I noticed something white back in the cove where the splash had occurred, so I fumbled in a storage box, dug out a pair of binoculars, and saw a softball-size bit of foam moving in a gentle breeze. That, of course, meant that some water was spilling somewhere back in the weeds, so I cranked up, idled over to the scene, and saw that there was a brisk run-in of surface water making a miniature waterfall back in there. Very shallow where it came in.

I accepted this calmly, as I had been throwing popping bugs at such dribbles all afternoon without result, but I did throw a Number Six frog imitation as close as I could to where the water came in, and it was sucked under as if an ambitious but undersized bluegill was trying to assert himself. It was a bass, though, maybe weighing a pound, and after that I hooked twenty-three largemouths from the same spot, one of which was around five pounds. I believe I caught bass on six consecutive casts once during my little orgy.

The little, green frog had rubber legs, and it certainly didn't match the tiny minnows that were coming in, but since I threw no more than three casts without a strike I saw no point in changing lures. I guess I either caught or stuck all of them, because when they quit I couldn't raise one on anything in the box. The little run-in looked like other run-ins, but evidently it came from some puddle that had withstood the drought and was carrying bait with it.

I was back there the next day, and when nothing touched the little, green frog, I tried a streamer that should match small baitfish. Nothing. A heron was standing expectantly by the little run-in, and I recalled that he had grouchily left the day before when I moved in, but I never saw him strike at anything on the second day, and he flapped off with a disgusted squawk. Things were back to normal, so I worked a half mile of shoreline and caught two small bass. I heard some wood ducks squeal as they changed course to get through a bunch of oaks. I wasn't even late for dinner.

Run-ins following heavy rains are well worth fishing, but not all of them are carrying bait. When they bring bait, it isn't necessarily big enough to attract a bass. It may attract minnows, which do attract bass in a sort of concentrated food chain. Any moving water about a lake is worth special attention, especially when it's one of those "saucer" lakes that isn't fed by a full-fledged stream.

Now in a few thousand bass-fishing trips, there are going to be some outstanding ones, some through luck and some through good management, but as I look back I can't think of many that resulted from my expertise in locating fish. Oh, I figure they're in one place because the water temperature is just right, or the spawning areas are nearby and it's the right time of year, or a certain baitfish is schooled up here or there, but it's seldom anything spectacular. In the South I keep an eye on places where water "comes out of the woods."

When I first began to sniff through learned works on black bass, I read an opinion that one of the main features of good bass water was a stabilized depth and current. Then, years later, I learned that the experimental "drawdown" of lakes would expose large areas of shoreline to the sun, preparing them to accommodate more bass when the lakes filled up again—a planned procedure that duplicates (repeatedly) what happens in a newly filled reservoir.

But less spectacular are the year-in-and-year-out ups and downs of slow-moving streams with low banks that repeatedly flood large areas of swamp or forest and then recede into their banks again, bringing back the bass that had worked their way into new territory. And as the water recedes, it brings with it all sorts of food gathered from its recent flooding. I would like to say this is a really foolproof rule for catching bass on flies, but sometimes the period of good fishing is critical and doesn't last long. Most likely it is merely an upsurge in the catches, although I have seen spectacular results a few times—as when Marcus Crosby took me up a broad river channel in the South—St. Johns River, Florida—at what was *almost* the right time.

We knew the water was "coming out of the swamp," probably hurried a little by winds that were moving downcurrent. Marcus was in the bow of the boat with a plugging outfit, and I was waving a fly rod and popping bug from the stern. We went with the ghostly movement of a silent electric motor along a wooded bank.

Marcus and I almost blew it. We worked the bank carefully, and I went from my popping bug to a shallow-running streamer, but nothing happened. We tried another sector without result, and it was almost time to go home.

There is a feature of the St. Johns River that is disturbing to visiting bass anglers. The place is loaded with mullet, a saltwater fish that seldom touches a lure or bait, lives on minute organisms, and is a commercial food fish of considerable value. It jumps high and wide at intervals for reasons known only to mullet and has caused near-apoplexy in newcomers who take it for bass. When I first fished the river, it was my second trip before I really knew what those things were.

Marcus started his traveling engine, and we pulled out of our side channel to where it joined another channel, still half a mile from the river proper. I fiddled with my tackle while the big engine sang importantly. It was good mullet country, and there were splashes all over the place.

Marcus cut the throttle and I nearly fell on my face.

"Those aren't mullet!" Marcus yelled, and dived for his rod. He threw a big plug at a swirl fifty feet away and a two-pound bass beat his friends to it. I was fast-stripping line from my reel but there was really no hurry, and when I got my bug over a boil, a bass grabbed it. Now I don't know how many we caught. It couldn't have been as many as it seemed. They were not particular. Any bug or plug worked fine—streamers too.

The term "school bass" is pretty loose. It began as a description of surface-feeding fish that attacked bait schools together, and in most areas it's a matter of violent action for a few seconds, after which the bait scatters and the bass re-form for another attack when a new school comes along or when the shattered one re-forms. But we had something different. We had largemouths, some of them up to three pounds or more, simply cruising near the surface, far from any visible cover, and striking baitfish that had somehow gotten scattered over an area a hundred yards across.

The fish struck hard and fast or gently and slow. They splashed or came in silent swirls, and for once I guess I had too many bass. I used bugs mostly, but streamers worked too, and finally things began to slow down a little. We'd moved the boat around for some time and must have put down a large share of the fish. Anyway, Marcus caught a bass and unhooked it carefully, watched it swim away, and said we might as well be going in. So I looked around for a moment, noted a swirl back past the stern, and flipped a bug back there. *Chug!* I tightened up and said I guessed we'd had enough.

We think we figured it out. Water outside the riverbanks had gotten lower rather suddenly—lower than the bait (mostly threadfin shad, I guess) could handle, so they simply moved out, for some reason not in tight schools. And the bass from shorelines anywhere near the flat had left shelter to feed. I have never found fish there since. I've sure tried.

From time to time someone used to write that there were more smallmouth bass in Virginia's Shenandoah River than anywhere else in the country. I approach the Shenandoah with reverence because Harry Murray (who wrote a very, very good book on smallmouth fishing) has been fly fishing it since he was a kid, and when I catch a bass there I feel I am trespassing.

"Over there by that big rock," Harry will say, "the current sort of sweeps down into a deep little run, and there should be a fish on the edge of it just a little downstream. You can drift a streamer or big nymph down through there without any trouble at all. Just dead drift it."

So I wade over to the big rock and dead drift a sport model Woolly Worm down through the fast water, and when it swings out a little to the edge of the run as the water slows, a feisty little smallmouth grabs it like money from home. I tighten up and look over toward Harry, who is very high and very wide and is nursing a streamer between a rock and some weeds. I am tempted to ask him if I did good, but that would be rather silly, so I unhook the bass and look around as if I knew what was going on.

Harry is one of those people who would fish with a rod in each hand if he could, and when his son, Jeff, was too small to wade the Shenandoah on his own, Harry carried him on his shoulders. Jeff would use a spinning rod and Harry would continue to cast flies. It somehow seemed unfair to the bass.

The Shenandoah slides through some backcountry, where you might see a wild turkey or some deer if you aren't too engrossed in your fishing. I guess the most thorough way to work it is to drift it in a canoe, but when I've fished there, Harry has simply taken me to good spots by devious routes requiring the good will of various farmers. It really isn't as thrilling as it used to be, because Harry no longer drives his old Jeep, a loosely related collection of parts that gave forth grating sounds of complaint at every chuckhole but always seemed to get home at the end of the day. Harry finally bought a sharp, new four-wheel-drive, setting to rest the suspicion that his fishing career would have ended if the old Jeep disintegrated on some mountain road. It hadn't been a matter of poverty. I think the old Jeep had just been an added challenge.

I love canoes and have long preached that youth is safer in a canoe than on a street corner, but like other fly fishermen, I have sometimes found the recreation canoeists (no fishing tackle) to be a special challenge on well-traveled streams. Harry placed me on a fishing spot where he said I might see some canoes, but I had not expected twenty-four of them in a bunch—a cheery crowd of teenagers who parted to slide past me with courteous inquiries as to how fishing had been. I moved my rod tip to avoid one of the rigs and produced a fixed smile as I prepared to wade to shore, feeling all bass had gone to hidey holes. Lots of canoe liveries around there.

Now I've always thought of the Shenandoah as a small-fish stream, despite stories of really big smallmouths occasionally taken there. I have fished four types of lures—hair bugs, popping bugs, streamers, and nymphs, and have had no great breakthrough. On one occasion Harry placed me on a run that seemed made for bass, well upstream where the river wasn't very wide, and I threw a bug over near a fallen tree, where it was taken instantly. It was a half-pound bass, which suits me just fine on a light rod, and I watched my fish swing downstream in the current, little glimpses of bronze flashing in the bubbly, rough water. Then, as I began to pump him back upstream, it seemed he made an especially large swirl, and it soaked in that there were two fish, so I concluded a second one was trying to swipe my hair bug from the first one (who by then would undoubtedly have given it up gladly). Then, of course, I saw the largest smallmouth bass I have ever raised, who wasn't after the bug at all but was obviously considering making a meal of Fish Number One.

Evidently the big bass saw me and left. This kind of story has been told by the thousands and is a real yawner, so I promise not to do it again—but there are some big smallmouths in the Shenandoah. I am convinced that in that river, as in many other smallmouth streams, a big,

A canal and backwater give canoeists a chance at water seldom visited by larger craft.

deep-fished nymph, imitation crawfish, or whatever, is the best bet for the bigger fish.

"School bass" come in many forms, and this has come to mean almost any situation in which fish gang up to strike bait on the surface, whether on impoundments, natural lakes, or rivers. I first heard of them on the St. Johns in Florida, and at one time there was a cult of school-bass fishermen who weren't much interested in any other kind of angling. Most of them used small, fast boats and threw lures with plugging rods. There are still schooling bass on many lakes and rivers, but the heyday of the school-bass fisherman on the St. Johns probably began when fast outboards became available at reasonable prices and seemed to fade out about 1975.

More fishermen and heavy boat traffic have made the traditional "school grounds" less productive, and most of the school fishing I've done there in recent years has been almost by accident. On many rivers and lakes of the South, however, there are little-advertised schooling spots, well known to a few regulars. Sometimes, as in the case of the fish found by Marcus Crosby and me on an earlier page, such areas are only occasionally active and the particular conditions that make them productive might not occur again for years. In the meantime, the bass are behaving as bass are supposed to behave, loafing in tight cover or in deep areas and emerging to feed as individuals when they feel like it.

In some parts of the country they are called "jump bass," or "bar bass," or simply "schoolies," but the South has more than its share of them. Most big impoundments have them from time to time, even if on a small scale. With some hesitation I say that river schooling is nearly always a southern phenomenon, feeling that it's being kept secret in some parts of the world.

When jump fishing was at its peak years ago, the fly rod wasn't a particularly good choice, simply because a school ground might be pretty well loaded up with fishermen, and their boats would be very close together at the spot, even though there might not be another boat for miles. This sounds strange, but it's not as silly as it seems at first. There was a sort of underground telephone network of school fishermen, and they'd pass the word every evening as to where the fish were jumping. In more recent years when there is no immediate competition, the fly rod is a top tool for the job.

It would take supernatural powers to predict where a schooling ground would appear, but once you have found jump bass in action, you can almost invariably tell why they are doing it where they are, especially on a river. There are schooling grounds I know of that were active for half a century, and although most of those have pretty well faded out, they may still have action occasionally. Happily, even though a spot may not have "jumpers," it is likely to attract some semiresident fish.

Schooling generally involves something that causes schools of baitfish to either compress or become confused. For example, in a river with migratory baitfish headed for salt water, a school of bait may be compacted by a bottom that shelves up to make a shallow area. There may be an obstruction that causes a steadily moving school to change its course completely or become confused. A tributary stream may bring in bait from a big area and concentrate the schools in a narrow passage. A narrow place in a river may simply condense the bait and make it more vulnerable. An attractive kind of cover may cause baitfish to hole up or scatter.

You'll generally find something like those conditions where schooling takes place, but you'll find many such spots that never have schooling bass. So I end up rather lamely without seeming to be sure of anything.

It's been a long time since I saw half a dozen boats anchored against each other with deadeye casters poised for the next jump, which might be "up" for only a few seconds. The perfect cast is one that lays a lure between a fish and a baitfish it is already pursuing, but any cast that hits the general area where the bass are striking is likely to produce if it arrives quickly. For the fly fisherman, the problem is getting the lure into action *fast,* which means no more than one quick false cast. It is the same condition faced by the saltwater angler on shallow flats who must lay his fly to the exact position for a moving bonefish.

You need a weight-forward line for school-bass fishing, which is generally (not always) done from a boat, and you need to handle your running line with special care, since too much false casting leaves you throwing at smooth water. It's a good time for a garbage can for coiling line, although any kind of a "doily" is good on a boat deck. After the fish are "down," you won't have much chance.

It's good to have a fly or bug that approximates the size of the bait, but in many cases the fish are in such a feeding frenzy that they actually prefer something larger, picking it out of a swarm of lesser targets. Since the surviving bait generally goes back down after the massacre, I used to insist on some sort of streamer for school fishing, retrieving it fast. When the bait is very small, three or four small and shiny streamers on the same leader can "create your own school." A bug can be left on station for a while and may get a second pass before a fish retires to wherever he's been ambushing. And if there's no one else fishing the spot, you can sometimes leave a bug floating downstream and be extra quick on the next rise. A bug doesn't have to be a close match. Generally, I like a "Marm," without wings, with a slender body, short tail, and a popping cup. This book has a picture of it along with some other bugs.

But to my utter frustration, I have found times when bass that have been whacking shiny little minnows preferred big frog imitations with rubber legs. Keeps me humble.

Chasing schooling bass on lakes requires the same kind of fly presentation as on a river, of course, but there is the added business of following the fish, and when the schools are fairly tight and move fast, there is an element of boatmanship that must be kept under restraint. I still blush to recall one experience I had on a small lake no more than a mile across and two miles long. Fish would follow schools of shad all over the place, underwater most of the time but breaking the surface at intervals—a break sometimes coming considerable distance from the previous one.

By accident, at that time I had a fast boat. It was a Penn Yan Swift, product of a revered boat company, and the light hull of wood and fabric was made for racing. It was pretty seaworthy and could be used as a cartopper, but when it came to chasing schooling bass, it was quite a bomb. One spring we used it hard on the lake mentioned, and I guess we made a little better time than most of the other skiffs. When we saw fish break, we could get to top speed almost instantly with a pretty big motor. The boat (by accident) was bright red, a bit too gaudy for the other bass fishermen.

One day, for a forgotten reason, I visited a resort on the lake shore and saw three boats racing about after schoolers.

"Man, look at 'em go!" I mentioned.

"That's nothing!" commented the resort owner. "You should be here when that damn fool with the red boat is out there!"

In the South, "schooling" is a pretty loose term, and I find myself using it to describe any situation in which bass continue to strike on top over a small area. Occasionally a busy striking zone, even on a lake, is very small and will have intermittent action for days or weeks. Apparently when one bait school disappears, another moves in.

On one lake where Debie and I have fished for years, there's a little colony of fly fishermen who are always good for the latest information. Two years ago I checked with one of the local authorities, and he said the fish were taking every evening "in the bonnets." The lake has acres of lily pads, called "bonnets" locally, so we set forth in a boat and fished lily pads energetically all evening, producing one yearling bass. Our informant apologized.

"I didn't explain it right," he said. "We've been talking about it so long, I thought everyone knew. The pads we're talking about are just a round patch out there two hundred yards from that old duck blind on the point. They start there just about sundown or a little earlier."

So the next evening we were there a little before sundown, and there were two bass boats pointing the patch of bonnets like bird dogs. Anchors out. The bonnet patch was almost round and less than a hundred yards across. As the sun dipped, a heartfelt blast occurred at the edge nearest one of the bass boats, and two plugs headed that way immediately.

We picked a spot a polite distance from one of the bass boats, slid over the anchor, and waited. Two minutes later a pair of frantic shad minnows skipped along the bonnet edge, followed by ominous swirls, and there was a pair of loud strikes. We were a little slow that time, but a few minutes later one of us put a popping bug behind an airborne minnow, and there was a soul-satisfying bang and yank.

Most of the bass were small, but now and then there would be a two-pounder, and we saw at least one six-pounder caught on a friend's bug several evenings later. The fishing went on for weeks, usually only two or three bass chasing bait at a time—and sometimes it was a single, harder to fool because he had no competition.

A few regulars visited the place regularly, but we were so hooked on the program that we became almost as much a landmark as the old duck blind. Much of the time we left the boat and waded, as the water was about waist-deep. There would be a preferred bug or streamer for a couple of trips, and then something else would work better. The irritating part from the viewpoint of someone trying to get scientific about the program was that some of the most successful lures bore no visible relationship to the bait, and one evening's winner would be followed by something entirely different twenty-four hours later.

Other fishing in the general area began to get pretty good, and occasionally there would be quite a few boats in sight. Came one evening when the place was crowded, and since nothing much was doing at the pads, we decided to work a little stretch some distance away. When we moved we found three other boats idling so close to us we could have traded sandwiches.

"Why do they follow us?" Debie wondered. "We can't fish with that crowd breathing down our necks."

Finally a great truth dawned. When passing boats have noted the same people catching fish for a couple of weeks, I suppose it's natural to follow them when fishing is slow. It is a form of admiration we could do without. I guess I should try to justify the situation.

The pad patch was located near extensive eelgrass flats, it was not far from where there was a little river current, and it was at the mouth of a big cove that extended back for almost half a mile. I guess it was a logical spot for moving bait schools to hole up and rest, and it was an obvious place to try a few casts if you were looking for good cover. There have been busy bass there several different years. The ringbills still roar past at dusk, an osprey still sits on a post near the duck blind, and I've been asked why the fishing hasn't been good there lately. How should I know?

Anyone who chases bass for a lifetime has memorable trips that are recalled in detail, somehow treasured, even though the fishing may not have been very good. Drift fishing for bass on a briskly moving river as is found only in mountainous—or at least hilly—country receives little attention anymore, almost completely eclipsed by adventures on impoundments, where fast bass boats with their flashing and beeping electronics replace rustic wooden rigs with paddles or oars. And most of the canoeists in bass country seem to be travelers rather than fishermen. The drift boat and canoe now seem to be mainly tools of trout and salmon fishermen—or perhaps my education is incomplete and most of the good smallmouth rivers are simply secrets of those who fish them.

As a kid I thought the Ozark float trips must be the peak of angling adventure, and I reveled in what little of it I could manage. A khaki-clad sport from Chicago or St. Louis who drifted down the James or White River on a folding chair in a wooden johnboat had more glamour for me than any lion hunter. His guide, in the stern with a homemade paddle and bib overalls and sitting on a gunnysack that held his spare shirt, was my idea of a true outdoorsman of the Daniel Boone stamp. That guide, you know, not only ran the river rapids without missing a chew on his Horseshoe plug tobacco, but also could set up a quick camp at nightfall and serve bass fillets from a campfire that made only a slender wraith of smoke.

Well, the dams took over much of the best mountain float water, and below the dams the cold rivers held trout that I considered interlopers. The remaining streams were hard-pressed, and maybe the guided

At low water, smallmouth bass fishermen are likely to meet unforseen problems. This started out as a drift-fishing trip on the Ozark's famous Crooked Creek but turned into a series of portages done the hard way. A canoe would have been better.

float trip lost much of its glamour for bass fishermen. A man who wrote a comprehensive guide to many of the rivers said he wished he hadn't done it.

I went back to the Ozarks and took a float trip with a professional guide in about 1947, but we had a slow day. Then about 1955, my wife and I put an aluminum boat in one of the rivers at low water and spent much of the trip pulling and pushing the thing over the shoals—but we did catch some smallmouths. Something was missing. I decided to do it in the grand fashion, so I drove to a village on a bass river of long standing and asked for the local float-boat operator. A puzzled native finally directed me to a retiree who owned a johnboat. It was smaller than the modern ones over on the big trout rivers, but it looked sound.

There was a guide, but it was said he had been drunk for three days. His front door was very high above the ground, for the steps were missing. I wondered how a man who had been drunk for three days could make it but guessed there was a back entrance. Let's drop the alcoholic part right here, because the man paddled from dawn with mist on the river to dusk with a barred owl announcement and never complained.

I used a Number Seven rod, although I'm not sure they used that designation in those days, and I put a hair bug against the rocky banks, dropped it where there were little current seams, and twitched it above and below boulders. I paid special attention to a little stretch of willows in one quiet pool where the current didn't move us much, and the guide paddled grimly. That was where the little largemouth bass popped the bug to the paddler's approval.

"Li'l lineside," he announced judiciously, squinting with his red-rimmed eyes. "They're in these dead holes."

It was a busy day and a very long one. The man who had provided the johnboat had said it would be a hard day of paddling, but he seemed to take pleasure in that fact.

"Damn a drinking man," he had muttered as we launched the boat.

I caught big-mouthed green sunfish on the hair bug, and then some rock bass the guide called goggle-eye as the Ozark guides always have. I caught some little smallmouths, "black bass" to the guide, who seemed to perk up as the day went on. It was late in the afternoon when a better smallmouth took a bug, coming up as smallmouths are supposed to do in chunk-rock holes. When he was hooked, I saw his bronze flashes in the low sun and knew then the trip had been worthwhile. In some ways the river had not changed. But there was something missing, for I found no one to talk to about the good old days.

Bass are nearly always nearby, and I think that's why they come with sentiment. Almost everywhere I have lived or worked, I have had bass within a short drive—and when I go back to a bass-fishing spot I have not visited for years, I now realize that the place I fish for bass condenses some of the best memories of another time.

IN ADDITION TO its unique sawtooth pattern through the water, a streamer "breathes." The long, wavy hackles of feather-winged flies open and close with each rise and fall of the fly, and even the wings of bucktail streamers behave similarly underwater, opening and closing, opening and closing. Marabou-wing streamers have even more constant, more delicate action. Marabou really flutters in the water, and sometimes even when just sinking, without any action imparted by the angler, they have enough natural wiggle to draw strikes from bass.

Something else going for the bass fisherman using streamers is that streamer flies transfuse light. Many baitfish are nearly transparent, shiner minnows for example, or at least they seem so when observed in clear water against bright surface light, and there's no doubt whatever that bass most often hit streamers because they mistake them for minnows. . . .

And dry-fly fishing can be a dirty trick to play on stream smallmouths. In late summer and early fall, when the rivers are very low and clear, a ½-pound smallmouth can be as angler-wise as a 6-pound brown trout in a Pennsylvania limestone stream. Toss a spinning lure or heavy plastic plug in front of a smallmouth under the conditions of low, clear water and you'll see the fish spook right out of its scales.

Tom McNally
Fly Fishing

FIVE

Bug Business

WITH BASS BUGS we need a little romance. While some flies get colorful names like Queen of the Waters or Parmachene Belle, bass bug names tend to be something like the Gerbubble Bug or the Stunted Skunk. Anyway, I like the deer-hunting story as an origin for surface fly rod attractions.

The story is a little vague as to just where the deer hunt took place, and the time is a bit doubtful too. It seems this deer hunter killed a deer on the bank of a bass river or lake, and when he dragged it away from the shoreline, a little tuft of hair blew into the water and was really banged by a big bass. Since they have been using some sort of surface lure for bass for some time, I visualize the hunter as wearing buckskins and using a muzzleloader. I do not know if he developed into an expert fly tier or not. Anyway, I hope this adds a little class to one of the most delightful forms of fly fishing. It may not be the most delicate angling in the world, but for that matter, there is nothing particularly dainty about fly fishing for marlin.

Despite numerous revealing reports, no one knows when the bass bug business really got started. Historians believe early fly fishermen probably fastened big flies to bits of cork or wood to make them float, and the bass bug is as hard to date as the dry fly as used for trout and salmon. In the eighteenth century, breakthroughs in bass fishing were probably overshadowed by less colorful things like Indian raids and a push westward. And remember that we got our ideas of sport almost entirely from the British or mainland Europeans, and they didn't have black bass over there.

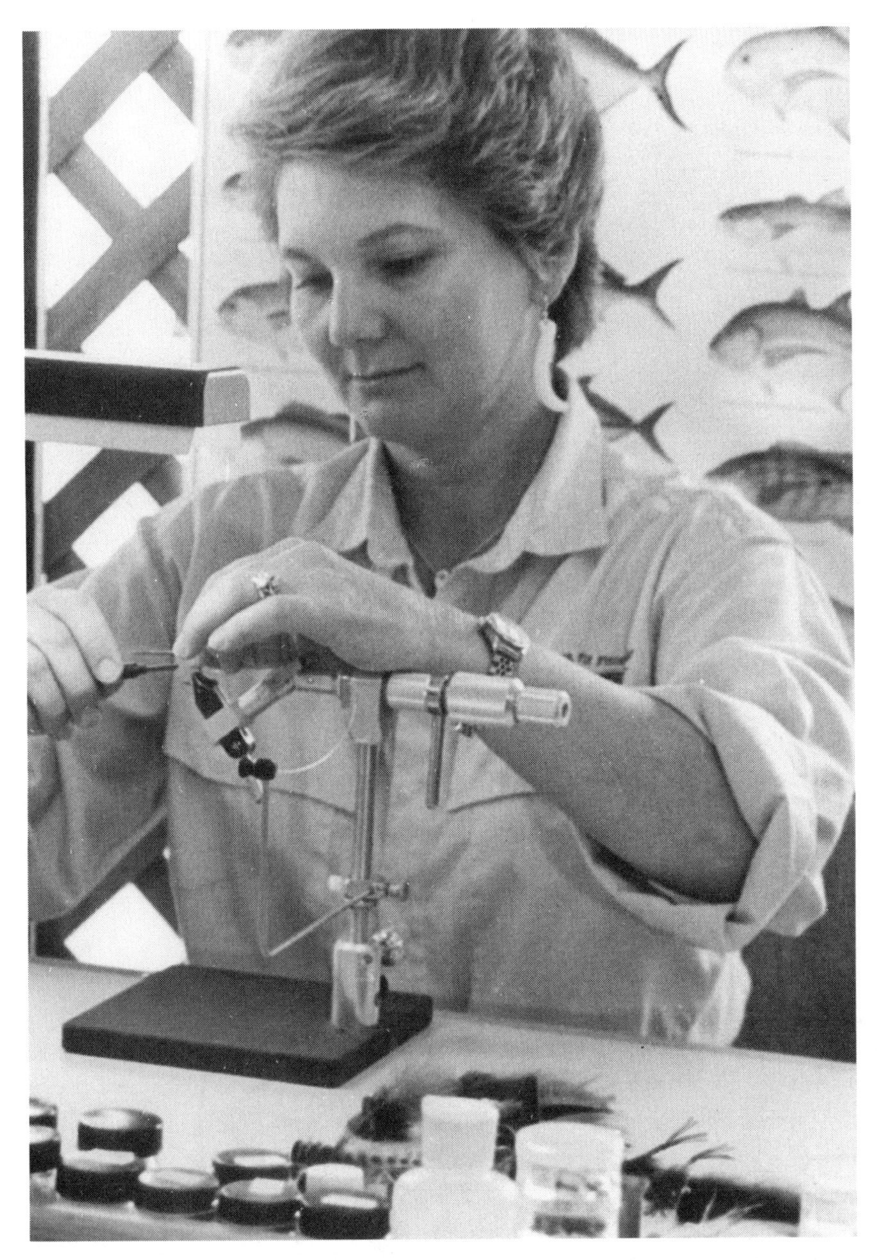

Bass lures are tied in endless variations. Liz Steele of The Fly Fisherman, Titusville, Florida, uses an advanced form of vise, produces custom flies, and instructs students of the art.

By far the majority of largemouth bass taken on fly rods are caught with surface bugs of some kind. This one struck what is probably the most popular design of all—a medium-sized popper with rubber legs and a feather tail.

There are longtime methods of bass fishing that contributed to development of the bass bug, and I dwell on some of them because they give food for thought about how a bug should be fished and how it should be built. I don't know if the Native Americans beat the Europeans to some of these methods or not.

One of the most intriguing facts about that early surface fishing for bass is the tendency to use a lure that moved constantly, was seldom retrieved at all, and was pretty big. What we have here is a gadget that made a continuous disturbance, its "wake" (for lack of a better word) roughing up the water enough to obscure the end of a pole and distorting the image of a boat or canoe with its bloodthirsty fishermen so that a bass wasn't scared off. Some of these methods are still in use—occasionally—and I have watched them with fascination. I even had a whirl at jigger-bobbing myself.

Most of these constantly active lures began their careers in the South. Dr. James A. Henshall, first of the great bass gurus and still widely respected as an authority, described "skittering" in his *Book of the Black Bass* (1904). In that, the fisherman uses a long cane pole (no reel) with a few inches of cord attached to some kind of spoon. As the boat or canoe is paddled, rowed, or poled along shallow bass cover, the lure is skittered along on the surface and is not picked up for considerable periods of time. The gimmick here is that the lure hides the end of the pole (and the rest of the fishing party) so that the fish has no distraction from the lure itself. Under some conditions I am convinced that a bass bug worked very fast in light weed cover accomplishes the same purpose. It doesn't happen very often, but it's good to remember. I believe that bass have a wider range of behavior than any other game fish.

The skittering business may have started with a spoon, but I doubt it. In the South I have seen it done with everything from a small, leather alligator to a tarpon streamer. There are a number of names for the process, and I've heard "jiggerbobbing" more than anything else. "Doodle-socking" is the same thing or a variation of it. It works, especially in seldom-fished waters, and I even tried it as an experiment on snook in brackish creeks. Since you simply pull in the catch hand over hand with the pole it isn't very sporty, but it sure is a novelty.

A few years back, a highly refined program of jiggerbobbing was chronicled and sold as a system, together with appropriate equipment. There were full-page ads in many sporting publications, and I'm sure it caught a lot of bass. It sounds a little weird to most anglers, but doodle-socking will catch fish, almost regardless of what is used as a lure. I don't think it will often work in the daytime where bass are fished hard and regularly.

The business that puzzles me is that known as "fishing the bob," very nearly the same thing but not involving the constant-wake principle. Bertram, the naturalist, tells of the bob being fished back in 1764. He says it was a bushy fly of white deer hair and was worked the same way as the more common skittering rig, except that it was simply waved on a short line a little above the surface and dipped to touch the water only occasionally. Now most bass fishermen have seen fish strike at birds, flying insects, or even airborne lures—occasionally. But the idea of using the flying lure for long periods leaves me with no explanation. I'd think only a very hungry or very cranky bass would strike it. I sure don't rec-

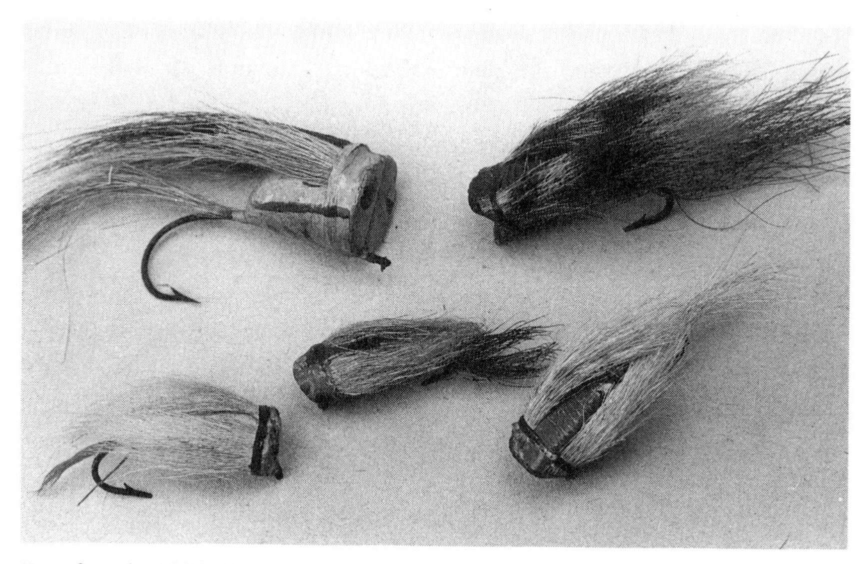

Bugs from the 1930s that greatly resemble the original Callmac. These have been designed with a variety of heads, and all of them have been made up with deer or squirrel hair instead of the feathers that made folded wings atop the original.

ommend it, but it is a little difficult to take issue with something written more than two centuries ago.

Fishermen being what they are, I am positive that many bass anglers worked big flies on top, either by doping them or simply putting them in the air again without letting them sink, many years before the bass bug got that name. The late A. J. McClane, one of the true authorities on angling, checked on some of the origins of modern commercial bass bugs and in his fishing encyclopedia reported what he learned from Ernest W. Peckinpaugh of Chattanooga, Tennessee. Peckinpaugh, considered father of the modern bass bug, started out with a lure for panfish and was using cork as a bug body around 1910. By 1913 or 1914, Peckinpaugh said, his "Night Bug" was featured in the catalog of the John J. Hildebrandt Company. He said Will H. Dilg popularized the cork-bodied bass bug. The first of Peckinpaugh's bugs were tied with two hooks, simply because it was easier to fasten the cork with two. Much later, of course, the hook with a hump in the shank handled that problem.

Whether the deer hunter with the muzzleloader started it or not, I am sure the deer-hair bug was used very early in the game, coming very close to the "bob" of cane-pole fame. We wouldn't learn much about it, of course, because it would be simply a matter of tying and wouldn't involve what might be termed "manufacture." Of course, there have been thousands of named cork or wooden bass bugs that have caught fish, almost everyone who has built one adding his or her own little feature, whether it made much difference or not.

The history of all kinds of fly fishing becomes an obsession with a very few. Most of the earliest bass bugs carried their maker's names, and some of the names have carried over to today, some of the bugs looking much as they did in the beginning, with the addition of modern materials. The original Callmac bass bug, a favorite of the twenties and thirties, came from the name of Call J. McCarthy of Chicago, who sold it. There is nothing wrong with the Callmac type, which can be made with almost unlimited dimensions. It appears as a large insect with its wings folded partway back, and I like it best with hair wings. That design planes well in the air. The nose can be shaped to get anything from a mild ripple to a resounding *pop.* In an ad in *Forest and Stream* for June 1920, I find Mr. McCarthy trying to protect his design: "Callmac bugs have proven such a success that several imitations are now being made. Insist on the original 'Callmac' bugs when making your purchases."

Since then, I'm sure the "several" imitations have become several

Most modern bass bugs developed from lures originated between 1910 and 1920. The original Callmac bug was generally made with two feather wings folded over its back. When the design was "improved," the wings were made of hair, giving added action in the water. By the 1930s, most of the bugs of this design used more hair than feathers for wings.

The Wilder-Dilg Feather Minnow is virtually unchanged in thousands of tackle stores and catalogs and is used in both fresh and salt water. It's generally just a "feather minnow" now in many colors, but the old Wilder-Dilg model can be quite at home. The true origin is doubtful.

thousand. In 1920 Noa Spears wrote in *Forest and Stream* of bass bugs, and the subhead for his column said, "A bass bug is a weird creature, resembling nothing that creeps or flies, but it certainly gets results."

A rough classification of bass bugs past and present might be a help.

The Callmac type of bass bug could be made to pop, especially if there was a broad nose, or it could be designed for gentler disturbances, with a rounded or nearly sharp front. That design may be the basis of other bugs with outspread wings of hair or feathers, some completely at right angles to the body. The very first of the Callmac types that I saw were made entirely of feathers and cork or of feathers and balsa wood.

The "feather minnow" type of bug was entirely different in that it appeared to represent a surfaced baitfish instead of an outsize insect. The head was bullet shaped, the most popular ones with the pointed end forward. A more modern name is the "slider." It has a long tail, usually with a long-shanked hook, and although most of the tails are made of feathers, bucktail works fine. If the head is simply turned around with the flat end forward, you have a pure popper, and if it is cupped it's a louder popper. Put a groove in the front (not a common design), and you have a feather minnow that dives and wiggles.

The hair bug evidently started as a floating fly of no particular species and has been woven into the "mouse" or "powder puff." It was the basis for later developments such as the "divers," which have been around for a long time in various forms but are greatly refined in current designs.

Hair has been used in a variety of ways in bug design. For many years the Devil Bug was very popular, generally the Tuttle Devil Bug. It was mouse shaped, but it was built with hair wings. The body did not have the hair ends spun into the usual puff but was made with the hairs laid down lengthwise of the lure. It sank or swam dependent upon the kind of hair used and how it was treated, and the body was fairly firm. I haven't seen it or imitations of it in recent years, although it's not unusual to see either wet or dry bugs with bodies made of longitudinal hair. Except for the Callmac bugs and the Peck's Feather Minnow, I think the Tuttle Devil Bug was commercialized more than any other top-water bass "fly."

The Muddler Minnow is often said to be the most popular and effective fly rod lure ever made—a combination of hair bug and streamer—and the variations are endless. It is much better known for trout than for bass. The original, made by Don Gapen as a trout fly, had a rather loose and shaggy head, and some will say the sloppy ones are best. It has been tied with natural deer-hair heads as well as with white and black ones. Most makers intended for it to be used wet, but when I got my first ones they looked like floaters to me, so I used them with line dressing on bass, trout, and panfish. They worked fine, but when I talked to other fisher-

The Tuttle design was one of the first of a vast number of "hair mouse" patterns. Simplified forms were simply called "powderpuffs" or "hair floaters" and remain the basis of hundreds of bass bugs.

The hair bug is tied in hundreds of forms. Some users insist the loosely tied and bushy ones will catch more fish under some circumstances—but the artistic ones sell better. The tightly tied one shown here was done by "Tap" Tapply.

men, I finally realized they were using theirs as streamers. The Muddler is truly versatile, and when one is rough finished, a nonconformist with scissors can have fun.

Gapen built his first Muddler as an imitation of the sculpin, a favorite bottom-dwelling target of large brook trout, and the date given is 1928. Dan Bailey developed it at his fly shop in Montana, and the ones he made were more tightly constructed and neater in appearance. It's the same old story as that of the first hair bugs. Sloppy Muddlers wouldn't sell well. Anyway, with an assortment of Muddler sizes to be fished both dry and wet and with all sorts of tails made from feather, hair, mylar, and whatnot, a bass fisherman could get by with nothing else and catch his share of fish. Of course, some of the things would look hardly at all like the original Muddlers.

A Muddler popper comes out simply as a Muddler with an especially large head, scissored to make a flat nose, and the tail is skimpy. The thing can be made to rest with its head high, and with a good twitch will bow and pop. An almost completely different Muddler can be made with leader-sinking dope (and possibly a very little lead) and used in an area of top-striking fish. If allowed to sink with only slight twitches, it is accepted as a damaged baitfish, I suppose. I caught some bass that way before I realized what I was doing. My Muddler just started sinking, and while I was gawking around for another striking fish to throw at, a bass tried to swallow it. In small sizes, the Muddler has been used as a trailer for loud bugs.

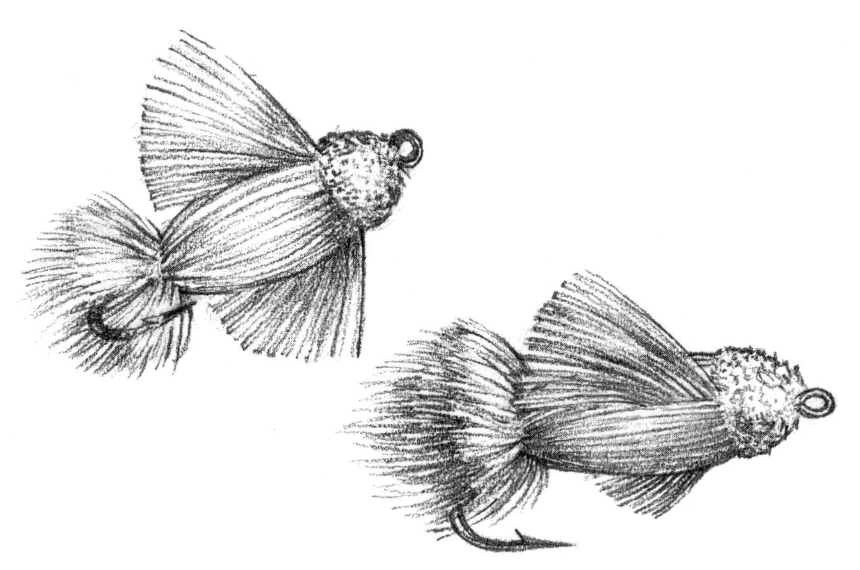

Tuttle's Devil Bug was highly successful for generations, and the pattern still takes a great many bass, whoever ties it.

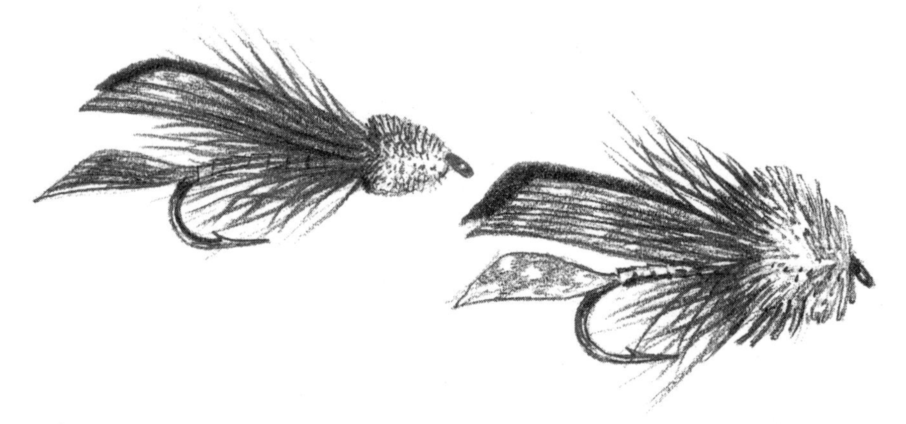

The Muddler Minnow is often said to be the most versatile fly rod lure of all time, made in a variety of shapes and colors and fished either wet or dry. The original by Don Gapen was loosely tied and rather bushy and was intended to imitate the sculpin or bullhead, a bottom dweller. The lure was then developed by Dan Bailey and tied with a "tight" head, and there have been dozens of offshoots. Originally, it was intended for deep fishing, but it has also been worked on top as a diver and grasshopper.

One bug type that merits more attention than it gets is the Marm, simply a slender piece of hard and high-floating material with a hook at the stern and a sprig of tail. I first used it on schooling bass, and it was plugcasters who introduced me to it. They were using it as a trailer on heavy plugs for bombarding distant striking fish. Some of the best of the Marms (relatives of the "stick-bait") have beautiful scale finishes. They are too slender to make very large *pops,* but they can make a *plip* if the nose is shaped for it. One of the best I've seen has a turkey quill body covered with mylar tubing. That was built by writer-angler Bill Parlasca, who has used smaller quill flies for a variety of purposes.

The simplest of homemade popping bugs have been made from bottle corks, but most bottles are closed some other way these days. If you do have some corks, all you need is hooks with humped shanks, glue, thread, and hair or feathers. I recently received a bunch of popping bugs with strangely striped bodies, and I couldn't even figure out what they were made of. The donor said he had rigged a sort of cookie cutter and was making bodies from thick, laminated sneaker soles. I caught bass with them, but I doubt if they'll put the maker in the category of world-famous fly tiers. The man just liked to make fishing lures from odds and ends, and in doing so, he probably learned a lot about bass and what they like. I firmly believe that if anything floats and isn't too heavy, someone will tie feathers to it and throw it at a bass.

The Dahlberg Diver has a really special action, coming on as part bug and part streamer. Many years ago, the late Roy Berry, a Kentucky fly-fishing perfectionist, showed me a hair creation that floated at rest but dived when retrieved. Roy had made a hair bug with a tail and had used glue to form a stiff collar at the front. If it was pulled briskly it would dive, and Roy said it had worked fine on Kentucky bass.

When I first got my hands on the Berry creations (probably too meticulous to be sold at reasonable prices), I was on a brackish-water fishing trip and had located a bunch of small tarpon that would swirl around my bugs but wouldn't take. Pop-and-stop routines didn't work, and streamers got nowhere either, but when I put one of Roy's bugs over these fish, retrieved it slowly and steadily while it half submerged and made a gentle wake, the tarpon became easy to catch. Continuous

The Pencil Popper has an elongated body and usually has only a short tail of feathers or hair. It is balanced so that it rides at an angle when at rest, popping when the leader pulls the cupped end against the surface. Its opposite number in a plugging lure generally uses propellerlike spinners without the popping cup and is called a "stickbait."

Popularity of diving bugs is the most recent development, and most of these are versions of the Dahlberg Diver. The bug that floats at rest and dives under when pulled has been so accepted that some anglers now use nothing else for bass.

motion sometimes works when stop-and-go won't. Some time later the Dahlberg Diver became famous, and I take nothing from it. One bass fisherman told me he had given up all other types of fly rod lure.

Then came the Desperate Diver, a carefully designed head of hard material, suitably finished and colored, with a short streamer behind it. It has been highly successful. It will pop, dive, and wiggle.

The diving type of lure has created some addicts who say they will never use any other kind.

I doubt if they'd let you into the U.S. Patent Office with a bass bug. The lure names I use are purely to isolate a type in most cases, and to say a certain angler made the very first of *anything* is a little like designating the inventor of the wheel. Some lures have been invented countless times, and most of those who claim credit do so innocently. Sometimes they have made something from their own ideas and don't realize it's been done before. Or perhaps they feel that some small addition or subtraction they have made has created a totally new item. Sometimes the "originator" has only come up with a catchy name that people remember.

Fishing lures, and especially flies and bugs, are not hard to make, and when an acquaintance of mine, Keith E. Perrault, made up a dictionary of fishing flies, he had sixteen thousand named flies on short order and said he was only getting started and that another edition was needed immediately. So how many little-known named flies are there? A million?

It's true that naming a fly or lure may carry a bit of prestige, and some fishermen have their names on a great many. I once found my name was used with a streamer I got from someone else. I made up a name for it, but I sure didn't invent it, a similar thing having been around for two hundred years or more. And my wife, Debie, found there was a "Debie Popper." She made some, all right, but said she had simply copied a nameless bug and gave some away. Anyway, don't be too sure an "inventor" is really producing something new.

Some simple bass bugs are easy to make, but even if you make up some for yourself, you'll probably buy a majority of what you use, simply because you want some variety and it sure isn't cost-efficient to dig up a

The Desperate Diver employs a hard head and is followed by a streamer type of body. The nose design causes it to wiggle when retrieved rapidly, and when used with a floating line it runs barely under the surface.

special design, find the proper paint and materials for it, and then build only two or three bugs after all that trouble.

There are some well-established bug-making companies, and you'll quickly become familiar with their names, beginning with Peck, which has survived through all these years. Some good bugs cast better than others, of course, because of their basic designs and the pick-up problems some give on the water, but there have been real dogs whomped up by unknown makers, some of whom simply didn't understand how the things were supposed to work.

Years ago I bought what appeared to be a supermouse. It appeared to be a takeoff on the venerable hair mouse or Powderpuff and had been rendered in such detail, down to mousy tail, eyes, ears, and whiskers, that it was worthy of display on the same shelf as your copy of Henshall's *Book of the Black Bass.* The thing was in a plastic bubble, so I didn't make a close examination, but aristocratic fishermen like me know quality when we see it. So I bought the mouse at three times what I'd generally pay for a bug, took it home, and found it wasn't made of deer hair at all but of some product of modern chemistry I instantly hailed as a breakthrough. It was a breakthrough all right. The damned thing sank.

Not only did the fancy mouse sink, but it quietly rolled over on its back, which evidently gave bass a view of the lifelike eyes and ears. Thoroughly waterlogged after the third cast, it went through the air like a sockful of mush. That was an extreme, but beware of premium-priced bugs with excessive detail.

When the Dahlberg Diver bug became popular a few years back, I tried some made by a top-notch fly tier and experienced fisherman I'd known for a long time. They worked fine, so I ordered a batch from the catalog of a well-known tackle dealer, and they were so bushy that the original diving process was almost forgotten. This type of thing happens frequently with bass bugs. A dealer in top-quality flies buys from numerous suppliers, and in the case of a bass bug it's hard to tell what it'll do until it hits the water. So a new type of bug goes into the catalog along with known winners, and it may never have been tested. In the case of the diving hair gadget, we were breaking new ground, and without trying it you'd have difficulty telling what it would do. Diving bugs (streamers?) were something new. I did improve the mail-order gadgets with some hair cropping.

Lately I have seen deliberately ornate bugs selling at collector's prices, and they're examples of what a careful workman and expert tier can do if he takes plenty of time. Most of them will catch fish, but the things that make them exceptional generally don't help them attract bass. Some of them are intended as novelties to begin with, and their makers might be surprised to see them actually fished with.

There are two very common faults with commercial bugs. First is the use of feather, fur, mylar, or ordinary tinsel in such a way that they simply don't cast well or twist the leader as they go. Twisting is generally a result of mismatched wings. Hair that doesn't float, of whatever kind, is likely to soak up water and change the casting and working attitudes of a bug. Generally it's a matter of lying too low in the water. Before there were especially produced mylar strips for flys and bugs, many of us tried to make our own — and strips that are just a little too wide will set up incredible air resistance in casting. On the first cast you'll probably *hear* that something's wrong. And there are some commercial bugs that are just too blamed heavy—or not streamlined enough. Huge popping cups in the bug heads are simply a nuisance, as they aren't needed for all the noise you could use, and if they aren't slanted and balanced properly, they can hook under on the pickup, killing a cast instantly. It looks simple, but sometimes casting and fishing are the only ways to tell if a design will work. Takes time.

The second really big problem with bass bugs is their hooking qualities, which vary from here to there. The way to get into this problem is the old stunt of filling a basin with water, submerging your hand in it, and then dropping in a bass bug, after which you try to grab it quickly from underneath, from different directions.

One main problem of hooking fish with a high-floating lure is that it has probably been making considerable noise and displacing a lot of water in its action but actually weighs a skimpy fraction of an ounce. All of the power that makes it dart around, pop, and throw water comes from the leader manipulated by a person who may weigh two hundred pounds or more. If any creature was able to make all that fuss under its own power, it would have considerable weight, so when a fish strikes hard, it probably wouldn't be pushed away by the attacker's bow wave.

It is ridiculously hard to catch that water basin bug with your hand at best, so the size and position of the hook is more important than it seems at first, especially if the bug has a hard body. There is an ancient test for a lure's hooking qualities. Simply try to put the hook into a piece of screen wire. If it won't catch in the wire, it's too small, too short, or positioned wrong in the bug's body. Some of the worst of commercial bugs could catch only contortionist bass.

We go into great detail about "rise forms" where trout are concerned, but not much has been said about the way a bass hits or misses a surface lure. Actually, it's especially important, because the bass usually has to grab something pretty large in such a way that it doesn't hop away from his bow wake. Bass strikes are commonly described as blasts, smashes, or explosions. Some of them sound like that, but there are other approaches.

If he comes very hard and is near the surface, it's obvious he has a good chance of missing. If he comes more slowly, he can take the bug into his mouth without a loud chug. A bass coming to a bug from near the surface, or rising gradually from some distance away and taking his time, will usually make a distinct *plop,* but he will not scare the local herons. In this case the fish's mouth is actually around the bug before we hear anything, although we might see him coming. That makes for pretty good hooking.

If he comes nearly straight up from underneath and doesn't hurry, he may take silently, considerable water going through his gills and allowing the bug to stay fairly still until he closes his mouth. You should hook that one if he doesn't flip the fly away by bumping the leader. That take sometimes comes with a sucking sound, which I think indicates he takes the bug for a big insect or other food of minimal weight. If he comes up fast from beneath, he may knock the bug away.

Of course, if the fish hits when the bug is moving pretty rapidly, he'll probably come fairly fast regardless of where he started from. And a fish that has followed and watched a bug for a while seems more likely to take softly, simply because he has evidently sized it up and figures it won't get away anyhow. Some of the most heartfelt strikes come when a fish is in heavy cover and a lure arrives in a small opening to surprise him—but some of the least tumultuous attacks come when he is sorting a lure out of thick vegetation and has no desire to swallow a small lily pad along with it.

If a current is flowing pretty fast (more likely with smallmouth bass than with largemouths), the takes are more prone to be brisk, simply because the fish probably has a feeding station and doesn't want his prey to drift out of it. Some of the hardest strikes come when bass have been chasing bait and competing with each other—simply being programmed for quick action. Needless to say, they'll sometimes take strange lures at such times.

I think the leader plays a considerable role in many strikes, and if it is fairly taut, it will flip a bug away, even when a fish is sincere. With a stop-and-go retrieve, or with a bug that lies quiet for considerable time, there's no telling what direction the fish will come from. Even so, you can't afford to have a lot of slack. Many a fisherman yanks mightily long after the fish has abandoned the whole project.

There is no doubt that a fish is more likely to spit out a hard bug than a soft one, even though there are times when the cork or balsa bug appears to have been nearly swallowed. In some cases, I suppose, the fish is trying to discharge it through his gills, but that's hard to believe in the case of the bigger apparitions.

You can't keep a leader completely taut unless you have the lure moving constantly, but you should take up slack after each twitch or jerk. That becomes automatic after a little practice—but if you want the bug to lie completely quiet, it requires a little slack. I have repeatedly read that the lure should be manipulated only with the line hand, but I think there are few experienced bug casters who don't flick the tip of the rod a little, automatically taking up excess slack by hand. With the rod tip I can get a crisper twitch, necessary with some lures.

In fishing a bug, I keep the rod tip about horizontal to the water, but I do not keep it pointed quite straight at the lure. Being right-handed, I point it just a little to the right in anticipation of a strike. Maybe I can't move it more quickly that way, but I *think* I can, and I set the hook with a movement that's up and to the right. The strike is brisk and is made simultaneously with the line hand and the rod tip. A truly vicious yank can be effectively slower than a brisk lift, because it will cause the rod tip to momentarily bend toward the lure, giving an instant of slack.

The most common fault of beginning bug fishermen is to work the bug almost entirely with the rod tip, gradually lifting it until when there's a strike there's nowhere for it to go. Such victims wallow in slack line, trying frantically to get it back with the line hand—and they never do get a solid pull on the fish, who has probably spit out the bug and gone back to where he was first interrupted.

"Keeping the rod tip down goes against human nature!" grumbled one beginner. "I can work the bug a lot better with the rod than with my hand."

Anyway, it is absolutely essential that you keep the rod tip down on a retrieve, so you might as well get used to it, and it's ready to pick up for the next cast if there's no fish involved. I think hook setting with a bug is pretty tricky. The very nature of the operation means you probably have a little slack, and a fish isn't likely to hang on to a bug very long. A minor advantage of fishing open water close to heavy cover is that the fish will probably head back toward the place he came from as soon as he takes. Even in the delicate operation of dry flies for trout, a client is apt to take more time before spitting the thing out. With a bug, he's likely to learn pretty early in the game that he's made a mistake. One of the biggest advantages of the hair bug is that it's soft enough that the fish may hang on longer. Another advantage is that a soft body is less likely to interfere with hook setting.

There are weed guards on a large percentage of the bass bugs sold today, and many more are installed by fishermen after they buy them. Generally, it's one of three kinds of guard: hair, wire, or monofilament. The most common fault is in getting too stiff a guard, and there's an ancient indictment saying that "weedless" and "fishless" are the same thing.

In most weedy uses, the bug can be worked gently in what appears to be pretty heavy cover without hanging up, even if there's no weed guard at all. A very light one will ward off most grass as the lure moves gently. The main need for a heavy weed guard comes when the rod is yanked hard as a hangup seems imminent or is already felt.

Some strikes can be hooked, even if a very heavy guard is used, but others, sometimes with good-size fish, are warded off. A bug that uses only a sprig of hair for barb protection can't be worked very hard in cover, even though application of some glue will stiffen the guard considerably.

A loop of monofilament is popular for bugs with hard bodies. In most cases I've found that cutting the loop, leaving two flexible pieces of mono, will do the work. There are some good bugs that have wide, flat bases and work with the hook riding up. Except that they often tip over and must be balanced carefully, these handle much light cover. Remember that in most bass fishing, we're warding off weeds rather than rigid objects.

In fishing real hayfields you'll need to make short casts, of course, whenever possible, but there is a problem with interlaced vegetation below the water line. A wader or boat can cause a commotion far ahead, and the disturbance may not be visible to the fisherman. Even if it's easy to shove through the weeds, you'll be wise to keep to the open spots as much as possible to avoid an underwater chain reaction. A fish cannot help noticing if his whole environment is moving, and that can happen out to twenty-five or thirty feet in an extreme case. You'd better cast farther than that.

Lily pads are real bug grabbers, and trouble happens when a lure is pulled into the corner at the juncture of the stem and leaf. When that happens it generally means a trip to get loose, and yanking simply makes things worse. Strangely, after fishing such water a great deal, you subconsciously learn to lay your line in the places least likely to get you snagged up, even though it falls across the pads themselves. I went fishing in Florida's Lake Okeechobee with a fine caster who had never fished bass before and found that although we used similar bugs, he was constantly getting hung up in the pads. I'd guess he hung up several times as often as I did, and since I sure didn't feel I was a better caster, I watched carefully. He was simply picking a spot and casting to it without thinking of where his line would fall in getting his bug there. I realized I was picking a path for my line on each cast, told him so, and watched my superiority disappear.

When it comes to hook size for largemouth bass bugs, I'd say the range is generally from 3/0 down to #6. Although I have seen a very few

4/0 hooks on bugs, I've used very few larger than 2/0, and generally the very large hooks are heavy enough to change the attitude of the bug in the water. Some bugs with insufficient hook bite are obviously wearing those with shanks that are too short, especially important with hard-bodied models.

In Florida, where you might meet extremely large bigmouths occasionally, I have found medium-size bugs do just as well as huge ones on the larger fish. Charlie Wiles, who fishes weedy water and often has his bug working over eelgrass, has held three different International Game Fish Association fly rod records on black bass in different leader classes. All of them were caught on bugs with #2 hooks. And lately, he has been using the same kind of bugs with #4 hooks. Remember, big hooks are generally harder to set and almost certainly need sharpening.

I have used #2 hooks more than any other size, although there was once when I thought it was time to change. We had a big eelgrass flat where prespawners seemed to go to fatten up before the annual event, and plugcasters were catching them on really big stuff for several years. I tried to rig up bugs with silhouettes as large as the plugs, but all I got was more work in casting, for the fish I caught were no larger than the ones I'd been taking with #2s.

One of the creations I tried on that big flat was a very long streamer-bug I christened the Slosher. Using a long-shank hook, we tied a batch of hackle around the front, then followed it with a long, oval, cork body and tied in long tail feathers in the brightest colors we could find. It was pretty scary, even when dry, but it was no bigger than the Al Foss Hawaiian Wigglers and pork rind or the big spinner plugs that were killing big bass that year. When it went through the water, it was an undulating, creepy-crawling apparition I was sure would skim the cream of the big female bass. With this thing, barely floating when all those feathers were wet, I used appropriate tackle—a saltwater fly rod taking a Number Ten weight-forward line—feeling I was treading the edge of good conservation policy.

I never did catch a big bass on the thing, although I did produce some ominous swirls my companions insisted were probably made by curious alligators. I had fallen in with a bunch of plugcasters who treated me with kindly tolerance and a little pity. Then along came Ray Donnersberger, the man who had all those fly rod records in salt water and who had caught all of those trout and salmon all over the country. Ray hadn't done much bass fishing.

I took Ray down to the flat and we fished for hours across the eel-grass, visible almost everywhere we drifted, with tendrils breaking the surface. At one edge of the big flat was a long-abandoned pier, by then just a row of haphazardly leaning posts, and since it had been a very slow day, I figured we'd go in a little early after a brief check of that spot. I had issued Ray a #2 bumblebee-finish popping bug, and he had his only strike of the trip. He said the fish pulled pretty hard, and it was not surprising, since it weighed more than 8 pounds. Didn't jump but once.

While I figure a #2 bug is probably big enough for any bass, I also have a limit on the small end. I simply don't believe one smaller than #6 is likely to catch an outsize bigmouth. We frequently use what we call a "compromise bug" to catch a mixture of bass and panfish, generally #6 or #10, and although we've taken a great many bass with those, I know of only one really large one. My wife was working a #10 bug with rubber legs along a hyacinth bank and caught a 6½-pounder—the only bass taken on a day when there were plenty of bluegills.

One of the best bass bugs we've used in the larger sizes is a little crude. It's simply a "feather minnow" with the popping end forward and with rubber legs on each side, long tail feathers or bucktail back of that. The gimmick is simply that we have used it with very light wire hooks, allowing it to ride very high in the water. Long silhouette.

That bug, made as either a slider or a popper according to how the head is turned, has caught a lot of bass and without the rubber legs has done very well on several saltwater species. It wouldn't be a good commercial model, because the hook is as light as we can get and it doesn't look durable. It rusts away quickly in salt or brackish water.

The hair bug can be made a thing of beauty, and an expert tier can spin the hair so tightly that someone who has never seen one will feel of it to see if it's solid. I've caught a lot of smallmouths with those near-perfect ties, and they often work on largemouths, generally when they're being worked fairly briskly. "Tap" Tapply, who is an artist on hair bugs, insists that his beautiful creations, which show all the colors of the rainbow in tasteful bands, are made to look pretty but would work just as well if they weren't so smooth. There are cases in which ragged hair bugs will do better, but you can put rubber legs or other disfiguring things on Tap's bugs for the same effects.

Russell Francis, who ran a fly shop in Kansas many years ago, trained his tiers to make beautiful hair bugs, and when he gave me some rejects I was not exactly enraptured. They were a shaggy lot beginners had sweated over.

"Oh," Russell said. "The rejects are better than the good ones. They wouldn't sell in stores, but they'll catch more fish. Look at what those ragged edges do when you move one in the water. The good ones keep their shape."

Russell was right. The ragged hair bugs worked better. When a shaggy hair bug is twitched or jerked on the surface and then left to rest, there are endless tiny water currents moving as the individual hairs straighten themselves slowly. Many years later I was using some near-perfect examples of the tier's art supplied by a top-notch fly manufacturer. They were colorful, bouncy, and firm to the touch. They had slender hair tails, but the bodies were nearly solid. They floated high in the water.

We were fishing a largemouth lake where the fish had shown a preference for surface things, but it was a slow day, and except for some half-hearted swirls and a few bluegill strikes, the hair bugs hadn't produced. As an experiment, we tied some rubber legs to one of them, and business picked up immediately. So we ran a test with one rod using the original bugs and the other using the ones with added rubber legs. It was no contest, the rubber legs winning hands down, catching several bass to none.

Filled with self-importance and helpfulness, I contacted the manufacturer and told him that his bugs would be much more effective if he'd have some rubber legs installed—or leave some whiskery hair to wave in the water. He was duly appreciative of my attention, but he explained that he couldn't compete with other hair bugs if his looked ragged and said he'd continue to make them in the old artistic way.

There have been countless hair attractions that appear ragged and fuzzy and are great fish catchers, but most of them are not as well known as the neat and shapely mouse type, a simple matter of the fishermen outvoting the fish in many cases. The average angler seems to have more aesthetic taste than the bass has.

This tirade about fuzzy bugs is not quite original. The fishing writer Noa Spears was a little ahead of most of us in wanting bugs to be fuzzy. For example, he wrote, "Never cut the outer ends off the hairs if they seem too long as they are tapered and their wonderfully live appearance in the water is dependent on preserving the tapering end . . . cut off at the root end if you must reduce their length."

As I say, he beat me to this business a little, since he wrote these instructions in 1919. He was not speaking of the spun hair bug but of those with cork bodies. Same principle. They didn't use rubber legs in those days as far as I know.

These details aren't so important if you keep a lure moving, but a resting bug certainly appears alive if kinked rubber legs straighten snakily and individual hairs decide to separate from each other while a bunch of tiny bubbles show that the thing really is alive. There are days when the resting bug gets most of the strikes and tiny movements are a great attraction, giving an illusion of life. A bass may strike a weird thing—if he thinks it's living.

Some of the most ornate bass bugs have all the detail on top with nothing on the bottom but a hook and possibly a trademark, and it's obvious their eyes, scales, or whatever are made to please the fisherman rather than the fish. Laughing at them for that reason is good, clean fun, but it simply isn't true that the fish can't see anything above the water line. It's distorted, all right, but if there's any ripple at all, he can see the whole works in a strangely distorted way—and under almost any water conditions he's likely to see some reflection.

I don't mean he can note whether the eyes have lashes or not, and delicate scale finishes may be wasted on him, but he'll see the color of the upper part, whether it's hair, feathers, or enamel. There's nothing mysterious about this, and you can prove it by ducking under the water and looking at a floating lure.

The importance of bug color is good for all sorts of argument, and it's been argued for centuries whether fish can detect colors. The intellectual conclusion is invariably that they can see color but not as we see it, and the "as we see it" part makes it purely academic. I don't care what green looks like to him, but if he likes to eat green things, I'd like to show him a green bug. And on one Michigan lake, smallmouths didn't like a

Some of the elite bugs have prominent eyes as added attractions. These were tied by Randy Morgan of The Fly Fisherman in Titusville, Florida.

natural deer hair bug but struck white bugs as if there had been a shortage. That was proven, even if they insisted on gray next time.

There is no logical human reason for some of the colors that appear on surface bugs. Undoubtedly, many bass feed occasionally on green frogs, and the undersides of many baitfish are white or nearly so. There is the old story that red is the color of blood and should mean easy pickings, but I am a little doubtful as to whether bright orange is very common on the bass menu. Gray or tan can be accepted as mouse colors, although many a big bass has probably never seen an aquatic mouse—depends on where he lives. Bumblebee color, complete with black and yellow stripes, is the only enamel some bass fishermen will use—but I don't think bass eat very many bumblebees. Incidentally, one bunch of dedicated bass operators used nothing but bumblebee bugs for years and then went to frog finish exclusively.

This doesn't mean that certain colors aren't highly superior *sometimes,* but it's pretty hard to justify them. It's a little different below the surface, and the Scarlet Ibis wet fly was preferred by some bass fishermen almost a hundred years ago. I do believe that an assortment of several colors may be helpful in the long run, and it seems certain waters prefer certain ones most of the time. Some of the bright colors are touted because of their visibility, but unless the water's very murky and you're pulling bass up from great distance, I don't see how that's important. I personally like yellow and white bugs and frog-finish bugs, but I can't give good reasons—and I don't use fluorescent bugs much.

A great many bass strike a bug that has been perfectly still for some time, but few of us have that kind of patience. A. J. McClane once wrote that the ideal retrieve for a bass bug would take from twenty to forty seconds—and he knew how long that was. Few fishermen leave it on the water that long, and there is some sensible argument about it. If you leave the bug down for forty seconds, it sure limits the amount of water you can cover in an hour. So if the fish take well on a faster retrieve, you'll probably do better with it, and drifting boats sometimes limit your cast time anyway. Stop-and-go, even if the go is only slight movement, nearly always beats a steady retrieve, and today's routine may not work well tomorrow.

Still fishing a bass bug is almost unheard of, I suppose, but I encountered it under embarrassing circumstances on a small, weedy lake in the Midwest. I was alone, went to the lake with a cartop boat, and was launching it when another fisherman arrived with an obviously homemade skiff and a fly rod. He said he fished bass bugs.

The wind came up and I didn't have enough anchor for the cartopper, so I decided I'd just drift and cast over the weeds. The other fellow paddled out near the middle of the pond, put out his anchor, cast a hair-winged bug out about thirty feet, and poured himself a cup of coffee. He never twitched the bug or made another cast until a bass took. Then he put down his coffee and put the bass on a stringer.

I'd say the waves were running about six inches high, and I'll confess I was drifting a little too fast. I had exactly one strike, a good fish that came unbuttoned quickly. The still fisherman continued to string bass, good-sized bass, until he had all he wanted.

Now his bug was making a wake all of the time, and its hair wings and tail probably breathed a little, although the leader pressure was uniform. There may have been a special move as the bug came off the top of each wave, but it was anchored firmly and he didn't manipulate it at all. It may be he had some special knowledge of a bottom formation at that spot, but it certainly couldn't have been very prominent, as it was simply a shallow impoundment in prairie country.

Now there have been many times when a bass has struck a bug that I have left on the water for a while as I untangled my line, dug for a new lure, or looked for my sandwich. I've caught a number of these fish, although most of them had left by the time I could set the hook. I do not recall this happening on a stream, and I have always wondered how long a bass would study such a setup before striking. Does he do it in passing, or has he been watching for a while? Has he been sneaking up on it? Where are those scuba divers when I need them? I am sure that nearly all of us fish bugs too fast, but there's always the tradeoff concerning water coverage.

I believe there's a bug-working routine that's almost foolproof on still water, and it involves the imaginary bass I have cited from time to time in a childish approach to the subject. Cast the bug to where you want it and let it lie there for a while (make it ten seconds or so to begin with), and then retrieve it very gently for a foot or so. Then twitch it hard enough to produce a little plop or a quick movement, let it lie for a few seconds, and move it for two or three feet in your version of a swimming motion. Then pop it a little louder than before and let it lie for a few seconds. Finally, yank the stew out of it, making it dart, throw water, or both, and pop enough to scare a shorebird.

Thus you've pretty well explored the whole repertoire of manipulation, starting with the gentle touch and ending with a racket that may send the real or imaginary bass you're working on under the nearest rock. You've approached him gently to satisfy a desire for an easy meal; you've shown him that the thing will get away if he doesn't catch it; and finally, you challenge him to kill something that's tearing up his whole neighborhood. Any one of these stages is likely to raise a bass, and when you get rough with the bug at the end, there's no harm done if he panics, for you've given him those other chances and you're going on to another spot anyway. Any successful top-water fisherman is going to get bored if he doesn't think each cast is aimed at a particular fish, whether it's a real fish or not. Silly but true.

A lake fisherman going to moving water finds some new problems with bugs, but he finds some new possibilities for manipulation. One of the cuter tricks is a sort of supercharged dead drift involving a whole series of line mends to satisfy the most rabid dry-fly angler. You cast the bug upstream, and as it comes down with the current, you give it little twitches without changing its course more than absolutely necessary. The effect is something alive but overcome by the moving water and kicking feebly. To work it right you may have to do some fancy line mending; in effect, you may make two or three different "drifts" on the same cast.

Experienced trout fishermen will find that in most cases the bass likes a little more artificial action than trout want. In moderate flows you can simply retrieve a bass bug cross-stream with the usual starts and stops and catch fish, but I never had much success actually swimming a bug nearly straight upstream with twitches and tugs. That's a bit too far from natural, since few bugs are expected to represent a healthy creature likely to head upcurrent with a lot of splashing. I've always felt nearly all bugs represent something in trouble.

Underwater lures may come close to something real, but bugs tend to be purely impressionistic, and most of them bear little resemblance to any living thing except as to size and color. The few exact imitations I've seen didn't work well.

Bug action that catches fish today may cause an evacuation tomorrow. The most confusing situation comes when an unusual preference lasts for a considerable period, and there's a tendency to feel you've solved all the world's bass bug problems.

A beginning bug waver seemed to have the magic touch on one largemouth lake, and some veteran fly fishermen watched him catch several times as many bass as anyone else. They studied his approach, which could be heard as well as seen, for the man had completely skipped the niceties of fly casting. He thrashed the water, yanked his bugs into frightening blasts, ripped his pickups, waded like a charging bull moose, and cursed the bass, which he apparently considered the enemy. He kept catching fish.

After a head-shaking conference, the experts had to conclude that the commotion was what attracted the bass, and it continued to work for some time. Such occurrences assure that no one will ever be able to predict bass performance. There have been times when the slam-bang attack would have driven the fish into seclusion.

But the slash and smash approach is understandably related to what I call the "popping cork business." Saltwater anglers using spinning or plugging tackle have long used floats with popping cups when fishing natural baits. The idea is that the noisy cork attracts fish that think other fish are striking bait. The bait itself is suspended below.

I think the riotous approach of the greenhorn fly fisherman simply stirred up fish who thought their associates were in a bait-working orgy on the surface. I have always thought the louder popping lures represented striking fish rather than escaping bait. In plotting against gamefish, we tend to exaggerate their mentalities and minimize their instincts. On some days the extraloud popping sounds trigger a feeding program—but don't count on it.

A fly fisherman named Neil Allinger caught especially large Florida bass some years back, winning national contests. As far as I know, he always fished a large and noisy popper and used a small, nondescript trailer bug that followed soggily some eighteen inches to the rear. He said his strikes were about equally divided between the two, but some of the really big bass weren't interested in striking the big bug. The little one evidently looked more palatable.

There's no doubt that individual fish turn foolishly aggressive at times, and I was once attacked by a largemouth bass. I was paddling a little wooden boat while my friend was casting from the bow. It was dusk on a Midwestern river—so small a river that it wasn't running that hot, dry summer.

I rested on the paddle and trailed my fingers in the slightly cool water. The bass hit my hand pretty hard, but I was disappointed to find no abrasions to go with my story. That particular bass, which weighed about a pound, was on a real tear. I am sure it was the same one my friend caught on the next cast.

Now here we have a fish that grabbed a hand trailed from a ten-foot boat, apparently paying no attention to the paddle—or had the paddle brought him in the first place? How many bass in that pool had no interest in the boat or were afraid of it? If the hand grabber was always that gung ho, I doubt if he could have lived as long as he had.

With all the tiptoe approaches we employ in presenting flies to fish, I'm regularly amazed at the seeming stupidity of occasional fish—even good-size bass. When I was a kid, I set some bank lines for channel catfish on the old James River in Missouri. I was wading in fairly fast water and fastening short lines to springy undercut roots. In one place the bait wouldn't swing back under the bank, and thinking it might stay if I pushed it back there, I took hold of the hook shank and reached under the bank for a couple of feet. I thought I'd hung up on something, so I pulled the hook and bait back out—with a smallmouth bass attached. That shiner had looked so good he ignored the hand and arm. These instances of fishy bravado would seem to indicate wide-eyed and starving bass, but at the time fishing was very slow.

Someone built a casting lure called the Dying Quiver, and loose hair and writhing rubber legs produce something similar when a bug is at rest. Some of the very best presentations involve special attention to what the lure does then, with the theory that there should be some signs of life at all times. A. D. Livingston reports that he causes a bug to quiver by tapping his rod butt and that little jar *does* provide an effect hard to get any other way. You can do it with your line hand with very little effort. A dainty move can be made by simply tightening the leader on a resting bug.

When fishing a short line, it's possible to throw a half-hearted roll cast, which causes the bug to hop off the water and come back down, but it's hard to do without creating considerable fuss with the rolling line. I've seen bug operators who moved their rod tips from right to left and back again as they went through a twitching routine. That's fine on a very short cast, but if you have considerable line out, the minor change in the lure's direction is hardly worthwhile.

These things seem strange, I suppose, when advocated along with procedures that throw water and sound like shots, but the bass that attacks a 6-inch casting plug today may prefer a little fuzzy bug tomorrow. If there is a single rule for manipulation, it is that until a preference is established, variety is the logical way to go. I think changing bugs is often less effective than changing presentations.

In surface bass fishing, the leader goes from being completely unimportant to being a major factor. In weedy waters or when there's considerable wind disturbance on the surface, I think you can use almost anything that doesn't cramp the lure's style. But when the surface is calm and there's no thick cover, the leader becomes a major factor, especially in sunny weather.

Remember the fish you're after is probably no more than three or four feet deep—possibly only a couple of feet down. There's no doubt he can see a big leader either in the air or on the water—and although it may not bother him today, it may cause him to change coves tomorrow. Since we're speaking of pretty big material, I won't use the X designations but will stick to pound tests of monofilament. I think most largemouth fishermen tend toward something like 10-pound test, which shows up like a falling cable on a calm day but is very comforting when hauling fish out of their favorite garden plots. It is seldom that largemouth fishermen use anything much smaller than 6-pound test. In smallmouth fishing, requirements are sometimes much the same as those for trout, and 4-pound tippets are logical if the water is open and the flies are small. In addition to their visibility, extraheavy leaders restrict the action of anything you twitch, jiggle, or vibrate. With the more dainty surface things, some sort of loop knot is better than simply tightening up hard on the hook eye.

A shiny leader in the air doesn't appear very dangerous to me, but a fish doesn't get an especially good look at it and is likely to simply record a shiny thing several feet long. Flashing lines and leaders over shallows have frightened hundred-pound tarpon, and I figure they just get a distorted look at the rig and may take it for a twenty-foot-long osprey, simply noting the length in a sketchy view. I am sure bass do the same thing sometimes, although their retreats are not as notable as those of hundred-pound fish.

Very light leaders give trouble with big bugs, tending to fold up if a cast isn't exactly timed, and a little stiffness will straighten things out. Probably the best results come with a tapered leader of 7 feet or more. Many of us like to make up our own from varying lengths of monofilament, but any kind of knot is likely to give trouble in bass waters, picking up all sorts of debris and being a nuisance to clean.

Probably the best working outfit is a knotless taper. You can buy any kind of knotless tapered leader and then trim off the tip if it's too small. A heavy butt is helpful, and 25- or 30-pound mono there will help turn over the casts. Too small a leader butt forms a troublesome hinge where it's tied to the line, and if you make a sloppy cast, it folds. Most leader breaks come at knots, and it's generally a matter of neglecting to check them regularly. If they're trimmed close, they may work a little, and it's easy to ignore them for a season.

Anything as big as a bass bug demands some special casting methods. The bug taper lines pretty well take care of their part of it, but the caster taking his first whirl at bugs should remember he'll generally need a somewhat wider loop than that used for small flies. Just call it a "slower" cast. You can throw it a long way, all right, but it takes a little gear shifting. Feeling amateurish and clumsy, I once took a world-class trout and steelhead angler bass fishing. He had never thrown a bass bug. Maybe he was too good a caster. His timing had been adjusted to small flies (even though some of them had been weighted) through the years, and it was some time before he could adapt to the big bugs we needed for that particular spot.

At first he rebelled at the bugs, saying they simply wouldn't cast well, and he thought he'd use a small streamer. I finally got him to stay with the bugs for a while and things went better. Here was a case of a timing so strongly built in that it rebelled against the wind-resistant things. You can learn to throw big things all right as long as they aren't too heavy, but the smooth cast of a big bug has a resident curse: It simply can't be used for pinpoint accuracy when there is high wind. It's going pretty slowly and can be blown off course for two or three feet in a stiff breeze. You'll have to learn to allow for that as you go. I try to use something that's streamlined when the wind blows, and I frequently throw tight loops, which are extra work.

The ancient Dragon Fly bug, which I seem to be obsessed with, has its big wings straight out at right angles to the body and is an offshoot of the Callmac, I suppose. It's very hard to cast accurately in the larger sizes, tending to twist the leader and strike the water upside down, after which it may turn over as the leader straightens itself. No matter how seductive this spooky business is to the fish, I sure don't care for those widespread wings for really big bugs. The regular Callmac type (wings folded back) casts pretty easily.

The bullet-headed feather minnows (sliders) cast very well when properly built, and most of the hair bugs go easily unless allowed to soak up too much water. The hair diving rigs can get pretty sloppy with some of the exotic odds and ends used to decorate them. If the diving part works properly, the rest of the lure can be pretty water-resistant.

In all bug designs, we need to consider their planing qualities in the air. A big, bare hook doesn't cast well and works better when you build it into a well-designed lure. Within reason, the weight of a bug is a lot less important than its planing quality in the air when it comes to casting. If it's too big, the air resistance kills your cast. If it's too small and heavy, you're getting near the bare hook category. Anyway, good-size lures don't go well on rods with flippy tips. We need something that works pretty well down into the butt section, and probably the most representative big-bug rod would be a Number Eight about 9 feet long.

In most bug operations the high-floating line is a help, but there's a trick with a sinking-tip combination. With that, a floating bug will sit briefly on the surface and can be pulled under with a quick jerk. The effect you get is similar to that of a bug designed to dive, although the sink tip probably gets it deeper and gets it there quickly. This whole procedure depends on how buoyant the lure is, and the combination of leader, lure, and tip gets pretty complicated, but you can make the thing do a lot of maneuvers with proper manipulation and line choice.

A seldom-used setup involves a very small spinner ahead of a big, high-riding bug. Generally this rig is hard to cast and may make the weak of heart think rebelliously of spinning or plugging tackle, but it'll work if the spinner is light enough. A bug so equipped needs to be kept moving pretty steadily and a little faster than I like to retrieve surface things.

In many of these far-out methods, we again get into the question of whether some of them are fly casting or not, and there's a point where we're stretching things to be able to say we're fly fishing. With some fishermen it's a game of doing something with gear that wasn't intended for it, and with others even the larger bugs are suspect. They'll say you might as well be throwing a plug. I'm sure not taking a side in these arguments. I'm just pointing out some of the things that can be done with a fly rod—appropriate or not.

AS A GENERAL RULE, largemouth show a marked preference for grass beds and other forms of vegetation. They will go deep—and I've caught 8-pounders at 35 feet—but they don't usually go as deep as the smallmouth and the spotted bass. Because the largemouth is more likely, day in and day out, to hit on or near the surface, I'd have to rate it a tad above the smallmouth as a fly-rod fish. But a lot of anglers, and especially those who fish for smallmouth in streams, will take issue with that statement, and rather hotly so. . . .

I do have a definite opinion on which is the better bass for the *fly-rodder.* It's neither the largemouth nor the smallmouth. It's a little redeye, a relatively unimportant species that I will discuss in due course. . . .

The black bass is considered to be one of the more intelligent freshwater game fish in the country. I'm not sure, however, that intelligence is the right word, and anyone who thinks that a bass is smarter than he is will never have enough confidence to make an expert fisherman. I think that too many anglers overrate the intelligence of bass—and underrate their senses. . . .

In my opinion, no bass boat is complete without at least one depth finder aboard . . . Although the fly-rodder will usually fish in rather shallow water, depth finders are still very helpful. . . .

A.D. Livingston
Fly-rodding for Bass

SIX

A Little Deeper

UNDERWATER OPERATIONS CAN be very simple—a matter of just casting something and bringing it back—but the complications can be endless, crafty, and a bit scientific, so I'll give you an example.

Forrest Ware, a successful fly fisherman for bass, starts with a built-in advantage: He is a fisheries biologist. When he announces a fishing procedure, I listen very carefully and with due humility. He said he had a method for working an artificial pit in central Florida and it was working very well. He added that for a time it had been touch and go, with disappointing results, but that he had worked out something a little different. So I drove a hundred miles, thankful that this trip had not called for my meeting him at some out-of-the-way crossroads at 2 A.M.

It was an ordinary artificial pit, produced in phosphate-mining operations. There was a fringe of weeds around the edge, and there was a pair of small islands. The boat was rather ordinary, with an electric motor and more gasoline engine than was needed for such a spot. Forrest stopped the big engine in what appeared to be open water, although not too far from the shoreline. He made a cast with something that looked pretty big and black, and he took on the expression of someone dealing with the occult, staring fixedly at where his line sank well up ahead. I realized it was a sink-tip outfit. It would have been less fun to ask questions. He said the water was nine to twelve feet deep.

Forrest's conversation then became rather spotty and took on the dreamy tone of someone thinking of something else and trying to be polite. I threw a popping bug about the place, getting nothing but casting practice. Forrest nursed his line with his fingertips, and I thought of asking him if he had sanded them but thought better of it. He lifted his rod tip, it bowed jerkily, and a 5-pound bass jumped well out from the boat. I used the net and had a look at what Forrest was using.

It was a line with a fast-sinking tip, clean dressed so the floating part sat high on the water. At the other end of the sinking tip were a few inches of lead-core line. Then came a short leader, stepped down in two sections, and a huge, burr-headed, black streamer, 7 inches long.

Forrest continued to catch bass, carefully putting them on a stringer. For once, he said, he was going to show a really heavy stringer of bass caught with flies. I gave up on the bugs, and Forrest asked me to act as a control, using a baitcasting rod.

"I want to test this method carefully, and this is an ideal setup for a worm fisherman. You fish the worm, and if you catch a bunch of fish while I'm not getting any, I'll know my setup needs changing," he explained.

Not only was that an overly formal statement for Forrest, but it also carried what I thought was a bit of overconfidence. Also, while I have the utmost regard for plastic-worm operators, I just don't get too excited about that kind of fishing. Nevertheless, I dutifully started humping the worm along the bottom with great care. I caught bass, too. But in areas where Forrest didn't catch any, I didn't catch any either, so I was helping prove his method. As a matter of fact, I caught one fish that weighed 9 pounds and something, but I was a lot more excited over what he was doing, and I figured I could use a sinking fly line very gently and do just as well.

So I tried the sinking line and never felt a strike, having to agree with Forrest that his setup with the floating section of line detected takes that I simply couldn't feel with my rig. The key to success lay not only in working right at the bottom, but also in getting some indication that a fish was chomping on the lure. I still wish I knew if I had many unfelt takers.

When Forrest had a real wrist cracker of a stringer of bass, he had me take a picture of them, recorded the whole bunch as to weight and length, and released them carefully. The whole thing was scientific, all right.

Now that bottom was ideal for working with that sort of lure. The lure went very slowly and seldom got hung up. The exact design of the streamer may not have been important except for one thing: Its head was made of hair and was softly chewable. What he had was a sort of giant, black Muddler Minnow with a very long fuselage. He explained that the nameless giant felt lifelike enough that the fish would take it into their mouths and be slow to put it down, sending chewy messages to the floating fly line. I think very small strike indicators popularized by nymph fishermen might be a help in some cases.

I don't think it was critical, but the hook size was 1/0. It wasn't a delicate leader, Forrest feeling its length wasn't critical, and it was 20-pound test, stepped down to 12-pound test. I am not introducing this as a method that will work everywhere there is a fairly smooth bottom. My whole point is that underwater fishing can be a highly technical business, and fooling a largemouth can be just as touchy as catching a thoughtful brown trout. Only a handful of serious fly fishermen will go into this type of venture, which has endless controllable factors to fit endless slightly different fishing situations.

It may be an anticlimax to the story, but I want to make a point with something else that happened. Remember, I had almost worn out my rod grip throwing popping bugs everywhere I could see a little bit of vegetation and had not had so much as a looker. As we were getting ready to leave, Forrest saw something move over by a half-drowned bush on one of the little islands. Up to that point he had caught nothing on top-water lures, but the little boil by the bush looked interesting; so he threw a popping bug over there, and a bass took it as if he had been waiting all day for it. It weighed more than 5 pounds, and my point is that a bass fisherman doesn't do his best wearing blinders. No matter what had gone before, *that* bass was ready for a bug, and Forrest saw it.

Bottom bumping with a fly rod is a pretty complicated operation. One setup that's almost unheard of is a sinking line with a short leader and a floating fly or bug. When the line sinks to the bottom, the floater holds the leader up and can be worked along at a measured depth, dependent on the leader length. That takes thought and patience, things I am often a little short on. And some of the sinkers and sections of lead-core line used by bottom bumpers can be replaced by the variety of sinking tips now available. Floating lures can be made to do a lot of things when held below the surface. Fly lines are expensive, but the true experimenter can achieve almost unlimited depth control and lure action.

While many underwater flies are tied to represent specific living creatures, there are certain moves that seem to have attraction in themselves, regardless of the lure. Probably the most productive of all is what I'll call "jigging action." The original jigs were evidently used several thousand years ago, but the more modern operations gained recognition only a few hundred years ago when the blue water commercial fishermen jigged lures straight up and down for all sorts of saltwater fish. Some of these up-and-down gadgets carried natural bait with them, and others were just jigs with scant decoration or none at all.

Use of jigs by name in fresh water is a very recent thing, and I can recall when a saltwater angler ventured into black bass territory and confessed that on a slow day he had tried a jig, bringing forth considerable merriment from his friends. Just a few years after that, various kinds of jig lures became common for bass. Other freshwater fish had been victimized by the up-and-down moves long before that.

It's a little difficult to explain why the jigging action attracts bass, since I can't think of many bass foods that do their navigation in a vertical plane. The best I can do is guess that when a supposedly living object starts toward the bottom, it appears out of control and possibly seeking a place to hide. One of the wildest demonstrations of the jig fly I have ever seen occurred forty years ago on a pier at Lake Monroe in central Florida.

I was spending the night in a Sanford motel just a couple of blocks from the pier, and I stepped out toward the lake to get some air. I wasn't a Florida resident, and the hot midsummer was crushingly humid for me. The pier was dimly lighted, and there were no boats tied up there. Some wild splashing and a single human figure at the pier's edge got my attention, and I almost ran to see what was going on.

The guy on the pier had a little cane pole ("cracker pole" in local parlance) and was heaving on it. The water was several feet below him, and as I arrived he hoisted a big largemouth bass into the light, unhooked it, and threw it into a pile of incredibly big bass lying behind him.

"Wind blew hard against this place all day," he explained, "and smashed all kinds of minnows against it. I was just tryin' to catch me a couple of speckled perch [crappie] and I found out there was every damn big bass in the lake stacked up down there. I had some little old speck flies, but I've busted most of them off. I can't hoist the real big ones!"

He would just lower his fly to the water and pump it slowly up and down as he walked along the edge. I watched him grimly break off his last "speck fly" and throw his pole down near his feet. I figured then that Florida must be a sort of fly fisherman's dream world. Things have changed and Lake Monroe hasn't been much of a bass lake lately, but I always grin when I drive on the busy street that passes the old pier.

I doubt that many bass fishermen actually jig their flies straight down, but any stop-and-go retrieve of any streamer or nymph includes a series of periods in which the lure starts to sink a little. This little dip seems attractive to all sorts of game fish. Regardless of the pattern for bass streamers, I believe a heavy head helps produce the jigging action, however slight. When I add lead to any streamer, I want it at the front end, and I think the addition of heavy imitation eyes help the action of an otherwise unweighted one. Remember, though, that we're still fly fishing and this is very little weight we're dealing with.

Without even mentioning streamer patterns, we can note some other generally attractive features. The "breather" streamers have two or more long feathers tied so that they tend to curve slightly outward when the lure is dry and at rest. As they are pulled through the water, the feathers go straight back, and when there's a pause, they bend outward in a lifelike movement. They "swim" or "breathe." If they're properly flexible, they offer little resistance in casting and aid in the streamer's planing qualities. The hackles forming a streamer's collar have their own way of breathing, and they too get in their licks when there's a pause in the retrieve. They begin to straighten and then flatten down again as the pulling is resumed. Many hair flies made to use down deep have loose hair ends that definitely breathe as the thing is worked. They might look prettier without them.

There are what I call "lineside" flies (I have to call them something). Here again is an imitation of nature, however crude. In rather conventional bass streamers, I like to have a dark line of some kind running along the side. Assuming the streamer pretends to imitate a baitfish, we remember a great many species have a lateral line that shows pretty plainly. Some of the streamers I like best for fairly rapid retrieves have streaks of peacock herl down their sides. Others have a darker area gained by a choice of other feathers or hair.

There are a lot of scale finishes on floating bugs, and, though we don't paint scales on feathers, there are many mottled ones that may give an impression of scale "patterns"—that is, they give a blotchy appearance a little similar to the uneven colors of some live fish.

"Exact imitation" is no more practical in bass fishing than with trout. Through the years, for example, the most successful casting plugs have looked like nothing that ever lived, and the scientific souls who have tried to fashion casting lures or flies by making duplicate casts of actual flies or minnows don't have a very good batting average. Evidently an "impression" is better than an exact imitation, but some of the impressions are eerily lifelike, especially when in motion. Some of the best may represent something alive but nothing that ever lived. Forrest Ware's aforementioned enormous, black, creepy, crawly thing is an example.

There are thousands of streamers with local names and dozens nationally known. One reason is that they're very easy to tie. Since most of them represent nothing in particular, it's a good place for imagination and strange components. Early in my smallmouth career, I was told the Gray Ghost pattern was a good one, and it caught fish for me, all right. But somewhere along the line I thought it needed something more and something less, and I ended up with a nameless thing that caught bass pretty well in specific instances, although it was probably not as good as the original pattern for general use. Now I can't find it in my fly boxes, and I've forgotten what my dramatic breakthrough was supposed to be.

The old, traditional patterns are often spiced up with tying materials that weren't around when they were first introduced. Generally the additions are made to produce more flash. Early in the mylar business, we cut up some sheets of it to make gleaming bodies and folded wings for some streamers. It shines, all right, but unless the pieces are very small, it becomes an abomination to cast; if you want some extra glitter, you'll do a lot better with the strands sold for the purpose by dealers in fly components. To work properly, mylar has to be used in very narrow strips. Just a little too wide and your casting goes to pot. In fact, any streamer that makes much noise as it passes overhead is setting up wind resistance—and flutter is worst of all.

Similar to trout fishing, the deep nymph or streamer is worked in fairly rapid water for smallmouth bass. This angler deals with a variety of current speeds and depths.

Flashabou is probably the best-known name for mylar strips to be used for flies, and it comes in a great many colors, even some that glow in the dark. But any that we have added to streamers have generally been silver or gold. A more recent kind of glitter strand is Krystal Flash, which carries reflective bubbles in its makeup. It comes in both solid and pearlescent colors, and you can get it in fluorescent, too.

Some of the best streamers my friends and I ever used were fashioned from Pogo hair, a white and rather shiny material that held together well under hard use. Unfortunately, after a long and illustrious career, Pogo passed to his reward, and my fishing friend replaced him with another dog whose hair had no particular attraction at all.

I guess my favorite streamer is the Silver Outcast, which is a modified form of the ancient Silver Doctor and has changed with the addition and subtraction of various things through the years. I certainly didn't invent it, although I chose the name when the late Dan Bailey said the streamer I was using, which I thought was a Silver Doctor, didn't look like any Silver Doctor he ever produced at his fly shop. The Outcast just developed on its own. It has a white, blue, and yellow bucktail wing; a silver mylar body; and wing topping of peacock herl, which makes a fishy streak down the side as the streamer travels. I like it tied pretty skimpily, and it casts easily, looking like no baitfish in particular and a lot of them in general. It takes no master craftsman to produce it.

Streamers represent two distinct classes of bait: those that are likely to be at midlevel or near surface and those that are found almost entirely

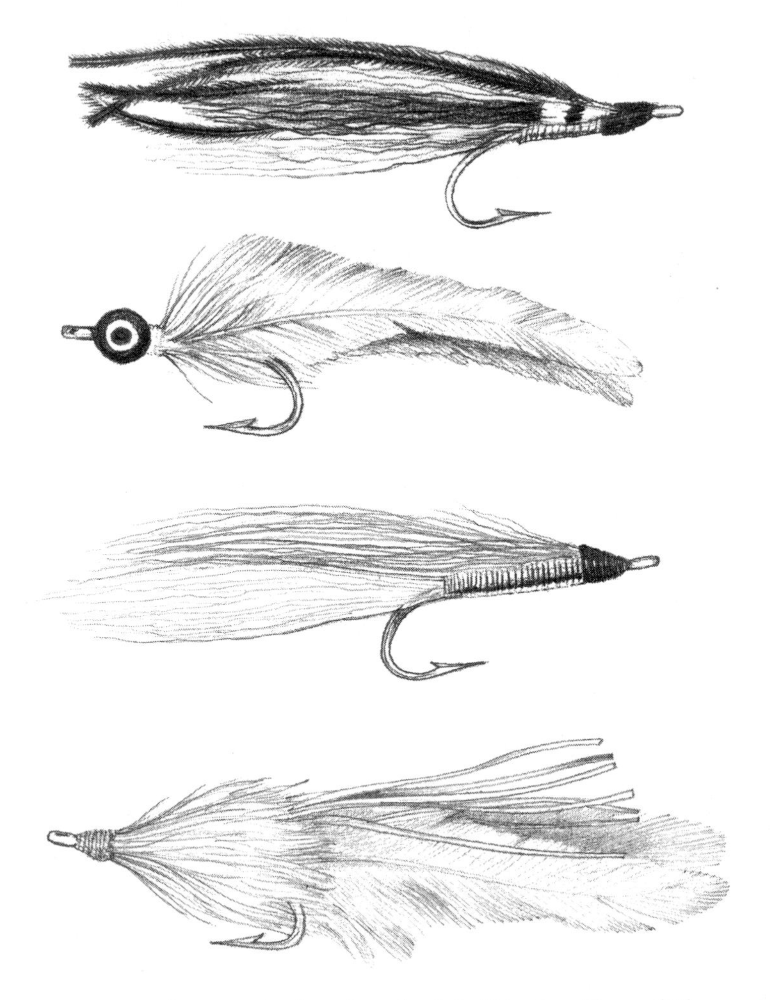

Bass streamers are often very simple and can be tied efficiently with very little experience. The one at top is a Silver Outcast, a simplified version of the Silver Doctor. The bottom streamer is one of the Blonde flies popularized by the late Joe Brooks and made completely of hair with two sections for added length.

near the bottom. The ones used over shallows have considerable color, usually have an overall light appearance, and are generally retrieved at fast or moderate speed. They represent a great many baitfish and the young of a number of game fish. The shiners fall into that class, as do the shad, chubs, and an assortment of panfish from green sunfish to bluegills.

Streamers (?) in the other general class are meant to imitate the colors, actions, and shapes of things that live on or near the bottom. The one perhaps most mentioned is the sculpin (also called a "bullhead"), because it was the inspiration for the Muddler Minnow, which is a streamer, a bug, or a nymph, depending on how it is tied or used. Most of the deep-working things are fairly dark in color, as the bottom-dwelling fish, nymphs, and whatever.

Generally, fishing a near-surface streamer is much simpler than operating something that follows the bottom. Much of the time you can pretty well see what your streamer is doing, and most strikes, if not seen, are generally felt pretty promptly. When you work the bottom, you need a gentle touch, a great deal of patience, and even a little extra imagination. Good bottom bouncers aren't likely to be very strong on nature watching while they fish, and they wear bemused and faraway expressions. Very poor conversationalists.

A conventional streamer that goes no more than two or three feet below the surface in still water is generally stripped fairly fast, about one pull by the line hand for every second and a half. That really isn't as fast as it sounds. As in working bugs, the line is pulled under a finger of the rod hand, and there's a pause between strips, which can be accentuated by use of the rod hand. In some kinds of fishing, it's considered bad form to move the rod tip while stripping. But in bass fishing, as my line hand ends its downward and sideways pull, I generally flick the rod tip upward and to the right a little, giving a moment's slack in which the streamer generally makes a little dip toward the bottom, an abbreviated jigging effect. Of course, some streamers have a little side-to-side motion of their own. In some cases this actually becomes a wiggle that demands longer and faster strips.

With unweighted or very slightly weighted streamers, the depth is largely controlled by speed of the retrieve, and many of them never get more than a few inches beneath the surface. Some fish are caught while

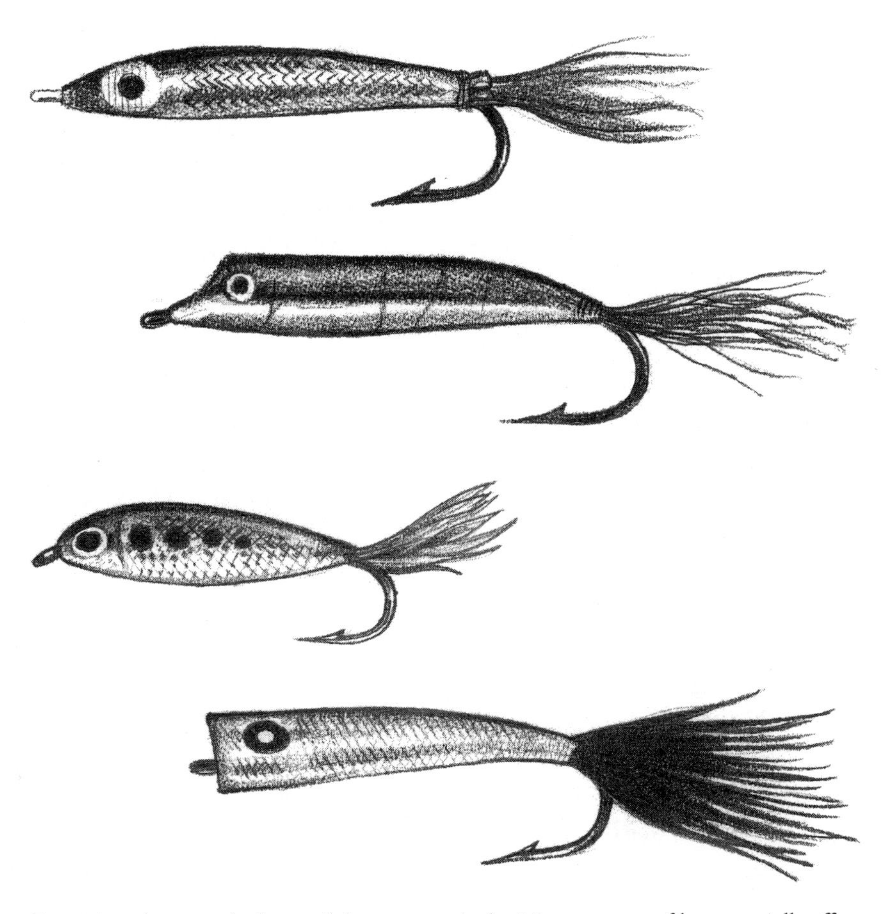

Somewhere between the bug and the streamer is the Marm, a type of lure especially effective when schooling bass are striking small bait. Made from a variety of materials, some of the most artistic are done with quill bodies.

the streamer is sinking, immediately after it strikes the water. If you let it sink for a few seconds, a single quick flip of the rod tip and tug by the line hand is likely to get action from a curious fish that has been standing by and apparently thinks the thing is escaping. These maneuvers become a little more complicated when the water is moving fairly fast.

Generally fifteen or twenty feet of operation will enable you to get all there is to be had from a surface bug, going from dainty quivers to strident pops, but you may want to move a streamer a lot farther. On quiet water I generally end up making longer casts with streamers, so that after working one for some distance, I still have room to pick it up and throw again with a minimum of false casting. Its depth is likely to change greatly as you bring it in. There's the business of letting it sink and possibly feeding it a little line immediately after it strikes the water. Then most streamers won't go much deeper and will start coming up as they near the rod tip—so if you pay attention, you can work one through a considerable range of depths on the way in. You can even violate that often-screamed rule of rod operation and put the tip up pretty high as the lure nears the pickup point. You have a fairly tight line, and it isn't like gathering up a lot of slack after you do get a strike.

You're constantly checking depths in your stillwater streamer operations. There are many times when suspended fish simply don't want to go up or down. I got a lesson in that on a new impoundment in California. I got out of a boat and was casting from a steep, rocky shoreline when I saw a small school of largemouth bass cruising about forty feet out from the bank and about six feet deep. The water was clear, the sun was just right, and the fish paid no attention to me but moved past me fairly slowly and without pause.

With my usual composure, I slapped my streamer just ahead of them as if trying to kill a snake. That didn't give it a chance to sink before they had tooled on past, and they seemed not to notice it. I stood on my boulder muttering to myself, but what happened next reminds me of that old quote from the poem *Casey's Revenge:* "And Fate, though fickle, sometimes gives another chance to men."

The bass were coming back, all six of them, sliding along in water almost as clear as air, still about six feet deep. This time I threw well ahead, and when the fish arrived, the streamer was only a foot or two above them. One of the 2-pounders rose lazily and gulped it. I congratulated myself upon my good fortune and brilliant casting, but by the time I had unhooked and released my fish, the other five were coming back.

This time I was a little sloppy and the streamer didn't get down far enough. But when they came by a third time, I caught a second fish, and some time later I hooked one of the last two to swim by. The lone survivor shoved off, obviously noting something was not right about that area. It was a perfect example of fish insisting on a lure being within a foot or two of their depth—and in water clear enough that they could see the lure for fifty feet or more. It was the cleanest lake water I can recall catching bass in, water that was being backed up from mountain rivers as the impoundment filled. I don't think the kind of lure was important. Depth was.

With streamers, the various types of sinking tips and whole sinking lines really begin to come into their own, and leader length becomes important, aside from deceiving the fish. I was lucky on that California lake to have a setup that would sink far enough fast enough, and I had a good day despite my simian blunders. There are faster-sinking lines today that would have made it simpler, but I had a lure and line heavy enough to do the job. Lest we get carried away, though, I don't believe I caught another fish that day. It was no magic depth—just the depth that little bunch of cruising fish preferred. That's interesting in itself.

I recall the two dead-serious bass fishermen who were working a small river and wanted to rake the bottom. So one of them stood on a high bank across from the other, who did the test casting with various streamers. They learned a lot, but both of them were surprised. A sunken lure is seldom doing what you wishfully think it is. I learned a few things ,just watching and listening to them.

It's easier to do it most of the time with sinking tips of various densities, which can be quite an investment, but there are times when you need weighted flies in moving water, and a weighted streamer or big nymph that goes down fast requires some special methods in casting—methods that many fly fishermen feel simply aren't worth fighting. For the loyal few who are willing to do things the hard way in the name of keeping the reel below the hand, I'll elaborate.

Strip casting with a fly rod is simply throwing a heavy lure or bait by peeling line off the reel and then shooting it with the weight of whatever you want a fish to take, and it has been done with everything from wooden plugs to live minnows. It isn't really fly fishing, of course, but it does use fly tackle. True fly casting, though, is concerned with the weight of the line, and the fly goes along for the ride.

When we cast heavily weighted streamers or nymphs, there's just a little of the strip-casting business mixed with true fly casting. The weight of the line is still the prime mover, but the heavy lure has a lot to do with direction and distance. Jim McLennan, the Alberta fly rod master, is one of the best at fishing weighted flies and has done a good job of instructing on the subject. McLennan, who doesn't beat around the bush on such things, says that two necessities for that type of fishing are shockproof eyeglasses and a hat or cap, for you'll hit yourself with the thing sooner or later. And he wrote that you should always use a fairly long rod in case of a miscue.

You'll probably use the same rod you use for your other streamer fishing, and it shouldn't have a tippy action. The line should be as heavy as or a bit heavier than that ordinarily recommended for your rod, and when I get into the heavy-lure business, I feel a little the way I did when I used to throw tandem spinners for bass. Keep an open loop and don't hurry.

In casting, you tilt the rod a little away from your person, but I wouldn't try to sideswipe except in dire circumstances, when obstacles are reaching for you. The tip is tilted away so that if there's a flub, the heavy thing won't find your ear. Now you start the cast with a sort of exaggerated pickup. It's always necessary to start the pickup slowly and get the line and lure moving well before they come off the water, but you can get by with a little sloppiness as long as the fly isn't heavy. With a heavy streamer or nymph, the timing must be precise, and as you feel it gaining speed, you soon learn just when to hurry the pickup to throw your backcast. You make the loop go high and wide in back, and your forward cast must start just when the loop begins to straighten out, for after your forward cast starts, the heavy thing will head down the instant tension slacks off.

On the fishing cast, the fly probably won't go as high as you feel it will, as there's not much planing involved. It wants to drop. If you aim an ordinary fly three feet above your mark, aim the heavy one about nine feet up. On the fishing cast, resist the temptation to drive too fast too hard, because your cast will then go too low. All of this sounds very complicated, but a competent caster will do pretty well with very little practice. I wouldn't want to make a career of throwing heavy flies, but there are times when it helps, and on the next trip you can get back to conventional moves.

A lot of bass fishing, especially largemouth fishing, is done at the very edge of above-surface cover, ranging from lily pads and algae blankets to half-sunken logs. Many streamer fishermen make beautiful casts to such edges and then don't show the fish their lures at all. Assuming the fish is under the obstacle and a streamer strikes right at the edge and moves away immediately, the lure may be several feet from the cover before it goes down near the fish's level. He probably isn't interested in going that far for it.

The remedy is simple: Allow the thing to sink a little before retrieving. It's slightly different with a surface bug, since it may make considerable disturbance before it moves more than a few inches and may "call up" a fish. Even so, it's common to work a bug too close to some kinds of cover, and the fish "back under" isn't interested. He can't even see it.

Even when we aren't dealing with current, it's possible to do a spectacular job of casting to cover without showing the lure to the occupants. A fallen tree is the outstanding example, as the fish are likely to be under the trunk and the larger branches. If the layout permits, you can cast over and past the cover and gradually work the streamer deeper until it reaches the edge, then let it sink with a few twitches, which is the jigging effect—in spades. Hundreds of years of fishermen have noted that fish taking jigs generally strike when the lure is sinking.

I've always felt that a weed guard on a streamer could be a little stiffer than those used on bugs, simply because I think a fish is more likely to take a streamer well into its mouth, while a bug has all sorts of ways of escaping. You can watch a bug pretty well and steer it gently away from obstacles much of the time, but the streamer is operating on its own and finding things down there that you haven't seen. When a streamer bumps something, you try to set the hook into whatever it hit, whether it's a bass or a stump, and a good weed guard may help some.

In moving water, especially on the brisk smallmouth streams, streamer use is complicated, but you have some fish-catching options provided by the current itself. There's the dead-drift business, which in the case of bass probably isn't a dead drift at all. You cast across some likely water that's moving pretty well, and although you want the streamer to go with the flow, you want it to appear alive. This can involve a lot of line mending (flipping your line upstream or downstream without taking the streamer out of the water) in order to keep the thing from swinging clear out of the fish picture. I have found that bass usually ac-

In "bonnet water," waders have distinct advantages over boats, as a little commotion from a boat can be telegraphed for long distances.

cept more twitching and darting on a drifing object than trout care for. This is different from the dead drift of a trout dry fly. If you're fishing current and aren't particularly concerned with a dead drift, casting up and across can give a very different effect from casting down and across. And you can always mend.

True undercut banks are hard to fish, because, much as they look alike, they all seem to handle the current a little differently. It's pretty hard to cast a streamer so it will actually swing back into an undercut, although you can often manage it. I have caught more fish at the edge of the undercut than back in there, though I can't say exactly why. The best guess is that the fish is lying (the accepted word is "lurking") in the undercut and is actually watching for food coming by in the open. From a boat, the undercut is a tough assignment, because whatever your means of propulsion—motor, oars, or paddle—you'll probably have trouble getting anything back past the edge without more commotion than a marine landing. If you're wading, you can use more finesse and can actually watch a leaf or twig to see just what the current is doing.

"Reading" moving water can be complex, but there are some obvious things you shouldn't miss. A boulder in the current has a pad of somewhat slower water upstream from it, and a streamer should swing past that or drift twitchily into it. There is a patch of either dead or confused water below a boulder, and bass will hold there, although the *edge* of the undecided water is better than the part directly below the boulder. The theory is that the fish hold below the rock but are looking for things that drift by to right or left. Anywhere two current speeds run together you may get what the intellectuals call a "seam," and there is likely to be holding water where a fish can comfortably await food.

Nymphs are simply immature insects living underwater. Smallmouth bass are frequently caught on them, of course, and largemouths sometimes, but most of that type of fishing for bass is simply a matter of using a deep-going thing that acts like a nymph. For smallmouths I have fished some true nymph imitations, but for largemouths (usually in stillwater) I have leaned toward imaginative offspring of the Woolly Worm and snaky things with fuzzy heads. Some of them were frankly designed to take the place of the plastic worms that have revolutionized spinning and plugcasting.

Most fly fishermen for bass have at one time or another tried to cast a plastic worm with a fly rod. In my case it was hard both on the plastic worm and my disposition. Sure, it will work. Using a sinking-tip line or a full-sinking line, you can lob one of the smaller worms and retrieve it well enough to catch bass, but this turns into a sort of tip-toe strip casting and I classify it as a stunt.

The San Juan Worm is generally quite small, works well in some

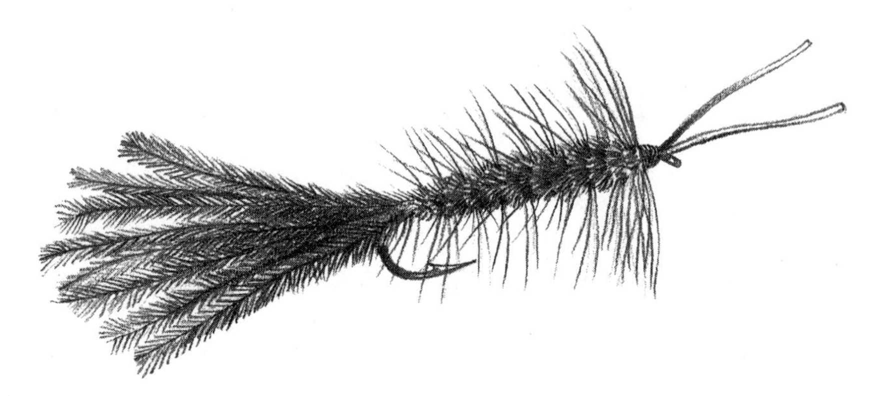

A Woolly Worm with rubber feelers and a feather tail becomes an imitation hellgrammite, but the creepy-crawly characteristics of these deep-going flies will work on bass and panfish in areas where the living hellgrammite isn't present. The real thing is the larva of the dobson fly.

trout situations, and will catch bass. It can be cast, but in making it tough enough to stay on the hook, I'm afraid they've lost some of the squashy, squirmy look and feel preferred by bass. I have no doubt there will some day be a material that works, but I don't care much for that kind of fishing. Fishair (a commercial product that came from what we used to call "doll hair") has a breathing look in the water and can be cast in long, wormy lengths.

Deep-water bass lures are generally dark in color, as are most of the weird little things that live near the bottom. Generally, we're told, a fish can see something black down there better than it can see colors, and we know that colors begin to lose their definition as they go down. It has been proven repeatedly that black streamers work well at night on many varieties of game fish, especially when they're at or near the bottom. I suppose if the water is stained or clouded by suspended material, the black lure is more visible.

When it comes to the matter of a lure being audible down deep, we're pretty confused. Sound is vibration, we're told, and that's closely related to anything that sets up little currents in water. The fish's lateral line accepts all sorts of vibrations and possibly some sensations of which we have no idea at all. My point is that in dark water, a bass may hear or feel lure movement from some distance. While he can undoubtedly make out all sorts of vibrations from a metal, plastic, or wooden lure, I doubt if he can "feel" the gentle waving of rubber legs or a feather tail. There is no doubt that bass somehow sense the presence of some lures in water so muddy they certainly couldn't see them. Fish can be caught occasionally in that muddy water, but the specialists think the lure has to pass very

The original Woolly Worm has been altered into a wide variety of deep-going lures, most of which vaguely imitate some sort of nymph and some of which come very near to the real thing. Some of the vague but fuzzy creations will work on bass and panfish almost anywhere.

close to them and go very slowly. Slow movement is the first requirement of deep fly rod lures where there is no current.

Ninety percent of underwater bass lures are cast toward cover and worked away from it. That's often the only way we can do it from a boat or when wading, and most banks aren't very good as casting platforms. Very few American fishing streams or lakes have manicured shorelines. I love what I once heard a British angler say:

"I have been to the Rocky Mountains, where the Americans walk right up the middle of the rivers. Right up the middle of the bloody rivers!"

It isn't possible most of the time, but the logical retrieve of a lure is toward cover rather than away from it, for we assume most living food is looking for a hideout. When I can wade to a floating bed of algae, a patch of grass, or a midstream island, I like to cast from it and retrieve toward it, especially when there's running water. Fish holding at the edges of current are used to seeing their prey heading toward concealment. I think it's more important with streamers than with bugs. On southern rivers, this works with hyacinth jams—and in these cases you can often push a light boat to a good casting site.

Raking an underwater lure of any kind along the edge of a bank of weeds or other cover can be deadly, although you may have trouble holding a fish out of the stuff. In moving water, I think it's more logical to work the lure downstream, even though it's more trouble and makes hookups harder. Most lures represent something unlikely to go sprinting upcurrent.

Wherever possible, underwater lures should be presented broadside to the fish, and it becomes a delicate operation in moving water. Dead-drift techniques, which have reached their peak in trout streams, are generally somewhat modified for bass. Few bass fishermen cast straight upstream and hope to keep a reasonably tight line on a nymph sliding down toward them—and the stop-and-go type of retrieve is a pretty good compromise. You simply cast the fly upstream at an angle, let it dead-drift for a little way, and then tighten up so it does the same thing again but changes its attitude in the water. You do this several times until it swings below you, and if you're wading there is a point directly downstream where you'll get quite a few strikes—even though the thing isn't behaving naturally and appears about to go against the current. My learned explanation for this is that the fish has been following the nymph through a couple of route changes and is shaken into action when it suddenly stops dead still and holds against the flow. It sure isn't a natural situation.

When truly bouncing a nymph on the bottom, you'll need a pretty short line, and I have no idea what percentage of drifting-nymph strikes are actually felt or seen by the angler. If the nymph is heavy enough or there is enough sinker on the leader ahead of it, you can feel its bumpy

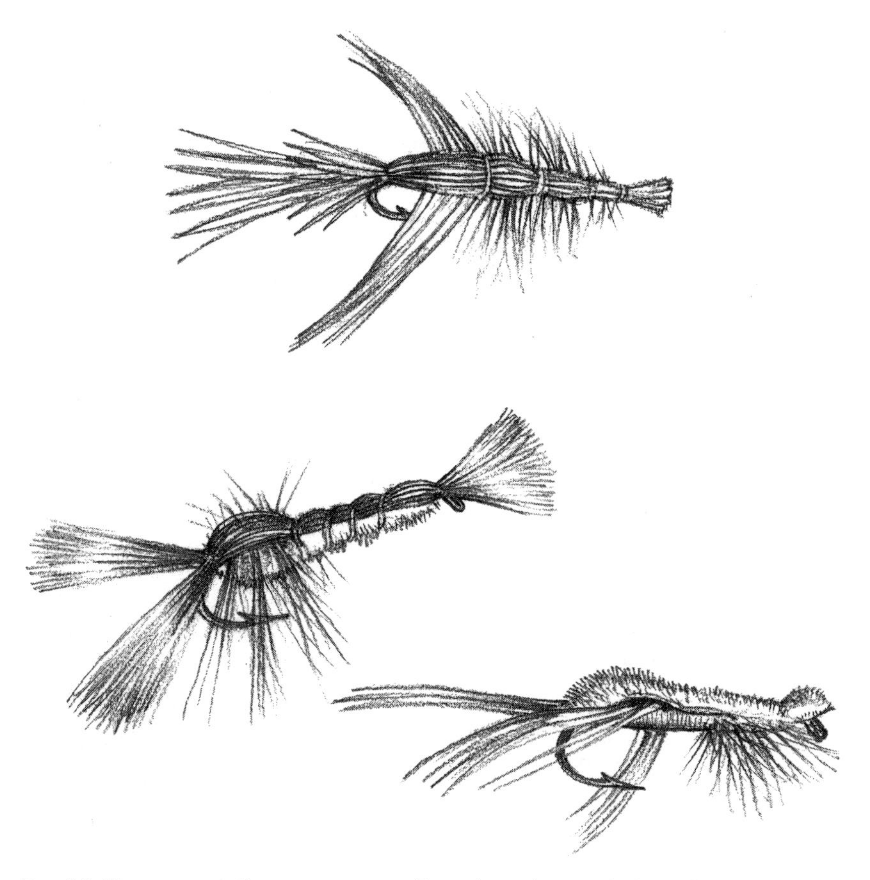

Crayfish flies are especially attractive to smallmouths and are worked rapidly and erratically near the bottom. Generally speaking, the impression crayfish are more successful than exact imitations. Harry Murray, designer of those shown here, emphasizes that fairly short "pincers" work best. Crayfish crawl forward but swim rapidly in reverse.

travel downstream and will detect a take. It takes concentration, for a "strike" is generally just a pause.

Some of the bottom bumpers can be manipulated without leading them out of character. The crayfish, a favorite food of bass, especially smallmouths, appears in numerous lures made mainly of hair and can move pretty fast just above the bottom. A few quick pulls on one of those won't upset the dead-drift impression. Waders can cover more water from the same spot if they use what's often called a "reach retrieve," simply extending the rod well out to either side as the bottom lure is swept down. This is such a simple maneuver it is embarrassing to realize you haven't been using it.

It is very rare for any bottom streamer or nymph (or crossbred fuzzy-wuzzy) to work well ten feet deep, although it can be handled in quiet water. Catching a bass in the act of tasting something down there requires full attention and carefully adjusted tackle. More and more fly fishermen are using strike indicators for that, the name being considerably more dignified than the word "bobber." Generally—not always—the indicator doesn't provide any flotation, and I think the simple stick-on orange tape is most popular of all, although many colored gadgets have been tried. It is generally fastened to the upper leader, and it is sometimes used submerged. The sinking-tip line used with both streamers and nymphs is sometimes misunderstood. A sinking tip is not necessarily the only part of the line that sinks, since it helps to pull the floating part down, and a weighted bullhead imitation or nymph gets in its licks, too.

In most bottom-bumping techniques, a large share of the strikes are seen before they are felt, and even an expert misses some of them, especially when the lure is traveling downstream after an upstream or cross-stream cast. The line and the strike indicator must be watched carefully, and the slightest hesitation in their drift should bring an attempt at setting the hook, which frequently sticks into bottom debris or wedges between rocks but sometimes catches a bass.

The terminal tackle for this fishing may not appear complicated at first, but as current speed and water depth change, it must be altered. I have watched expert bottom fishermen who could change leader lengths and sinker weights so quickly it appeared to be sleight of hand. Sinking tips, of course, come in different weights, cataloged by the number of inches they sink per second, and the bottom-bumping addict may have several reel spools containing lines of varied sink rates. Then there is the device of adding weight at the end of the sinking part, as with the short sections of lead-core line described earlier. All of these complications are necessary only when the water is deep, say more than five feet.

One effective bottom technique involves attaching a sinker to the leader several inches above a fairly light nymph so that the lure swings freely in the current—but the sinker is carried along by water pushing against the line and leader. It is almost impossible to use for long casts.

The choice of method—top-water or deep—can separate consistently successful anglers from those who fail regularly. I once made a trip with a man, however, who felt a fish didn't really count unless you made it strike on top. We fished a deep largemouth lake for some time with popping bugs without a strike, whereupon he put on a streamer and caught two bass within a few minutes. Then he reeled in and reached for the canoe paddle.

"If we have to use *wet bait,*" he said, "I'd just as soon go back to town."

But there are other experts who feel the skills of probing the depths are more refined, and I know a fly caster who says "Anybody can catch fish when he can watch them hit. I know how to feel for them."

THE COAXER, DEVELOPED by a Chicagoan named William Jamison before 1910, may have been the first commercial bug; it had a cork body, red-felt wings, and a feather hiding the hook. . . .

In 1919, Orley Tuttle, who lived near Old Forge in the Adirondacks, was fishing for bass one evening when he noticed that large beetles that fell into the lake were quickly gobbled up by smallmouths. He soon tied up an all-deer-hair bug, with a body made of a large bundle of the hair tied down over the hook and the head trimmed to shape and the tail left longer. When he showed it to his wife, the story goes, she said, "Looks like the devil to me," inspiring Orley to name his creation the Tuttle Devil Bug. . . .

I am an enthusiastic admirer of Dave Whitlock and other modern masters of deer-hair fly tying, but at the same time the work done in deer-hair forty or more years ago shows us most of the modern techniques. Joe Messinger's frogs and poppers, the mice from Weber and Tuttle, and the assortment of frogs and crayfish in books such as William Sturgis's *Fly-tying* (1940) are all as finished and refined as any bass fisherman (or bass) probably needs.

Paul Schullery
American Fly Fishing

SEVEN

Strange Waters

AS BLACK BASS have spread unheralded around the world, the true bass angler is surprised to find them in distant lands, and he is sometimes just as pleased to find them near home in places where bass are not supposed to be.

Bass, especially the largemouths, have tolerance for varied waters but are subject to automatic migrations that follow the waters they prefer. And often the best bass fishing occurs where they have been pushed by changing fortunes, sometimes setting up a temporary fishery that lives for months or years, only to disappear with changes in rainfall or water quality. And such fishing areas may then reappear to meet a new generation of anglers who are surprised to find them. These fishing windfalls come and go in a variety of places, but probably the most dramatic is the brackish water fishery that exists precariously on many coasts. "Brackish" is no longer a bad word to the biologist, who once thought of it as an undesirable mixture of fresh and salt water with the advantages of neither.

Florida's Everglades has almost lost its "River of Grass," the great flowing expanse that has covered much of the southern part of the peninsula. Channeling, damming, agricultural exploitation, and general misunderstanding of what the freshwater Everglades consisted of have done their damage, causing a chain of unpredicted changes. To me, the most fascinating part has been the ever-changing area where fresh water meets the sea, gradually and unpredictably, on Florida's lower west coast. For forty years we have fished the mangrove rivers, bays, and outer islands there, Everglades National Park enclosing a large share of it.

The mangrove rivers become narrow as you go up them toward the

In the 1950s and 1960s brackish water camping in the mangrove Everglades required some special methods. This tent was erected in a boat after equipment was hung in tree branches for the night. The best bass fishing was at the heads of rivers a long way from the dock.

saw-grass Everglades and fresh water, and long before the boat trails were marked we would run a boat almost two hundred miles in a day's fly fishing, guided by ancient Army Air Corps aerial maps from the 1920s. We fished for snook, tarpon, redfish, and other saltwater fish—and finally we fished for largemouth bass, but they came as a surprise.

Up a little-known creek we idled the boat, looking for tarpon rolls or moving snook, when we gradually came to what looked like fragile freshwater vegetation that hadn't been there the year before. As I had done thousands of times through the years, I was casting a streamer to the edges of the mangrove roots for snook, and the strike was a brisk tug that somehow seemed familiar but hard to catalog. The bass jumped and shook his head, plump and sassy, silver and green.

Back at Everglades City, forty miles to the north, I told veteran guide Ted Smallwood I'd caught a bass. For years we'd fished for them in what we called the freshwater Everglades, but I'd drawn a mental boundary between the freshwater grassy lakes, creeks, and swamps and the brackish coastal rivers. Smallwood wasn't surprised.

It was hard to predict, he said, but some of the country's best bass fishing could come where the fresh water met the salt—and the line was ill defined under circumstances that could involve heavy rains interspersed by drought periods. And here, any bass fisherman who throws his flies near a coast must either be his own authority or find a rare observer willing to report on brackish developments.

If there is a period of plentiful rain in the grassy Everglades, the bass will prosper in a thousand pools, sluggish creeks, and alligator holes, and it may be a stable condition for years at a time, largemouths generally undisturbed in waters reachable only by airboat or hard labor. Then comes drought and the fresh water begins to dry up, forcing the fish ever downstream until they are at the heads of the famous tarpon rivers where they may meet saltwater predators. If the drought continues, the bass will die as the water turns salt. If the rains come, they can work their way back to their natural haunts.

There are other conditions that can bring some of the world's best fly fishing for bass to the overlap of fresh and salt. When there is high water in the grass for years, the fresh currents hold back the salt, and high tide from the Gulf of Mexico is deadened and reversed by a steady flow from far above the mangrove edges. Then the freshwater species thrive, and bass and bluegills expand their range to river heads that in more normal times host only fish from the Gulf. So it is the extremes that bring bass to the tarpon rivers, and it was the wet-weather extreme that took us on our first brackish bass trip.

"Let's go way up there tomorrow," Smallwood suggested. "It ought to be pretty good if you caught a bass close to Gator Bay."

So we went up a river, fifty miles from the dock, past the wide parts where the bluebills made their running takeoffs, and then past the mudbank where an alligator reluctantly slid down from his slippery sundeck. Five of us were running two outboard boats, quick aluminum skiffs that drew little water.

We came to floating freshwater vegetation, and Smallwood cut his engine and set up his oars. I did the same and we slipped on upstream, as quiet as five people can be in two aluminum boats. There came a familiar

Bass fishing is good where swamp water feeds into a canal under just the right dry weather conditions.

swishing as a traveling flock of white ibis came around a bend in the little river and curved up and away when they saw the boats. When they find a headwind up higher they fly the mangrove streams, sheltered by the trees. Shortly after that there was a splashy strike against the shoreline.

"They're right where they should be," Smallwood said. "There'll be more of them farther up."

A man riding with me cast a streamer against the mangrove bank—a three-foot open strip between the mangrove roots and the water growth that clung to my oars and had made a shapeless bundle of my propeller. A bass struck the yellow bucktail almost instantly. Smallwood said he thought there would be bigger ones a little farther up, and there were. Then the river became two creeks, and we took separate courses. Once a single cast of a popping bug brought four wakes for the man casting from the bow of my boat, and once when my wife cast a big bug to where she had seen a bulge and swirl there was a blasting strike—too big for a bass—and a tarpon jumped and threw the lure. The saltwater predators had come to meet their neighbors. But most of the strikes were bass.

Most of the bass were less than 2 pounds, although Smallwood displayed a 5-pounder he'd caught on a saltwater fly rod and big popper somewhere in the other creek. A snook came into plain sight chasing a bluegill, the race ending in a booming splash. There were more bass, but we wanted to run home in daylight so we quit early. Short day. As I tooled the boat through the labyrinth of bays, rivers, and islands, I decided that for once I wanted to catch bass on flies until I was tired of doing it. Debie said we should go back for a longer trip, so we did. We camped with the bass.

Our system was a little different from that of those who usually say casually that "we spent the night on the boat." Such reports imply a yacht—or at least a cabin cruiser. Our fishing boat was sixteen feet long with a wide beam. Not even the gas tanks were built in, but there was room for a plywood deck that rested on the aluminum seats. At night we could take out all unnecessary equipment, including gasoline tanks, and hang it in mangrove trees, leaving room to set up an aluminum-framed tent on the temporary deck. We could cook on an alcohol stove that was perched on a carhop's tray fastened to the gunwale and sitting out over the water for safety's sake. There were no National Park Service platforms in that country in those days.

We left early and had a full day's fishing near one of the river heads, and at dusk we set up our camp in a broad and shallow part of the stream, far enough away from the mangroves that a welcome breeze thinned out the mosquitoes. The freshwater vegetation was almost a mat on the surface. That night the bass continued their foraging, often striking bait so near the aluminum boat that the hull thumped, and once the rig lifted on a gentle swell as something big, probably a tarpon, went by next to the shoreline.

The bass fishing was almost too good the next morning, and a yellow bug became a ragged scrap. I waded in one stretch and found a sandy ridge near the middle of a tiny bay, part of the river that was a creek that far up.

Along that little underwater ridge, and everywhere else I found a minor variation in the bottom depth and a slight break in the floating carpet of greenery, the bass were ready and raced for bugs. It was no longer a matter of whether there would be a strike but whether the larger fish would win the race, and sometime in midmorning I stopped and told myself the whole thing was getting silly. I told Debie that every fly fisherman deserves one day when he could catch more bass than he wanted, but enough was enough. I think of those times on days when I catch nothing and wait for a single half-hearted rise.

At risk of seeming wedded to one small area of the bass world, I must speak more of the Everglades country. I have found similar things elsewhere, but the Everglades make up a microcosm of black bass feast and famine in high and low water, perhaps an exaggeration of what I have watched in fishing such places as the extremities of San Francisco Bay and North Carolina's Currituck Sound.

In enormous flood control efforts there came a series of dams and canals that made feast or famine for bass anglers in some sections of the Glades. For one period, possibly to be repeated, there was one "conservation district" that contained chest-deep water and vegetation that made travel almost impossible except by airboat, and it held a water level that allowed several years of bass growth. Later the water fell, but there were opportunists—with airboats.

I got in there with two fisheries biologists in a pseudoscientific study of the welfare of bass in this temporary bass heaven. We've long known the largemouth bass thrives best when his lake bed changes with high and low water. The two biologists were happy to fill me in on long Latin words and observed many things I did not understand, but they carried fly rods and they obviously thought this would be more pleasant than netting specimens or using rotenone.

The airboat was a gleaming, high-powered beast that rode over walls of vegetation that lesser boats would circle, and we picked the most likely of an endless series of relatively open places. The bass were ready and seemingly offended by any loud bug that invaded their territories. One of the scientists caught a 9-pounder, but I didn't do very well. You see, I am not built for basketball, and the waders I brought were not what I'd use in a deep river. They were not the kind that come up under my chin, and when I stepped into the water I found I had about three inches of freeboard. This condition is often displayed in advertising for waders but is hardly acceptable when the water is chilly and you are walking through occasionally clinging bottom shrubbery. My predicament was not distressing to my companions, both of whom were well over six feet and had armpit waders. We were away from dry ground for two days, much of which I spent on tiptoe.

The bottom was pretty even, but the prospect of facing a hundred square miles of water three inches from my waders cast a blight over my fishing. I did some casting from the boat, a futile effort after the first few minutes in each spot, and once, when I was abandoned by the jovial biologists, I set forth on foot for an attractive clump of grass I didn't recognize. I used a frog popper, threw it clear across the patch of grass, and worked it with what I felt was a seductive series of starts and stops. The whole grass patch seemed to come apart, and when I convulsively set the hook, I saw a cavernous mouth as a fish vainly tried to jump in the clinging greenery. I misjudged the fish's size, and when I finally wrestled it into submission, aided by tangled weeds and some small pads, I found it only weighed less than 5 pounds. For a fish that size on a fly, I am not inclined to use the word "only," but I was a bit frustrated.

I got back to the airboat, having shipped but a very little water, and released the fish, and when my friends returned they refused to believe my story. It was just as well, for they then kindly went off to a "ridge" where the water was not quite so deep, making a point of the fact that they were making the concession for my welfare. In the two days of cruising the conservation district I saw no other airboats, and if I hadn't known we were fishing in an enormous pond formed by manmade dikes, I could have felt we were in a virgin wilderness of water and greenery.

In airboat backcountry there has been a sort of communal use of stilt-legged cottages built at great expense and effort far from dry ground. Bass fishermen, duck hunters, and other water wanderers simply pull up at somebody's unoccupied shack, move in their sleeping bags, make themselves at home, and end their stay by cleaning the place up and possibly leaving some nonperishable food supplies for whoever comes in next—who might possibly be the owner or owners.

Although I had done a bit of airboat bass chasing before, my trip with the biologists was my first overnight experience, and I was a little surprised that the cottage we stopped at that evening was so clean and well equipped. Only one minor distraction kept it from being perfect: Just inside the door was a large, freshly shed snakeskin.

"Corn snake," said one of the biologists. "Lots of the guys keep a snake around these cabins to handle the mice and rats."

Now a corn snake is about as harmless as a wild snake can be, and I am not a snake fainter or screamer, but the weather was a little chilly and I know a good old corn snake is likely to crawl in bed with you for warmth. Since a five-foot snake puts out no warmth at all, as far as I know, I have always felt the arrangement is one-sided. As a result of this attitude, I chose one of the top bunks. The corn snake, however, spent the night under my rucksack instead of in my bed.

Such temporary bass waters are some of the best in the world. When the water begins to recede, the fish are concentrated in ever smaller areas, and when such an area can be found, it is a concentration of good fishing, whether in the North or South. Then there comes the time when the reduced habitat is too small and the fish are crowded and thin, a discouraging time to cast a fly to slender fish that don't quite measure up in fighting qualities. And then the whole thing can be gone.

Some years after I went with the two biologists, I called one of them to learn how things were going in the conservation area. Any chance of getting in a little fishing trip sometime soon?

"It's all over," he told me. "The other guy doesn't even fish for bass anymore. If we ever get enough water back in that country again, I'll let you know."

I haven't heard from him.

But there is other opportunism in big lowlands—the canals holding the water that's left—and many such canals have sluggish tributary creeks.

Next to them are temporary or semipermanent run-ins that are used by fish probing as far as possible from the relatively sterile canal banks. Of course, as years pass, most of the canals abandon their ditch characteristics and become more and more like natural rivers or creeks. They're sometimes hard to get to, and I have retained a rather tame version of the pioneer spirit.

West of Miami, Florida, on the cross-state road known as the Tamiami Trail, there is an almost endless series of access points to fishing on the north side of the busy highway. All of the water looks good, and in fact, it has bass almost everywhere you get into it. I heard about a particular canal that ran north for some distance, deep into the swamp, and got in there with my favorite canal boat, a small aluminum rig that sacrificed a little lightness for a tough bottom. The tough bottom part is good to remember for anyone who takes to the backcountry—and not just for warding off stumps and stones.

The canal was a bit low, and there were a few places where I ran slow, but most of the time I was up on top and getting the most of a battered but faithful 9½-horse motor. I stopped to fish now and then, catching a small largemouth and a few warmouth perch, the South's answer to the rock bass. I used a medium-size yellow popping bug with rubber legs, and a Number Six rod. On one side I was passing flat grassland with occasional small cypress trees, but the dam was on the right, and when my ditch finally petered out, there was a pretty good stand of cypress on the right, across another canal that wasn't even attached to mine. These seemingly haphazard cut-and-patch ditches and dams begin to make sense when viewed from the air or when examined on a map, but the casual wanderer is generally surprised at what he finds. I pulled ashore and began to unbutton my outboard motor.

So that's when the tough bottom was handy. I carried my motor across to the other ditch, along with my gas tank and other odds and ends, but I dragged the boat. There was grass over the dike, and it went pretty easily. When I started to launch it on the other ditch, there were marks on the ground that showed someone else had had the same idea recently. That, as usual, brought mixed feelings. First, I certainly wasn't getting into any virgin waters. But second, there must be something worthwhile over in that other canal or no one would have hauled his rig across the dike.

Of course, the first reaction is that it would be ideal for a canoe, but I'd been on the first canal for quite a few miles—a long haul with a paddle for one day's fishing. I clamped on the motor, hoped there wouldn't be any more portages, and ran slowly on in the same direction the first ditch had led me. The second canal was well on the way back to nature, the banks green and even bushy, and there were some lily pads along the edges. My fishing picked up almost immediately, the bass darting out

Portaging over a dike to reach one canal from another. For this work the boat must be light but have a rugged bottom.

from cover (it was near midday) and taking bugs worked gently. A small streamer, worked jerkily, caught a bass or two, but I went back to the top-water things. The tall cypress was close to the edge in most areas, but it soaked in that I had dry weather with falling water levels and that wherever there were gaps in the cypress there was likely to be a creek leading to fertile shallows among the knees.

At one of the cypress gaps, I let the little boat drift in a trace of breeze and threw a bug well back from where the shallow water entered the deeper ditch. A bass came toward me, seeming to take the bug on his way to the deeper water, and leaving a little V as he came—not a big bass, although that would make a better story. But he hadn't disturbed the shallow water much, and there was another fish waiting when I put the bug in there again. This one stirred things up and closed that operation—but I thought I had the picture then, and I hurried on to another cypress gap. After that, time slipped up on me a little, and by the time I had wrestled my boat up over the dike and run back to the highway launch site, the Everglades residents had begun their dark-time noises, and I heard a night frogger's airboat cough and start somewhere over toward the moon.

That was some years back, but I overheard a discussion recently. It was at a lunchroom off the Tamiami Trail road.

"You run up Canal Number . . . " (I didn't get the rest because he noticed me listening and dropped his voice almost to a whisper). I had to grin, for when he walked out I noticed he had bass bugs in his hat. There are many canals in many places where you never hear a competition bass boat's big engine, but remember you have to work them gently because they are not used to boats—and maybe you should lighten up your leader a little.

There is a feeling among the world's fishermen that the larger the water, the larger the fish, and they tend to bypass roadside ditches, prairie puddles, and farm ponds. Having found this premise to be frequently false, I take the position that every puddle has a bass until it has been proved differently.

Debie and I pulled to the side of a road because there was a tarp or something flapping back in the boat we were towing. "That ditch is full of fish," Debie mentioned. "You don't suppose some of them are bass, do you?"

We strung a fly rod and followed our rule of "when in doubt, tie on a popping bug." The first cast brought a bluegill charge, but the second attracted an eager largemouth bass. I guess we could have done pretty well if we'd kept fishing there, but the ditch was low and the fish were gaunt. Some other time I'd like to try that one when there's been some rain—but who knows? Given some rain, those fish might have found another place to live.

With my first bass-weight fly rod, I went fishing on a prairie creek with two local celebrities who had a reputation for catching fish where no one else could find any. We planned to wade, and when we arrived at our creek, I went charging off, politely leaving considerable fishing territory to my senior associates. It was one of those creeks that ran only during wet weather, and it had degenerated into a series of pools with dry ground between them.

I waded where there was water enough, and I did it pretty carefully, making short casts ahead with a small hair bug. That was a Size Six shaggy one with a band of red somewhere around the middle. The pools were full of big green sunfish that we called "black perch" for no reason I have been able to figure. They whacked the bug with eager pops, and I put them on a chain fish stringer. It never occurred to me to release them under the circumstances, for this was show and tell as far as I was concerned. I only hoped I would have almost as many black perch as the veterans I had left back at the car. Youthful pride can be a crushing weight.

I worked hard. The sun was hot, and I stumbled through shoulder-high weeds and bushes much of the time. I knew there would be chiggers (red bugs) in that stuff. I approached each pool with panting stealth and assessed it for the best casting spot regarding backcast, sun, and probable water depth. It was lunchtime but I held off a little, wishing there was some drinking water. I didn't want my friends to think I quit early. ("Damn kid won't stick with it!")

Then the bass, a pretty good bass, struck against a bank where long grass would have meant sweepers if there had been higher water. I held him hard from a rotting stump, and he went to the deepest part of the pool, shook his head, and jumped once. I netted him in a floundering charge over a patch of mud bottom, put him on my stringer, and began picking my way back, sticking to the winding creekbed.

When I came to the stretch of water I had left for my friends, there was no one there, so I hurried a little and saw the car through the elms. I glanced down to make sure my bass and the big sunfish looked their best, adopted a casual appearance, and sauntered up to the car. My friends were sleeping on the grass in the shade but heard me arrive.

"How'd you guys do?" I asked, trying to appear as relaxed as a young guy can when trying to hold a stringer of fish in full view without seeming to.

One of the men yawned, looked for his hat with all the bass bugs stuck in it, and tried not to be surprised when he saw my fish.

"Aw, we didn't string up," he said. "Water's too low to fish."

Such creeks in pasture country can demand a stealthy approach, and sometimes the fishing is best at night—but it's pretty hard to handle a rod and line in close quarters and darkness. There are some such places where livestock have destroyed most of the cover, not only sloshing in to get a drink but wading deep in hot weather. But sometimes livestock are a well-disguised aid, for fish used to their splashing may be tolerant of a wading fisherman or two. Fish can get used to routine disturbances on any water, and if they won't strike immediately when you splash in, they may return to normal quickly as they habitually do after a herd of Herefords has had a drink.

Any freshly flooded reservoir has a character of its own, the very submersion of uplands producing unique cover, ranging from an abandoned filling station to a rocky mountainside. And the bass that occupy such strange places may behave strangely themselves—sometimes hard to recognize as the same fish that live in mature cover. New "structure," as the modern bass seekers call it, can produce, at least temporarily, perfectly healthy bass that won't quite follow the rules.

I fished some mountain reservoirs as they filled, and although there were plenty of fish, generally fairly easy to catch, the methods were sometimes a little strange. I felt at home in the shallow ends of coves, where the usual bass bugs and streamers would catch fish, but I didn't do too well off the rocky points where clean, blue water seemed to have no bottom. At one reservoir I mumbled around a boat dock about how I simply couldn't seem to get anything near the surface on the deep shorelines. It was discouraging to work streamers or bugs tight against a bank when I could generally see there were no fish near them.

"They're deep most of the time," said the cook at the local lunchroom. "It takes a lot of fuss to bring up a bass that's living way down there, and I doubt if your bugs will do it. You better stick to the shallow pockets where the coves are just filling up—or sink something clear down the shore for twenty or thirty feet."

I grumbled into my coffee, and the cook grinned and said he was catching fish off those deep points, and although he didn't use a fly rod, maybe his methods might give me some ideas. He said he caught his fish trolling, and I visualized a heavily weighted spoon or plug slow-bumping the bottom farther down than I cared to fish. I asked him how and what he trolled, and he said he used a surface plug and ran his boat "about ten or twelve miles an hour." I had nothing at all to say to that, and he laughed at me. He said he wasn't much of a bass fisherman, but that he had accidentally found that a ten-mile-an-hour plug would catch "quite a few." He invited me to come and see.

So I went with him, and I suppose it is anticlimactic to report that he drove his outboard boat at about ten miles an hour past some deep points. The plug he used was much like the old South Bend Bass Oreno, although it was made of plastic by a firm that specialized in imitations. The thing yanked the rod tip violently and occasionally sailed clear out of the water. It was in the boat's wake and about forty feet back. He was running about twenty feet off the points. The bass would strike and the reel would scream. Heavy line. I have hesitated to report this, as it makes me look bad when I recommend delicacy, stealth, and slow lure operation. He said the boat and motor made a hell of a noise and the bass came up to see what was going on, and the plug would come flipping along and the bass would decide they might as well grab it.

I'd like to say that I put on a really loud popper and drifted around those points yanking it until my wrist hurt and catching largemouths, but I caught only one fish that way, and for all I know it was just loafing near the surface.

I guess the most productive way for a fly rod under such circumstances is to get out on the shore, cast a sinking rig out, and let it go down until you can retrieve it up the bank, keeping the lure a fairly uniform distance from the "bottom," which is set at a steep angle. Now if the bass are twenty feet down the slope, you can say they're "twenty feet deep." You're really bottom fishing as it comes up the steep slope, but there's no telling how deep the lake is at that spot. The late Ted Trueblood successfully worked steep shorelines that way. It is tougher than it sounds, because there are generally obstructions such as trees and boulders on the banks, and you'd probably make a career of roll casting. I have done it enough to describe it, but I'm no real authority.

Now before we are convinced that the ten-mile-an-hour bass actually came out from the point or up from great depth to hit the trolled plug, let's contemplate the fact that the bass's top speed wouldn't get him to it from very far, and he'd have to figure a lead like a duck hunter. I am guessing that the bass were loafing offshore and for some unusual bass reason were not alarmed by a fourteen-foot boat going ten miles an hour. Maybe you should clip this part out of the book. It proves only that the largemouth bass is an unusual fish.

Joe Brooks, who knew the East and was raised there, spoke of Currituck Sound largemouth bass with respect for tradition. Brooks was a lover of tradition, even in his tackle. Sometimes when a new fly rod method or fly would appear as a deviation from standard practice, Brooks would say, "It catches fish but it isn't fly fishing."

Currituck Sound on the North Carolina coast had enough tradition, even for Joe Brooks, though the bass fishing was known to very few in his early days. He fished the duck blinds, and he cast bass bugs beneath the stilted ones. He liked the Gerbubble Bug, which has appeared in many forms. Not all of them today actually have holes through the body, but the ones he liked had holes that produced chains of bubbles added to the disturbances of hair or feathers and a rather blunt nose.

It is brackish water, and like most estuarine bass fisheries, the salinity changes wildly with rainfall and the fierce Atlantic storms that regularly alter the long string of barrier islands. The significant words for most Americans are "Cape Hatteras," a sort of breakwater against the great storms and just a little south of Currituck Sound. The duck blinds themselves have been a tradition, permission to build them passed down through Currituck generations in an involved process of seniority and

Credited by some experts as being the best bass bug fishing in the world, Currituck Sound angling comes and goes with the salinity of the water—and that depends upon rainfall and ocean storms. This angler is working a fly rod lure in very heavy cover, vegetation that might disappear if the water becomes too salty.

politics. For years they were the best bass hangouts on the sound, but when wind and weather made changes, the water weeds and grasses spread the cover.

We got to Currituck a little late. The bass fishing had been thoroughly discovered and was being exploited to a modest extent—but the storms and floods had somehow made what fly caster Lefty Kreh was to call the best bass bug fishing in America. We arranged a trip there with

Joel Arrington, who handled fishing promotions for the state in those days, and we moved into a guide's home. He was no youngster and had been born and raised on Currituck. His program was to tow a skiff with a small inboard cruiser and then fish from the skiff when the chosen area was reached. The skiff had its little, three-horse motor for minor maneuvers, and when we were casting, our host moved it with a strange tool I had never seen used elsewhere, half double-ended paddle and half push-pole. The Currituck guides used it as if running a kayak, and if it struck bottom, so much the better. If not, there was a blunt paddle blade on each end.

Much of the time we fished almost within a long rifle shot of the open sea on the other side of the narrow island chain. I asked the guide if he used his cruiser offshore much. It was only a short run to Oregon Inlet.

"No," he replied. "I've never been out there."

It proved to be a good place for fairly heavy bass tackle, and I used a Number Nine rod most of the time. There was likely to be wind, and the weedy strips and very shallow ridges caused plenty of hangups. The bass were shiny, hard strikers, and mostly medium-size—bass bug heaven.

Most of the time we were over water growth and casting to higher strands of it. On other trips we went with other guides with somewhat different equipment. The double-ended pole-paddle was still in use, but the flat-bottomed skiffs were used to reach the fishing areas with no cabin cruiser needed, and in the deeper channels there were modern bass boats with their growling engines and flashing electronics—the latter hardly needed where most bottom features were easily visible. And most guide boats had folding canvas cuddies in their bows to protect traveling fishermen when the wind came, which was almost daily.

Near where we cast bugs under duck blinds were Kitty Hawk and the Kill Devil Hills between us and the Atlantic, historical names involved with the Wright Brothers and their airplane. A little to the south was Oregon Inlet, where I had gone offshore to throw flies at eager dolphins and see the eerie little blobs of oil still rising from old wrecks that dot the coastal charts and now shelter a variety of saltwater fish. And there was Okracoke Island, where I had gone during World War II by mail boat on something highly classified and for the first time had heard

"Elizabethan English." The black bass were to me a strange link between Kansas tank ponds of my youth and the historical coast where heroic German submarine skippers had studied mainland lights.

Bass fishing has come and gone on Currituck Sound as it has on so many brackish watercourses, changing with the storms that breach the outer islands to rearrange the coast and the weather that makes Currituck waters too salty for largemouth bass. Like the other sometime fisheries, it should be watched and studied by serious fly fishermen. The last time I called up there, they told me fishing was down but was beginning to come back with "a lot of little bass" after some adverse weather that most of the country had forgotten.

The report sounded like some of those I get from the Florida Everglades and the upper reaches of San Francisco Bay. Watching such things are part of bass fishing. I like the reply when I spoke to someone about "strange bass waters."

"All bass waters are strange," he said.

I don't think that's true, but I like the sound of it.

"THE ARTIFICIAL FLY is a fish-hook to which variously colored feathers have been tied, and is supposed to be easily mistaken by a fish for a real fly. If this be true, it is strong proof that a fish hasn't sense enough to come in when it rains, and doesn't deserve to live. . . .

"Artificial flies are all named. There are the 'Professor,' the 'Hackle,' the 'Ibis,' the 'Yellow Sally,' and several other breeds. Whenever a bilious angler has no luck, and nothing to do, he sits down and concocts a new swindle in feathers, and christens it with a nine-jointed Indian name, and at once every angler in the country rushes in and pays $2 a dozen for samples."

Mary Orvis Marbury
Favorite Flies and their Histories, 1882,
in quoting from Henry Guy Carlton

EIGHT

Fellow Travelers

IN FLY FISHING for bass year in and year out, your incidental catches may well equal or outnumber your take of the main targets. From northern pike in the North to warmouth perch in the South, there are literally more than a dozen interlopers eager to grab something intended for bass.

Like others, I am apt to be a little irritated when a slashing strike turns out to be a chain pickerel or a popping strike is produced by a green sunfish, but without their fellow travelers there would be more disappointing bass days. I confess with humility that I have taken off a bass bug and installed a rubber spider when bass were uncooperative and bluegills particularly aggressive. And although I am likely to call a northern a "dam snake," I have tied on a heavy tippet and gunned for them with slit-eyed intensity when smallmouths were scarce. There are, of course, many fly fishermen who pursue panfish in bass country and accept the occasional stray bass as a premium. When I mentioned a bass book to a well-known fly angler, he wanted to be sure the panfish weren't left out, so they aren't.

I suppose the best known of the true panfish is the bluegill, generally listed without any special distinction along with the other small sunfishes. Most sunfishes can be caught with fly tackle, but I think the bluegill is a better taker than the others, especially in its love for top-water things. Since preschoolers heave bluegills on banks all over the United States, and probably in many other places, we tend to think the fish is no challenge for us angling intellectuals. It's true there are times and places where the only technical necessity is getting a rubber spider or

Best-known of America's panfish is the bluegill, which takes the same kinds of lures that catch bass. Miniature popping bugs with rubber legs are consistently successful.

a little Woolly Worm in the water, but bluegills (I refuse to use the term "lowly bluegill") can be tricky and even frustrating.

At a time when I thought the bluegill was a true peasant fish, I got into a strange situation on a little backwater of the Tuolumne River in California. I had seen some good-size bass loafing in plain sight and clear water, but they seemed to regard my bugs and streamers with tolerant amusement, and I finally gave up on them. Then I saw what appeared to be fins breaking the surface in a very shallow pocket, and decided I had cornered some bluegills and might as well save the day. So I put a small wet fly on my bass outfit and flipped it to them. The fish continued to move around their puddle but nothing touched the fly, so I changed to another color and tried again. It would have taken a second or so for the fresh fly to sink, and before it could, a bluegill grabbed it.

I thought it was the new color that was working, but the bluegills simply wanted a dry on top, regardless of color, and when I doped a fly and fished it on the surface I caught them with no trouble at all. This is true selectivity, because the sunken flies were no more than three or four inches down. Without getting into complex conclusions, I'd say the sunken fly was viewed in great detail and the floater was just an impression that fooled them.

Bluegills can be particular about depth, sometimes refusing to rise more than a few inches for a surface lure. I once got into a weird situation in the only head-to-head fly-fishing contest I ever indulged in. I don't care for fishing contests, but I found I was into one that seemed to be for blood and glory. I'd accepted an invitation to a fishing area with a "fishing contest" involving other guests, but I'd supposed it was simply one of those things where the largest bass would get you a gag trophy and a few laughs. Not so. It was for real, it lasted through several sessions, and each guest was to have a personal guide. I had no plans for winning, but I didn't want to take any booby award either.

The contest included not only bass but bluegills as well, and everybody would try to catch a limit of "bream" before getting after the bass at each session. Gave him a good start on the point total. We had different guides each day, and one of them said he had the bluegills really staked out for me.

He ran to where there were bluegill beds thick along a steep shoreline. The water was clear enough that I could make out the beds from a short casting distance, even though they were several feet down. I couldn't make out the spawners at first. I put on a small popping bug and began working the area carefully, catching one fish. My guide was restless.

"Very few of them will come up for that bug," he said. "I tie up a little weighted nymph that'll get one every cast, but you have to get it to the exact depth. Would you try that?"

I tolerantly tied on the nymph. It was dark green with a sprig of white tail. Call it a slightly weighted Woolly Worm of chenille with just a little "hair" made of feather hackle.

"Twitch it a little and count as it goes down," he advised. "When the fish takes, remember your count so you won't be wasting time. We should get a fish almost every cast. I'll put a nymph on your spare rod."

Using two rods alternately, I caught my limit of bluegills in a hurry. The fish were ready to strike, all right, but they wouldn't leave their nests very far, rising only a little to take the nymph. That was in the South, but the green nymph (known as "Greenie") has caught panfish for me almost everywhere I've tried it. It was an educational experience in sight fishing. We stayed just a comfortable short cast from the beds, and by easing over a little, I could make out the big bluegills just above their nests.

Any time bluegills are fished underwater, the depth can become touchy. It has been years since we caught the big ones during the fishing contest, but the count business is important. If you use anything that sinks, counting as it goes down will often establish a depth at which it will be welcomed. Most bluegill flies, whether dry or sinking, should be operated very slowly, many takes coming when they aren't moving. If you slowly count to ten to establish a depth, all you'll do when the time is up is simply twitch the thing a little and begin a very slow retrieve. A jigging action helps, but only a twitch may be just as good.

I often use what I call a "compromise bug" in about Size Ten or as large as Size Six. The bluegill has a very small mouth, but when he means business he'll take in a bigger lure than you'd think, largely through a sucking action. The Number Six bug will be a little too much for anything but the good-size "bream." The compromise bug will catch a lot of bass, and I find when both species are present the bluegills will take the very slow presentation. Before picking up, if you give the bug a few harder twitches, you may get more bass. Waving hackles or rubber legs are highly attractive to bluegills as a bug is resting. Of course, they work with bass, too, but may not be quite as essential as for the panfish. A small, rubber spider with rubber legs is one of the very best lures for bluegills but has caught few bass for me.

In some areas, half-pound bluegills are common. Although they survive in chilly water, they often feed best when it's quite warm, probably around 80 degrees Fahrenheit in some localities, but this may change greatly in different parts of the country. In many waters the big males have a rather blotchy coloration about the head, and there is the story of one eager fisheries biologist who attempted to develop an outsized subspecies from them, but it didn't work out because there were no females in his tank. A bluegill that weighs a pound is getting close to a fly rod record.

Bluegills are partial to quiet waters, even though there may be heavy

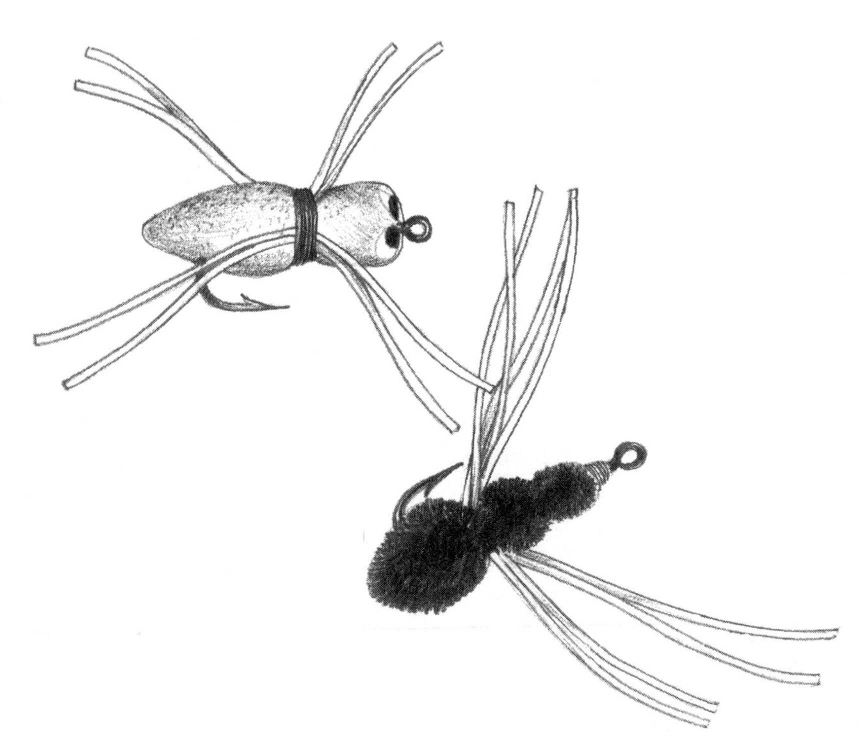

One of the simplest and deadliest panfish lures is the floating spider with rubber legs. Generally, these don't work consistently with black bass.

current not far away. They are notoriously evening feeders everywhere I have caught them. In Florida rivers I have found them coming to life with feeding pops along weedy edges somewhat later than largemouth bass. The busy bluegill is associated with frog noises, a disappearing sun, and roost-bound wading birds.

Although they are prolific in suitable waters, they can be a management problem, as there are some areas where there are swarms of undersize ones with hardly any worth catching. They're food for bass, but they delight in feeding on bass eggs, and a seemingly simple situation can gradually turn into a management problem. Overcrowded bluegills don't seem to be a help to bass, and I have heard several fisheries experts put on the spot by perplexed anglers trying to develop perfectly balanced farm pond populations.

When bass aren't expected, small dry or wet flies will take plenty of bluegills, but they tend to take such things deep and with so small a mouth it's almost impossible to release one alive, even with needle-nose pliers. In the best bluegill areas I haven't caught many bass on small trout flies, although there have been a few exceptions. I simply don't use them much, however deadly they may be under some conditions.

Since most panfish are the right size, it's natural to think of a whisper of a rod and the fun of truly miniature tackle. The trouble is that when you're using compromise bugs, a little Number Two or Number One rod isn't quite enough to cast them well—and bluegills and other panfish are likely to be caught in weedy cover.

Sunfish such as the pumpkinseed, redbreast, and longear will take about the same things the bluegills do. The redear sunfish, known as the shellcracker in the South, has different habits and feeds most regularly on the bottom. I had never caught many shellcrackers on a fly rod until I tried using some Woolly Worms and their relatives along shallow shorelines when the temperatures were just right. We'd let the fuzzy things, black or dark green (Greenie), sink to the bottom and twitch them very

An ultra-light trout outfit is used for panfish. This one is the red-ear sunfish or stump-knocker, which is often difficult to catch on flies.

gently, holding the boat pretty well off. We caught quite a few largemouth bass that way, although the bass ran pretty small. I never knew any fly fishermen who really specialized in shellcrackers.

I don't hear much about the green sunfish, which we used to call "black perch" in the Midwest. Those fish were real bug swatters and would take a Number Four bug almost as well as they'd strike a Number Six. When I was a beginning fly addict in Southeastern Kansas, some of them seemed pretty good fish to me, and sure enough, it wasn't just youthful enthusiasm. I found some old snapshots that showed they were better than hand size. I think the conditions were exactly right for them in some of those weedy lakes and prairie creeks. Their large mouths made them look a lot like bass. The rock bass has a similar silhouette and took bass bugs well along Ozark streams, where they were called goggle-eye and took bugs of smallmouth bass size. They lived close to fast water but preferred the quiet areas.

There's another fish with a big mouth and hearty appetite for bugs and wet flies: the warmouth of the South. I've caught them repeatedly in weedy water that they shared with gar and mudfish, and they have a reputation for surviving in stagnant areas with poor water quality. They have been caught over 2 pounds, but where I have fished they ran much smaller. They have good-size mouths and can hit with a *pop,* but I don't think they are particularly hard fighters, and their tail shape makes them look a little primitive. I've heard them described as a southern model of the rock bass. I've caught them when I'd given up on bass in small, landlocked backwaters and ditches.

The biggest crappie I ever caught hit a full-size bass bug where a wet-weather creek was feeding a sluggish river, but that isn't the best way to fish for them. At the time I was expecting bass, and a variety of fish had ganged up to intercept the windfall of bait. And although I've caught a lot of crappies on top, that's not the best way to go. Late evening is the best time for top water, but a slow-worked wet fly is more consistent.

The white crappie and black crappie have similar range over most of the United States, and the distribution maps show a gap between the Midwest and the Pacific mountain states, but they've been introduced in places the mapmakers probably don't know about. The whites are happy in murkier water, and they do not school up as much as the blacks. The schooling habits can make for feast or famine. A school of crappie doesn't make much disturbance on top, and this year's hot spot may be fishless next year—although the fish may not be far away.

Brush piles and submerged tree branches attract crappies, and I know lakes where there have been sunken brush piles that have been fished and replenished for human generations. It is not uncommon for a crappie lover to grumble that he has lost one or more of his brush piles, having forgotten where he put it and being unable to remember the shoreline objects he located it by. Most such stashes are pretty deep for fly fishing, although it can be done if you're stubborn.

There are times when the fish appear in shallow water along shorelines, generally just prior to spawning in late winter or early spring, dependent on the latitude. They prefer brushy spots, even then, and a small wet fly works. Generally they're deep enough that a jig fly goes best. That's simply a shiny, little fly tied on a miniature jig hook, and it can go several feet deep if you have the patience. A good rig is about a Number Six fly rod with a sinking-tip line, and the drill is to retrieve very slowly with repeated lifts of the rod tip. Most of the strikes come as the fly is "falling back" after a lift, and it is not a good time for nature study, as many a crappie tastes the fly, decides it isn't what he wants, and spits it

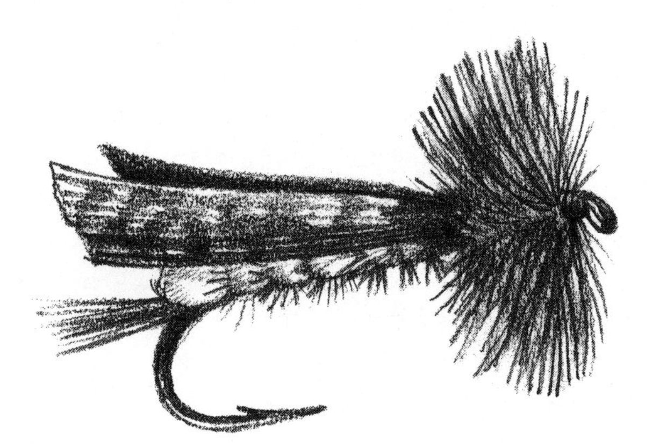

Hair and feather grasshoppers have, for the most part, been more successful than exact imitations of hard materials. This is Joe's Hopper, long successful with bass, panfish, and trout.

out. You set the hook at the slightest sign of hesitation, and though you'll catch considerable trash, you'll catch some crappies too.

In order to get the best jigging action from your fly, you'll need to make short casts so that the retrieve is largely vertical, and this is no place for the double haul. If I were going to make a career of crappie collecting, I'd prefer a long rod—at least nine feet—so that I could work the jig fly more nearly straight up and down without putting a boat over the fish. And this is almost always boat fishing for several reasons. The water's often pretty deep just off a shoreline bush or brushpile, you need to be up high to produce a jig action, and you may need to move frequently between spots. The casting is not artistic.

White bass live mainly in the eastern and midwestern parts of the United States, and much of the time they're not the best of fly-casting targets, as they stay deep, primarily in reservoirs, where trollers tend to be the big winners. But in summer and fall they school up to strike bait pods on the surface, making for considerable excitement and boat jockeying. It's much like school fishing for black bass, and the flies or bugs used can be adapted to the size of bait—but if the feeding frenzy is really under way, a bigger bug or streamer may be better.

True striped bass, formerly believed to live and reproduce only in salt and brackish water, are a fine fly rod fish but *generally* aren't found with black bass. A hybrid cross between the striper and the white bass often mingles with black bass, however, and has been pushed successfully by fish managers. For some time I fished the mouth of a river that hosted schooling activities of both hybrids and true black bass (with an occasional true striper) and found that when largemouths and hybrids were striking the same school of minnows, the black bass were easier to catch. That was purely unscientific and in only one area. For the most part, although the hybrids, appearing under several names, have prospered, they have not been easy to catch on flies, and fly fishermen have not dug into the project as far as they may in the future.

White perch have a limited range along the Atlantic seaboard and in isolated spots inland. They tolerate brackish water and will occasionally hit good-size surface things. At times they are thick in the very shallow parts of eastern waters, and I once fished a natural New England lake where they were taking the bugs I had chosen for bass in rocky places. I

The white perch, often found in smallmouth bass waters as well as with largemouths, is a true fly rod fish in some waters.

could sometimes see perch wakes. In that case, there were too many of them, and most of them were too small. After I had caught twenty or thirty I realized the native who had sent me there thought they were smallmouth bass—but the day was saved by a couple of good smallmouths that stormed up from their granite boulders just as the loons were tuning up for evening. Much of the time, white perch are too deep for entertaining fly fishing, but they are good streamer takers when moving upstream to spawn each spring.

Almost all of these panfish will take natural flies from the surface at some time during the year, so we can call them targets of opportunity. A bass fisherman is apt to run into a top-water feeding spree by other fish. A few bright streamers and some small bugs don't take up much room and are likely to come in handy. Generally you can keep the leader test down to around 6 pounds or lighter, heavy enough for bass in open water. The panfish aren't necessarily more leader shy than the bass, but

A mixed bag in weedy water includes a black bass and a pair of pickerel, which are noted for snipping off valuable surface bugs.

when we get into small lures, the big leaders cramp their style, and when the fish has time to really munch a lure, it's likely to notice something heavy.

Chain pickerel live with largemouth bass in much of their range, which includes most of the eastern United States, and will take most fly rod lures, especially near-surface streamers and those with small spinners. On a typical southern bass lake with plenty of weeds, they'll tend to concentrate in certain areas for no obvious reason. I wouldn't call this "schooling," but the strikes sometimes come in rapid succession. The surface strike is a slashing take easily recognized with a little experience. They tend to follow a rapidly moving lure at the surface or near it, whether they take it or not.

These fish, like other pikes, are ambushers, and when there's a border of weeds along a shoreline, you'll probably get the best results by working the bug or streamer parallel to the cover's edge, as the fish are likely to be just inside the weeds facing out and may hesitate to follow a lure that moves out away from cover. I suppose you should use a piece of heavy tippet to avoid cutoffs, but I seldom do, as it certainly cramps the style of the size of lure a pickerel prefers. In lakes the fish are pretty territorial, and you're likely to find the same fish in the same spot repeatedly—noticeable if its a big one. On the surface, I think a fast retrieve works best—certainly faster than you'd use for bluegills, and generally faster than a bass would prefer. There are pickerel specialists, but most bass fishermen take them incidentally while using bass lures.

Redfin and grass pickerel are the smallest members of the pickerel family, with the grass model living farther west, while the chain pickerel is along the Atlantic coast. Both redfin and grass pickerel take very small streamers and shiny items such as fly rod spoons and spinners. Their habits are roughly the same as those of the chain pickerel, their close relative.

The northern pike certainly can't be classified as a panfish, and although it lives in much northern bass water, it also holds forth farther north than the bass live. I am guilty of deliberate pike expeditions in waters where there were no known bass, but the northern and the bass, especially the smallmouths, are likely to live together. The pike is predatory in spades and will sometimes eat almost anything that doesn't eat him first, there being tales, undoubtedly true, of pike taking ducks and geese. It is good advice to keep your hands out of the water when pike are on a feeding binge.

The intriguing part is that the "snakes" can sometimes become uppity and refuse to strike anything you show them. I once went on a pike-fishing trip in an Alaskan backwater and found them ravenous and fearless for a few minutes, only to have them quit suddenly, and although we continued to paddle along the same type of shoreline for the rest of the afternoon, we had no more strikes at all. We tried deep and shallow streamers and several kinds of popping bugs—the same things they had charged wildly a little while before.

Having caught pike incidentally on various things, two of us decided on a true big-pike fly-fishing trip. We rigged heavy bass rods and lines with plenty of backing and told our desires to a Yukon guide with a top reputation. No problem, he said, he had the big pike staked out in a big backwater of a cold river, and in late afternoon he could promise plenty of action.

It certainly looked like pike water, weedy fringe and all, and on

Northern pike are frequent residents of black bass water but don't always live up to their reputations for ravenous appetites.

about the third cast I noted a frightening swell behind my streamer. Resisting the temptation to stop the lure and "feed it to him," I hurried my stripping, and the swell followed the fly to the boat, but then disappeared. Another cast produced the same result, and while the guide paddled unhappily, we watched a continuing series of great bulges without a single strike as darkness fell.

"I don't know what was wrong with them," the guide told us, "but they can be touchy. I'll tell you where they're stacked up and should be easy."

So the next morning we drove our truck until a bumpy trail faded out. Then we went on with an inflated boat we could use in some parts of a placid creek and across some marshy pools and over a beaver dam, until we reached a small woodland lake with weeds around the edges and a disgusted loon that left it with us. We started casting at a group of four visible pike and caught all of them, despite a rousing battle each time one was hooked.

So we paddled our little boat around the lake and watched the evil-eyed pike come storming up in the clear water to slash at anything we showed them. Like some other species, the pike has never really come into full respectability, and there are those who say it isn't worth eating. This latter seems to depend on the choice of chef. I've been releasing all of my bass in recent years, but some of the fellow travelers are almost as good at dinner time.

A long way from northern pike, in Georgia's Okefenokee Swamp, we slipped along in a little boat where the vegetation was knitted together in shallow water, sliding through little open paths. Fishing was slow. I flipped a yellow bug with rubber legs into one of few places where I wouldn't get hung up, and there was a glugging strike. A few tugs and a circular run, and I dragged the "bream" alongside and reached for it. It didn't look quite like a bluegill, and it was a stranger to me.

"That's a 'flier,'" said the man with the paddle. "I was raised with them. I guess almost everybody was raised with some kind of a sunfish."

I thought of the "black perch" and bluegills of my youth and agreed with him. I looked up "flier" in an identification text and found it fit in with the rest of them.

FOR THOSE OF us who are not particularly interested in fishing flies deep, alternatives are available for finding fish in summer. One of these is stream mouths where cold water pours in, usually providing compatible temperatures as well as a food supply. The channels of some streams continue out into the lake, so casts should be made far out, and perhaps deep, after trying the visible part of the mouth. Too many anglers anchor their boats to the visible part when the fish may be in deeper water. Other stream mouths may spread out in the form of a delta. In this case there probably is a sharp dropoff, and the best fishing usually is over this. . . .

Keel-fly hooks offer weighting alternatives that make fast-sinking patterns even more weedless . . . weights can be applied with sheet lead, trimmed as desired, or with split shot, to the bow of the hook or to the keel. Forward weighting of course makes the fly dip headfirst, while keel weighting causes it to settle. It has been recommended that the point and barb should be bent upward at an angle of about thirty degrees for better hooking. The weighting may or may not interfere with the body dressing, or may replace it, depending on how it is applied. This is a minor matter because the principal dressing is the wing, put on at the neck of the hook.

Joseph D. Bates, Jr.
Streamers & Bucktails

NINE

Boats, Boots, and Bubbles

WHEN BASS BOATS blossomed with fishing tournaments, the change was so abrupt as to startle veteran anglers. At the beginning of the big-time bass tournament, it was customary to start all of the boats together in a sort of headlong charge toward real or imagined hot spots. Even then, the boats were fast and getting faster. Eventually tournament managers had to put a ceiling on power for competitive bass boats.

But before the tournament starts were tamed, the takeoffs were spectacular, and Ray Scott, father of the modern bass tournament, told a story that seemed to cover the situation. The locale was mountain country where a great impoundment had filled the canyons, and it was the day's beginning for an entry list of some of the first professionals.

There was morning mist between the rocky and forested hills, and as thousands of horsepower growled and screamed ahead of dozens of roostertail wakes, the sounds bounced about the canyons. Indistinct in the mists and in midchannel, a lone fisherman stood in his little boat and tried frantically to start his stubborn outboard while the roaring apparitions bore down upon him. In one anecdote it tells the story of the "new" bass fishermen.

Tournament fishing and the big, fast bass boat have changed bass fishing so that it is seldom viewed as a contemplative sport anymore. And though fly fishermen grumble at the carnival atmosphere and the sacrilege of dollars for fish, they must admit that nothing has done so much to

This Skeeter was one of the first true bass boats and was extremely efficient although short on room.

encourage the study of their fish and its habits. The bass professionals have no intention of letting their meal ticket languish without management, and in the long run their input will have more effect than anything that could have happened without them.

The bass tournament doesn't work very well with fly fishing for a number of reasons, although it has been tried, but fly fishermen, it seems, are not interested in serious head-to-head competition anyway. It is the bass boat and its electronics that can help fly fishermen, and they haven't really taken advantage of it. For that matter, few of the bass boat manufacturers have made much effort at recruiting fly fishermen. They seldom include storage for long rods.

The fast bass boat is fine for large impoundments or other big water, but few fly fishermen show much interest in it, mainly because they operate a great deal in tight areas where a seventy-mile-an-hour bass boat would be a handicap. I've done years of fly casting from bass boats and have no complaint except that some of the gadgetry seems to be continually clutching at my running line. I have a reasonably fast compromise boat only a little more than fifteen feet long and pretty well dehorned for open space. Low console.

Fly fishermen tend to move about within a boat more than plug-casters or spin fishermen do, and I question the electric motor foot control, which tends to limit me to one spot, generally a high-mounted seat. Some tournament fishermen, of course, have the same feeling, even if they don't use fly rods. They feel it's easier just to reach over and make any direction change that's necessary. Some electrics can be rigged with a choice of hand or foot steering. Anyway, the fewer line grabbers you have, the better.

If the cost isn't important and you intend to travel long distances for your fly fishing, the saltwater "flats boat" is ideal, being wide open for running line and having secure full-length rod storage under the wide gunwales. A poling platform is good if you don't get carried away and use it when too close to bass in shallow water. The console should be low. In fact, a high silhouette is the curse of many expensive fishing boats.

The late Jason Lucas, highly opinionated but a fine bass fisherman who wrote for *Sports Afield,* was once asked what sort of boat would be usable for two fly fishermen to fish from simultaneously. He stated that

A true compromise boat, capable of handling rough water and with a usable poling platform consisting of an outsized cooler.

the battleship *Missouri* was just a little too short. But then, Lucas liked to fish alone, anyway, and didn't want to encourage companionship in that endeavor.

It's true that a careless fly caster can take up a lot of room, but it isn't necessarily so. Three of us once fished a lake where uncontrolled drifting was an ideal method—cross the lake, then go back and drift it again over slightly different water. Now we were not trick casters and we weren't tournament casters, but all of us had done a lot of it, often in confined spaces. In two days of drifting and casting, we tangled lines exactly once—all three of us standing up in a fifteen-foot boat. I confess we threw pretty much straight ahead, and there wasn't much wind, but I don't think I could have done any better if I had been alone. So I don't worry about two experienced casters in anything longer than twelve feet.

One advantage of the modern bass boat is that it lies low in the water, and few craft of its length keep you out of the horizon better. The otherwise near-perfect flats boat has a higher profile. Low profile is the main reason why waders sometimes catch fish while boaters draw blanks. The seaworthiness of the flats boat demands some freeboard.

Between the eighteen-foot bass boat with its big engine and the foot-powered floater bubble, there are some very light craft that work well in shallow backwaters and lakes, where they can be manhandled over shoals if necessary. Some of them will plane with moderate-size outboard engines, and all of them will go well with the smaller electric motors. They'll work with pole, paddle, or oars. The larger ones tend to be aluminum in the North and fiberglass in the South. Although they're not intended for offshore travel, they can live through heavy weather on most lakes. As they come from the factories, most of them are not convenient for fly fishing, but they can be customized with plywood to give spacious casting platforms. It may be difficult to attach electric motors to the bows of some of them.

For rivers and the smaller lakes, it's hard to beat the square-ended aluminum johnboat, preferably with a bow shaped to handle modest waves. An outgrowth of the standard shape is the aluminum bass boat, splitting the difference in cost between the big competition rigs and the unadorned johnboat. They can carry all the instruments and have plenty of room. Aluminum has many advantages and a few disadvantages. Mod-

A heavy-duty fourteen-foot aluminum johnboat is used to demonstrate a shoreline technique. The bug is being worked at the edge of a patch of small pads just under the surface. For a single angler, casting nearly parallel to the shoreline has many advantages over running the boat offshore and drawing lures directly away from the edge.

ern construction of heavy aluminum will take a beating and has come a long way in recent years. Here's a lot of go for a little power, and maintenance is at a minimum.

The plain and simple aluminum pram and aluminum johnboat are bare-bones efficiency for rivers, creeks, and small lakes, and I've owned half a dozen of them. I see them doing hard work from South America to Alaska, and it's hard to find anything to take their place. Right now we have a wide and heavily built fourteen-footer that goes faster than it needs to with a twenty-five-horse outboard. With a fifteen-horse engine, it will plane with three big adults aboard. We had a bracket built on the bow to hold a light electric motor. That's enough boat for two fly fishermen to use comfortably.

It's noisy, even in a little chop. We've insulated the interior with plywood and carpeting, however, so we can move around without sending vibrations to the shoreline. This type generally sits high in the water and is miserable to row or paddle in a high wind. If you expect to drag a boat over levees, you'd better stick to a twelve-footer or smaller. And it's possible to use aluminum that's too light, for you can wear out a bottom dragging the boat across rocks or gravel. I once let a grade-schooler borrow an ultralight eight-footer that I could carry under my arm to all sorts of backcountry puddles. Using a three-horse motor, he tried to see how far he could drive the thing up on a grassy bank, marking each new record. There was some gravel there, too, and the boat leaked copiously when he brought it back.

Some fine bass-fishing craft have almost disappeared with modern design, for it's hard to fasten a boat to a car top these days. I went through a lot of that, beginning with canvas and wood and ending up with aluminum. You can still fasten canoes on top, but it generally takes a little doing. The pickup truck is a marvel for the shorter johnboats and the semirigid inflatables, but the more comfortable the bigger boats get, the less likely the fisherman is willing to smash through brush and mud to get a little one in the water.

I like to fish from canoes, and the fiberglass ones are pretty quiet, though they may be somewhat heavier than similar aluminum rigs. I like about sixteen feet for a comfortable canoe to be used by two fishermen. Aluminum canoes are tough and light, although they tend to stick on

A canoe is a top-notch craft for backcountry areas like this river backwater, but it has suffered from being more difficult to car-top on modern automobiles.

rocks when used to run rivers. The beautiful handmade wooden ones of the true masters are not intended for the banging bass fishermen are likely to give them.

It's possible to fasten canoes atop many modern cars with suitable gadgets. Electric motors and small outboards work fine on them, and some of the best fishing rigs are square sterned. Those with really wide sterns are likely to be a mite big for carrying as cartoppers. In much of the backwoods North, the canoe remains a regular fixture, a good example of how location seems to have more influence than terrain when it comes to boat popularity. When I go to real canoe country of the northern United States and Canada, I am invariably surprised at what canoes can do.

Canoe poling is a neat trick, seldom used except in true canoe country. Maybe it's because standing up in one is considered bad form by those who feel a canoe is a touchy vehicle in which everybody should get as low as possible and stay put. In Canada I found myself with a Northwoods guide who looked like a Northwoods guide. He put our gear into his canoe and said we'd begin fishing about a quarter mile upstream. Since it was a fairly fast river, I had no comment but settled myself in the bow and awaited developments.

He brought out a pushpole and began sliding upcurrent. He read the water perfectly, slipping in below rocks that broke the heavy flow and now and then going out into the open river if there was a slow stretch or an eddy. We got to where we were headed with no problems and seemingly with no particular effort. Of course, with no one watching, I sneaked the canoe away from camp that night and tried it myself. It's a little like riding a bicycle—it has it's own special kind of balance. But within a few minutes I was doing pretty well. In a sort of backwater of the canoe business, there are upstream races in which the polers get surprising speed.

Canoes are highly efficient fly-fishing tools, easily transported and able to move in very shallow water, and if everybody stays seated when fishing, the silhouette is quite low. Generally a medium-size boat is most practical. A thirteen-footer can be pretty skittish and tiring over the long haul, and I've rolled a little one when my paddling became too eager.

Small gasoline outboards work fine on canoes, although they take a little balancing when set up on a stern bracket with a double-ender. Small electric motors will go surprisingly fast. Some states have confusing regulations regarding canoes if any kind of power is used. They license an eighteen-footer just as they would license an eighteen-foot bass boat or flats skiff.

The electric motor business isn't complicated with the larger boats, but it's easy to get too much motor on a really small johnboat or canoe. With a fourteen-foot johnboat we're using now, we have a little too much electric motor and have to keep turning it on and off when working a shoreline. Since fish seem to accept a steady purr and are easily scared by an on-and-off program, I'll get a smaller motor next time.

I've had a few repairs done on small electrics. But they aren't very expensive, and when one goes bad I tend to junk it and buy another, although I couldn't afford to do that with something that moves the bigger boats. At one time some of the small motors were intended only for fresh water, and when they got into brackish areas all sorts of things would go wrong. For one thing, the pin that held the propeller would disintegrate, though I don't think this is likely to happen now. From time to time there have been new electrics that had no parts program backing them, and twice I have found myself with a broken electric after manufacture had stopped. Better stick to well-known makes. There are several.

There is water growth you can't run an electric motor in any more than you can run a gasoline engine there. There have been some wonderful improvements in electric motor propellers, but the advertising is pretty carefree with regard to weeds. There are some kinds of weeds a "weedless" prop will go through and some kinds it won't. And the same goes for the guards that are installed to ward off weeds. These are good investments in most cases, but they aren't perfect.

Electric motors are frequently attached to the transoms of very small boats. The maneuvering isn't as brisk as when the electric pulls from the bow, but it keeps the motor farther away from the fish most of the time. It's hard to tell just how much effect electric motors, oars, paddles, poles, or idling gasoline engines have on bass.

I often hear someone say that such and such a disturbance has no effect on bass because they simply lie suspended and watch the noisemaker. Believe me, a lot of bass that lie and watch the machinery won't strike, and they're alerted, even if they don't squirt away. In clear water you can see smallmouth bass feeding within ten feet of your waders, but they have no intention of striking anything you throw to them. There are some otherwise normal bass fishermen who will throw a heavy anchor overboard, saying it doesn't scare bass—and it's true that the bass don't necessarily flush, but it can turn them off. I know, I know, sometimes a disturbance turns them on—but don't count on it.

In pristine waters bass are much more easily scared than where there's constant boat traffic. They learn to accept boats, water skis, and jet skis as part of the routine, and I once saw a man catching bass on a streamer fly in a spot where good-size boats were being launched and retrieved noisily only fifty feet away. Most of the time the quiet approach is better, and there are numerous resort lakes where the fishing doesn't really get good until the daytime traffic has subsided. The ten-mile-an-hour trolling mentioned earlier can't be counted on, but such exceptions make it harder to sell the gentle approach.

There is nothing wrong with the fish's hearing, and they can probably hear loud talk—but hearing is a matter of sound waves, and your falling over a tackle box or repairing a boat seat can cause scary vibrations. Insulation is a good investment on any boat, glass or aluminum. That we're sure of, but boat color is more complicated. White is fine when the boat is in shallow water and between the fish and a bright sun, but most of the serious bass fishermen feel that dull boat colors without too much gleam and glisten are better most of the time. A weathered, old olive-drab johnboat fits in with the scenery pretty well most of the time. Dull green and tan are pretty good bets. Boats are generally seen against the sky, and sky colors are endless. Try not to throw a shadow across the prey. There are many tricks, and keeping a low profile in a boat is good when you're close to fishy cover.

Much of my fly fishing, and possibly much of yours, is done in a boat with a spin fisherman or a plugcaster. When a boat moves along a shoreline, it's natural to assume the bow is the best spot to cast from, but some good fly and bug casters prefer the stern. In my experience, if fishing is very good, the bow is the best place. If it's slow, I'd rather be in the stern. The reasons are simple. If fish are striking well, they'll probably hit the first thing that comes along. But if they're not taking well, the bigger lures may stir them up a little and cause them to take a streamer or a bug coming along a cast or two later.

In fishing a shoreline there's a tendency to simply move the boat along a comfortable cast from it, and that works fine if there's cover extending out a considerable distance, for you can cast into pockets and keep your lure in fishy water for much of a long retrieve. But if you're fishing a steep bank with no extended cover, most of a long retrieve is generally wasted. The solution is to position the boat so that you can cast parallel to the shoreline and show your cast to more fish. That's a lot of extra work, and most of us tend to get tired of it pretty quickly and simply cruise along well off the bank and keep casting to the edge. Fly tackle has an advantage over other types here, because you can lay a lure against the bank briefly, pick it up, and drop it again just a short distance away, while the plugcaster or spin fisherman has to retrieve his lure all the way in.

In weedy water it's sometime possible to simply drift across a good place, motor back to the starting point, and do it again. This is pretty relaxing, but it's easy to be mesmerized by the routine, and I've found myself simply casting ahead rather than fanning the casts out to actually cover the water. A fly caster who minds his business can easily cover a swath of more than one hundred feet in drifting a flat—or he can just cast ahead mechanically and cover a ten-foot strip all the way across. When two casters are operating, of course, they can divide it up.

The float tube isn't exactly new, since it has been around ever since there were truck tires. Some of the latest models have all the comforts of home and make it easy to fish backcountry lakes or streams that are too deep to wade. The first ones I saw were simply truck tubes with homemade harnesses, but now they make them very comfortable—and safe—with some users towing second inflatables as tenders with everything from lunches to radios and beer. The best propulsion seems to be swim fins that enable you to move backward pretty fast. I've used other types that allow you to go forward, but they were harder to walk in. There have been horror stories of fishermen getting upside down in float tubes, but I don't think there's much danger of that and have moved across some deep, cold water. Once you get out of the water, you have quite a bundle to carry.

Deke Meyer, who wrote the book *Float Tube Fly Fishing,* points out some special benefits of float tubes. For one thing, being so close to the water, you can do very delicate things with flies. He points to the "neutral density fly," which can be manipulated at almost any depth when you and your rod are suspended just a few inches up.

Some of the tubes have most of the comforts of small boats and cost almost as much. At first I grumbled that there was too much built-in comfort and gadgetry, but when you spend an entire day paddling about in one, it's nice to be able to lean back and enjoy the scenery. The disadvantage, however, is that a fully equipped rig is a real load when you get to shore.

The float tube is as close to wading as you can get without actually doing it. I know fly fishermen who refuse to fish from a boat, saying that wading is part of the game. Unless you want to change locations frequently, wading is a good way to go, and in the South I see bug fishermen literally wading up to their necks during warm weather.

There isn't much place for hip boots. A man I used to fish with said that the only advantage of hip boots over knee boots was that they held more water. You need waders all right, and to be completely equipped you need some lightweight ones for cool water and neoprene ones for cold water. Most bass waters can be navigated with felt-soled shoes; only a few smallmouth streams demand cleats.

Bass are designed to see underwater, but they seem less afraid of someone wading than of someone standing high in a boat, and no one has been able to explain it to me. Often fish will bump against your legs when you're wading, but I'm not sure it has happened to me with bass. I do know that when wading trout streams, I've frequently had startled trout hurrying downstream that bumped hard into my legs, even though it was a wide stream with plenty of room to get by. Why any fish should bump accidentally into a man's legs in a broad creek has never been explained to me at all. At any rate, they must pay little attention to legs in the water.

But when you're fishing in weeds, there's a different situation. In some waters the growth is so knitted together that a wader can move it twenty feet from where he steps. In that case, you'd better not use extrashort casts, for you might be throwing to fish that are being yanked around by the plants you've moved.

Extra equipment becomes a nuisance, but nothing will take the place of a fishing vest for wading. It holds extra spools with different types of line, nippers, leaders, line- and bug-floating dope, a light raincoat, more bugs and streamers than you'll ever need, a small flashlight, leader straightener, something to drink, polarized glasses, a first-aid kit, insect dope, sunscreen, and possibly a sweater. That's only the beginning: Fishing vests gather things. When it grows to about twelve pounds, start taking out some of the stuff.

A THOROUGH COMMAND OF the rod and line is as essential and important as the wielding of the whip in the case of the tandem or four-in-hand drive. We are reminded of this analogy that the most skillful cast we ever knew wielded the whip. We refer to the famous coachman, Tom Bosworth.

Old Tom had, in the early part of his life, driven three successive British sovereigns, namely the Fourth George, the Fourth William, and finally, for a lengthened period, Her Majesty Queen Victoria. As a successful fisherman, old Tom, when known to the writer, was unsurpassed. . . . A favorite freak of his with the whip was to take the pipe from the teeth of a passing pedestrian by a calculated whirl of the whip, and his aptitude was as remarkably exemplified for a limited distance in the use of the rod. Bosworth originated the Coachman fly so much appreciated for night fishing. This artificial has recently been much used as a fancy fly for day fishing, and with considerable success.

David Foster
Scientific Angler,
on the origin of the Coachman flies

TEN

More Bass for Flies

IT TAKES NO science degree and no license to proclaim knowledge of black bass ecology. The layman's ideas of how to keep more bass healthy and happy in a few thousand rivers, lakes, and ponds range from lofty ideals of international environmentalism to ancient superstitions.

Unfortunately, some of the opinions of professional fish biologists have at times been only a little better than those of the unwashed multitude. There are devoted fish managers who would just as soon some of the accepted opinions of years ago could be forgotten. Probably there are some pseudoscientific papers they would like to see burned. In the black basses we have the best known of American game fish, but their failures and successes are still likely to come as surprises to conscientious experts.

Fly fishermen have a special corner in the bass welfare scheme. Of course, we want black bass to prosper in a variety of environments, but we particularly want shallow-water, fly-taking bass to multiply. We must remember that some kinds of successful bass fishing simply don't mean much to us.

There are several different types of black bass, although a fly fisherman could be happy and successful without knowing it. As we get into a little elementary biology, we'll get along better if we separate them now.

Largemouth Black Bass

The largemouth is best known, most plentiful, and most widely distributed. No one can now describe its range, as it has been established in thousands of lakes and streams around the world. The original range was in southeastern Canada, through the Mississippi valley and Florida, and along the Southern Atlantic coast. Late in the 1900s, the range was extended across the Rockies and then into New England.

There are true anatomical differences between northern largemouths and the Florida fish, but it takes scale counts to tell them apart. The Florida fish historically grow larger, but some of this has been because of the long growing season in the South. In recent years, Florida bass have been introduced in other states, and there have been some very large fish produced in California. Biologists are vague, however, as to which of the big ones were crosses with the northern fish and which were true Florida bass. Most of the biggest bass have been coming from Florida in recent years, mainly from central and northern Florida. Despite constant rumors of giants, Central America and Cuba have not produced anything bigger than southern U.S. fish.

The most common distinction in appearance between the largemouth and the smallmouth bass is that only the largemouth's mouth extends past the eye. There has been some question when largemouth bass have grown very plump, causing the mouth to appear relatively smaller, but the eye-to-mouth check remains valid. Another major difference is that the largemouth's dorsal fin is almost entirely separated from the soft-rays behind it, whereas the smallmouth's gives the impression of a single fin with only a shallow notch between the two sections. Usually there is a great deal of difference in the markings of the two fish, but certain water conditions can make that confusing.

The fish are so adaptable and live in such a wide variety of habitat that spawning temperatures and locations are only approximate. Largemouths prefer sandy or gravel bottoms for spawning, and the nests are in quite shallow areas, probably one to three feet deep. The males clear the beds, and the females (which typically grow much larger) deposit their eggs for fertilization. Females may leave eggs in more than one nest, and the whole procedure is less regimented than usually reported. After the eggs are fertilized, males guard the nests—but females may remain nearby for some time. Beds generally are near shore, but bottom characteristics regulate that. Eggs number in the thousands, the most frequent argument against planting small fry.

In general, largemouth bass like somewhat warmer and more shallow water than smallmouths and prefer water that flows slowly if at all. In some lakes and rivers accommodating both species, they tend to be separated by bottom and water conditions. But in other localities they live together, behaving the same for the fly fisherman. It may be unusual for them to spawn in exactly the same localities, but they're often not far apart.

Smallmouth Black Bass

The current range of the smallmouth bass can only be guessed at. Biologist Keen Buss, writing in McClane's *New Standard Fishing Encyclopedia,* says its range was once largely confined to the Lake Ontario and Ohio River drainage systems. Now the smallmouth is scattered over most of the United States. I do not believe it has spread to foreign countries as widely as the largemouth, being less adaptable to warm lakes.

An important part of the smallmouth's future will probably be in replacing trout in watercourses that have not maintained purity or temperatures demanded by salmonids. It has already filled enormous gaps in such areas.

The smallmouth's mouth does not extend past its eye, and there is only a notch between the two sections of its dorsal fin. Although its colors vary considerably, there is almost invariably a mottled bronze tone and some smoky streaks.

Smallmouths generally spawn in much deeper water than do largemouths and in very clear water are said to build nests more than twenty feet down. Perhaps seven or eight feet is nearer to the average. The male builds the nest, and several females may spawn in the same bed.

In general, the smallmouth demands purer and cooler water than does the largemouth. Probably the largest smallmouths available today are in the deep impoundments, where they are generally difficult for fly fishermen except for occasional shoreline forays, which are hard to predict.

Spotted Bass

The spotted bass, sometimes simply called the Kentucky bass, is apparently a hybrid between the largemouth and smallmouth. It displays some of the characteristics of each in its preferences for habitat and has been found in very deep water in impoundments. It is found through the

Caught from the same waters, largemouth and smallmouth bass appear similar in general outline. The largemouth, however, generally shows a mottled area along the lateral line. The smallmouth's bronze shading doesn't show in black-and-white.

Ohio and Mississippi River systems, in northwestern Florida, and in Oklahoma, Kansas, and Texas. Generally it is not a good fly rod fish but takes flies and bugs when in shallow water. Spawning is in shallow water, similar to that of the largemouth and smallmouth. Some biologists have stated that the spotted bass are more hardy than either the largemouth or smallmouth. As with the other types of bass, the hatching time depends largely on temperature, but it is especially short with the spotted bass.

Redeye Bass

Very near to the "regular" smallmouth bass, the redeye model is a fish of southern waters and is said to spawn only in streams. These are true fly fishermen's fish and are sometimes touchy as to terminal tackle. A. D. Livingston, who has fly-fished a great many bass in a great many waters, picks the redeye as the gamest of the group. Its red eye distinguishes this species.

A little-known fish, recognized as a subspecies of redeye, is often called the Flint River bass, named for a Georgia stream. It is found only in the Apalachicola drainage and is being scientifically considered for full species status. David Foster, a Georgia fly fisherman, tells of catching the Flint River fish by delicate nymph methods generally reserved for selective trout.

The largest redeye bass in the fly section of the International Game Fish Association record book, 1991 edition, was 2 pounds, 12 ounces, from Flat Shoals Creek, Georgia. But then, the largest smallmouth bass appearing in the fly section was less than 5 pounds.

Suwannee Bass

The Suwannee bass is something of a miniature, evidently not growing more than around a foot long and generally found only in the Suwannee River system of Georgia and Florida. In appearance it is much like a smallmouth.

Neosho Smallmouth

Apparently the Neosho smallmouth has interbred with the "northern smallmouth" but is native to Kansas, Oklahoma, Arkansas, and Missouri. It's probably the basic stock of Ozark rivers, preferring fairly fast water. It has a larger mouth than most smallmouths and is less distinctly marked. The Neosho River runs in Kansas and Oklahoma.

Guadalupe Bass

The Guadalupe is a small species found in Texas rivers and looks much like the smallmouth.

These notes have been simple bare-bones descriptions of the various types of black bass to enable us to discuss management achievements and problems in more detail. I simply wanted to make clear exactly what fish I am referring to—but for the most part, "smallmouth" and "largemouth" will cover it.

A great deal of fly-fishing water was lost in the original construction of many lakes in recent years. In fact, the most obvious losses are in the flooding of hundreds of rivers and their tributary creeks that were especially adapted to the fly rod approach. When a lake accommodates a hundred times as many fishermen as did the rivers it was made from, it is unlikely the complaints of a few fly fishermen will make much of an impression. We simply can't complain except to each other.

We do have legitimate complaints in the degradation of water quality in natural lakes and streams, a natural result of overpopulation, industrialization, and more and more chemicals used in agriculture. Depending upon how well we do with fly fishing in the big impoundments, we may or may not be losing ground overall. We must concede that although tackle is more pleasant to use, fly fishing has not increased in efficiency as much as have baitcasting and spinning.

Smallmouth bass streams may have been the greatest losses of all through damming, and like other ancients who have seen winding rivers turned into great lakes, I complain about the good old days. But in this case we tend to ignore the tremendous growth of fishing as a sport, and if our rivers had not been dammed, at least some of them would be badly overcrowded by fishermen.

Smallmouth fishing in deep impoundments is unreliable business, involving a watch for the times when fish move into the shoreline shallows, where water cools or warms first. Dawn and dusk have a special significance.

The smallmouth has always had a special appeal in rapidly moving water. Although all of the black bass varieties sometimes feed on insects, the smallmouth has been more likely to attend hatches and live in areas where they occur. Smallmouth fishing in many cases is much like trout angling and calls for light fly tackle. It is the smaller smallmouth stream that has suffered most from damming and pollution—and in some areas has deteriorated because of crowding by recreational "floaters," many of whom fish very little or none at all. This simply was not foreseen a few years back. The flotillas of canoeists crowding some rivers have made serious fishing almost impossible, even when the drifters don't take any fish themselves. The larger rivers can accommodate them, but the smaller ones are at the mercy of the rental canoe.

The actual harm done by floating traffic is impossible to measure and may be very slight, even though endless week-end parades sometimes make serious fly fishing almost impossible. There is, of course, some pollution and in extreme cases some damage to shallow bottoms. Outboard motors, where allowed and usable, can do serious damage in the smaller streams, which the boaters are most likely to enter from bigger water.

One touchy subject is the effect of dyed-in-the-wool nature lovers who accept fishing as a natural sideline of drifting and camping adventures. Although these people are accepted as the backbone of environmental movements, they are less likely to release fish than are serious anglers, especially fly fishermen. In many cases, "living off the land" is an important part of the outdoor experience in their view. These conditions can make their mark on the very small bass stream, just as they can on small trout waters.

With pride, we can call fly casters the elite of fishermen, but overall fish management must be aimed at satisfying the masses of outdoor people. Many a fly fisherman has found himself unpopular when he appeared to seek special concessions for his kind of fun. Our earlier examples of dislike for fly users by other fishermen are to a small degree our fault—not that I know of any way to change this. We cannot alter nature, and "fancy fishing" is not appreciated by those who think anything but bait is effete.

We have improved very few rivers since we first began to fish them, although there is a bit of wry optimism regarding "degraded" trout streams. The generality is that many trout streams that no longer support the favored fish became usable by smallmouth bass. This, of course, was most dramatic in the East (to the disgust of some natives), but the transition is still going on in some parts of the West. I'd predict that fly fishing for both largemouth and smallmouth bass will become more popular in the West—and some of the fly shops that scorn them now might come up with classy bass bugs.

Lakes are generally a little easier to classify. We have the standard classification of lakes, applied especially to northern ones. The historically young natural lakes are categorized as *oligotrophic.* These have skimpy populations of fish such as the lake trout. The *mesotrophic* lake is middle-aged, usually contains a variety of fish, and is found across the northern United States. It can be good smallmouth water. The *eutrophic* lake is one that has aged; it can be almost anywhere but is fading as a producer of game fish. In the earlier stages of its decline, it can be fine water for both largemouth and smallmouth bass, and it has a great deal of vegetation, for better or worse. Eventually it is degraded to the point that it is of no use to the fisherman. These classifications are very tidy but not always easy to use in assessing fly-fishing water.

The "aging" lake is confusing because the term can mean two very different things. The long-term aging can mean thousands of years of natural change or "development," in which man has no part—and cannot profitably alter. The other form of aging is a relatively short-term thing.

For example, a "new" lake in Canada (oligotrophic) is deep, has little vegetation, and has a minimum of water growth. Its fish (the lake trout is the best example) are scarce and tend to be deep-water residents. It ages through centuries.

Now let's take a shallow reservoir in the Midwest—the old tank pond is a perfect example. From the day it is dug, it begins to fill with whatever washes in from the wet-weather creek that was dammed to fill it. As bass habitat, it improves steadily for some years with the growth of desirable plant cover. Then, with the bottom heavily silted and deep in resultant muck as fifty years of plants decay, it begins to lose its bass population. It catches pollution from agricultural chemicals and possibly from industrial discharge or even sewage. It is so enriched that the surface is covered with emergent plants and what we simply call "scum." Eventually the pond will fill up, until it's only a depression. At least some of them have. There's an even faster program with small farm ponds and "the place where the old pond used to be" can be found on many farms and ranches. Routine.

Even in miniature lakes the process of aging can be extremely complicated, for no two are exactly alike. The water plants and the soil will be different, the weather will be different from year to year, and intentional or accidental introduction of fish species can change the picture. Even careful management is not a sure thing, and the layman's view is likely to be simplistic.

The big impoundment, usually above a power dam, has a well-known schedule: a few years of extremely fine bass fishing when it is new, a rapid fading of results as the water "uses up" the newly flooded ground, and a stabilization period that frustrates some fishermen who thought they were master anglers. When a big impoundment is new and still filling, the fly fisherman is likely to find excellent results over newly submerged rosebushes or cactus; then things get pretty tough as the lake's population, smallmouth or largemouth, changes its routine. Surface fishing becomes scarce and spotty, and electronic depth finders come into their own.

As years go by, some arms of the big lake remain fairly shallow and develop their own communities where bass are concerned. They have aged gracefully and take on most of the characteristics of natural lakes, and their bass populations can be permanent, with the normal fluctuations that go with the game. The general program is predictable, but there are too many variables for set forecasts of time periods.

The natural aging and deterioration of lakes is sometimes interrupted by some natural phenomenon that causes fishing to become good, or even exceptional. So, to make it more complicated, deterioration of a small lake is a stop-and-go business, often with professional biologists frantically trying to find just what made things get better or worse. Far from making fun of serious fish managers, I simply point out that their lot is often complicated greatly by a series of natural phenomena and made worse by the simplistic views of most fishermen, even you and me.

Many years ago, waiting in the office of a Michigan fisheries biologist, I overheard a hard-charging fly fisherman who was bound on developing a super bass fishery in a small, weedy natural lake he had control of.

He asked the biologist if bass liked to eat bluegills and certain other sunfishes. Yes, the biologist replied, they are staples of the bass diet. Whereupon the angler outlined a plan for getting more of all those kinds of fish into his lake through a netting program.

The biologist told him that the sunfishes could overcrowd, that they competed in some ways, and that they eat bass eggs, so the fisherman decided he'd introduce northern pike in order to keep the sunfish under control. But the biologist reminded him that the pike might eat some bass too. I have forgotten what was to control the pike, but after the angler left, the fish manager pillowed his face in his arms.

I am using "aging" in this chapter for lack of a better term. Anyway, as a lake goes through the years, unpredictable things can happen to it, for better or worse, and in some cases no management can change the process. There is the matter of the gizzard shad. I knew a fine black bass lake in the South that deteriorated rapidly, mainly because of various kinds of agricultural waste, and gizzard shad virtually took the place over.

Gizzard shad are not game fish and live on what they strain from mud, including organic debris and materials that might be considered pollutants in many cases. When they took over the big bass lake and bass virtually disappeared, they were cause, effect, and indicator. About thirty years ago, after the lake had been pretty well given up, I was there when fish management people rotenoned it and killed a lot of shad—shad by the ton.

With the typically inspired approach of an eager-beaver fisherman who thinks something dramatic is occurring, I asked what was going on.

"Aw, we're killing a jillion gizzard shad," reported a biologist.

"Aren't they good for anything?" I wondered.

"Yeah, bass like to eat them, but there aren't any bass and the shad have taken over. We never could kill them all. If the lake is that good for shad, it sure isn't much good for bass."

The other day, about thirty years after I first observed the shad crusade, I saw a television show on the lake in question. It seems there is a current effort at getting rid of the shad, and cooks trying to figure a way of making them palatable enough that people will eat them, even if the largemouth bass can't.

Now let's look at this situation. The badly degraded lake is evidently perfectly adapted to gizzard shad—a nearly inexhaustible supply. The lake apparently isn't suited to bass culture in any way, and no matter how many shad are destroyed, there is no indication it would improve the bass situation any more than it did thirty years ago. The only bass solution would be to stop the pollution and begin again. There is now a project for establishing suitable wetlands to help purify the lake. This is a big body of water, and such projects are truly big and expensive operations, whether they work or not.

I guess it's safe to say that improvement or saving of a lake is invariably more complicated than it appears at first. Even when we have a fish kill, it's seldom easy to put a finger on the cause—and sometimes a kill results from natural causes without the usual depredations of man. For example, a combination of weather and water plants can lead to a lack of oxygen hard to predict and impossible to forestall. Plants make oxygen, but they also destroy it.

The balances of any body of water are extremely complex, and the matter of oxygen is one of the most confusing. Plants renew oxygen when there is sufficient light. In darkness, plants use it. Decaying vegetable matter not only is destructive to the oxygen supply, but it also often produces a variety of poisonous materials.

When a body of water is overloaded with plant life and suffers exactly the wrong kind of weather, it can produce a fish kill. Since most of the fish die during the dark hours, the deaths often come as a surprise. Even a biologist may not have an immediate explanation, since lack of oxygen may be accompanied by various poisons, either formed by decaying matter or introduced by outside pollution.

A heavy bloom of algae causes water to appear cloudy but does not necessarily indicate a fish kill is imminent. At certain times of year, most warm-water lakes have considerable algae present, but when the water becomes nearly opaque and there is no flushing process, it is an indication of an unhealthy situation, frequently pollution.

Too much decay of plant matter in a bass lake causes a buildup of silt and sludge on the bottom, and though there may be no serious poisons in the material, it can prevent the growth of rooted plants that would ordinarily grow from the bottom. The life that thrives in bottom sludge is generally not beneficial to bass, the predator. It may be just what a gizzard shad wants, containing the organisms he lives on.

There are some sudden and often inaccurate conclusions coming from "bloom on the water." It's a matter of degree, and at a boat dock the other day, a fisherman told me the water was "clouding up" and good fishing was on the way. I suppose he had made some good catches when there was considerable suspended material. But fish managers are fearful of blue-green algae, which generally means poor water condition. I don't want bass water very cloudy, but when it becomes crystal clear in a strange lake, I'm suspicious, fearing the lake isn't fertile enough. Very cold weather tends to cause suspended material to disappear.

Water that "blooms" or simply carries considerable suspended organic material should not be confused with muddy or stained water. Some rivers are "black" with stain from shoreline vegetation, and the bass coming from them may be so dark their markings are mostly obscured. Black water doesn't necessarily mean it isn't good for fish. The same goes for reddish water. Frankly, simply looking at a lake never tells the whole story, although it can be a good indication.

We must remember that different sections of a large lake may be very different in cover and even in water condition. On one largemouth lake that was considered badly polluted, there was an angler who did well because he had figured what parts of the lake actually received major influxes of pollution—in this case chemical discharge from agriculture. He studied the lake's barely moving currents.

When an undesirable species becomes too plentiful in a bass lake, it is nearly always a matter of water quality. The unwanted species is generally a messenger instead of the problem itself. I once watched a sportsmen's club go to great effort in spearing garfish the members feared were taking over their bass water. What they were actually facing was a deterioration of their water purity, which was less favorable to largemouth bass and more favorable to garfish. The same thing has been done regarding the grindle, or mudfish, another common resident of inferior waters.

In the garfish business, a professional biologist stated it like this:

"Of course garfish are an undesirable fish here. It would be impossible to thin them down much unless we killed everything in the lake and started over. But garfish spearing is good for a sportsmen's club. It keeps the members interested and entertained—and when there's a project that can actually do some good, they're ready to go."

That sounded pretty cynical, and public relations was not the fish manager's field—but he was right. Lake or river improvement is almost invariably a very complex business that must be preceded by study from professionals, and it is a bitter truth that many such situations are so complex and far-reaching that the average fisherman is forced to give up before he gets to the bottom of his problem, and if he gets there he may lack the power to improve things.

I want to describe two management situations occurring in Florida. I happened to be near them and have heard details through the years. Florida is a good locale, because it lacks extremely cold weather and is a capsule of the ills of bass waters—and largemouth waters in particular. It has overpopulation, overdevelopment, and the pollution that goes with them.

At one time the Kissimmee River, which flowed southward into big Lake Okeechobee through something like one hundred miles of south-central Florida, was typical of subtropical watercourses going through nearly flat country. The main channel was hard to follow, often obscured by vegetation, and there were thousands of acres of wetlands with endless bays and unnamed little lakes—excellent weedy bass cover in shallow water.

In an effort at flood control, the Corps of Army Engineers dredged the entire river into a series of lakes and one deep channel, employing locks to maintain proper levels. Here we had a subtropical variation of the big power impoundments farther north. We drove our boats through the river (canal?) and worked the established lake shorelines with popping bugs and streamers. Things seemed to be working out just fine, even though the miles of weed beds had been destroyed. New agricultural areas prospered, and homes appeared where there had been marshland.

But downstream at one of our best bass lakes of all, huge Okeechobee, the chemistry went bad. Scientifically naive fishermen like me hadn't liked the channeling for various reasons, but we hadn't realized that one of America's big "purification plants" had been wiped out and the Everglades were being poisoned. Water growth destroyed when the mammoth dredge channelized the river had been holding its own with pollution for all those years, but when the river became a ditch and the marshes became short-grass pasture, the water began to go bad. For that matter, when the great dredge was still finishing its digging at the north end, there were furious environmentalists at the south end crying for the return of the river to its original state.

And now, the environmental catastrophe has been expensively studied, the dry land has been weighed against what was once considered worthless swamp, and there is a grim effort at regaining what has been lost. Now, it seems, the "new" land that was produced by the channelizing must be bought back for flooding by the proper management agencies and the building that has been done on it must be bought. This, of course, means multiple millions to undo what was accomplished by multiple millions. The black bass may be only incidentals in this business, but those who want to fish shallow bass water are campaigning for a new river, complete with side channels, swamps, and grassy bays. I describe this because it is a capsule (big capsule) of bad news for bass.

"Drawdown" is a fairly new word in bass management and brand new to most fishermen. I believe the Florida Game and Fresh Water Fish Commission has been a leader in the use of the drawdown as a fish management tool, although it has been used for several purposes on impoundments in many locales. To oversimplify, it is a routine of lowering the water in a reservoir until a great deal of the shallow bottom is exposed to the sun for considerable time. Then, when the reservoir is refilled, we have much of the effect of a new lake with greatly improved bass fishing in the shallows.

The drawdown works best when the banks of a lake slope gently and when a slight lowering of the overall level exposes a large area of bottom. Although the general effect would be the same in a mountain reservoir with steep banks, the amount of bottom exposed there would be relatively small, probably not enough to have a practical effect on the fishing.

The drawdown is not necessarily received with rejoicing by residents of the lake area. A fishing resort operator is not likely to be cheered when his dock is suddenly attached to dry land—so drawdowns must be handled in moderation and after thorough study. The more the pollution, of course, the more effect a drawdown has. In some cases it is practical to physically haul away exposed sludge that would never provide a good bottom—but that gets expensive. And a successful drawdown depends on some uncontrolled variables.

A large, shallow lake in central Florida made a good pilot project for the drawdown procedure. It has been drawn down three times—twice with great success. In all honesty, the third operation was less dramatic, emphasis of the fact that all management procedures must depend upon a long list of conditions.

The lake was drawn down in winter, and biologists conclude that the shallow bottom must be exposed for at least sixty days for habitat restoration. It is an educated guess that the process would run slower in every way in a colder climate and more time would be required. It is estimated that a drawdown every three years is nearly ideal in Florida, and perhaps drawdowns farther north should be spaced farther apart, as much as six or ten years, but might require more "down" time.

If this seems vague, I mean it that way. We're dealing here with a very new procedure, one of very few recent innovations in bass management. The drawdown in many areas has been used as a means of weed control, with any fish management as a secondary accomplishment, if it does occur. Bass management has a history of dramatic promises and frequent failures. At least the drawdown works, although it may be hard to sell to the public, even to some fishermen. I guess I have to use the anticlimactic old phrase—"further study is necessary"—but this one looks like a winner, and a lot of dedicated people have worked hard on it.

Much of the modern fish manager's job is overcoming sins of the past. A recent generation of biologists winces at many of the doctrines of fifty years ago, but the public often accepts rumor, superstition, and outdated practices as gospel. I came from an age when it was thought the way to have a lot of any kind of fish was to pour cans of little ones in and wait for them to become big ones.

Then there was a generation with some biologists who felt the best bass management was no management.

"Stock bass?" the man would say tolerantly. "A female bass lays twenty thousand eggs, and you expect us to put in more little bass?"

And the layman would have nothing much to say, but the biologist was preaching what he believed to be true. Today we believe there is no sense in stocking bass in a healthy river or lake with a solid resident population—but now we are beginning to learn there are exceptional cases where it just might be practical. And we know that stocking may save waters that have undergone catastrophic losses (generally through pollution of some sort).

I have seen mass meetings of sportsmen crying for the retention of large fish hatcheries devoted to bass, while the managers insisted they were no longer necessary. We know now that huge hatcheries are not the solution for all black bass ills, but we also know that well-managed hatcheries have their place in emergencies.

Fishing method can have considerable bearing on bass populations. There is the matter of "bed fishing," generally for largemouths, and it is possible for an angler to actually fish for bass that he or she sees on a bed, since the largemouth bass nests in such shallow water. Many bass boats have improvised flying bridges from which a spotter can watch while the boat is being poled. It can work for fly fishing, although that is not the best way of catching sighted bass. The fly fisherman *generally* does better by simply working the general bedding area.

There are all sorts of illegal contraptions that snag big females and all sorts of rigs intended specifically for bed fishing. Where I have fished, few of the true bed fishermen released their catches. I have disagreed with some fish managers on this subject. I argued that in prime big-bass waters the very large bass were skimmed off during spawning season—and if conditions were right, there simply wouldn't be big bass there the next year. Their argument was that in big-bass country an 8-pound female was nearing the end of her life anyway, and catching her was no loss to the overall population and might actually be a gain.

But, wups! Let them take the real wall-hanging whoppers. The loss is in the slightly younger fish that get caught, too, and aren't released. I have seen a dearth of big bass in a well-known spawning area where conditions had been perfect for bed fishing for a single season. Next year was slow.

Given proper purity and spawning bottom (largemouths are less likely than smallmouths to be in rocky areas), the main problems are temperatures, predation, and fish density. The spawning program is dictated by both season and temperature, but mainly temperature, and 68 degrees Fahrenheit is about as near ideal as we can get. Smallmouths will spawn in cooler water than will largemouths—but not a whole lot cooler. In the North, spawning will run right into summer months. The earliest recorded *regular* spawning program in south Florida comes in January.

Now if cold weather continues too long, the female fish will resorb their eggs and not spawn at all for that year. The eggs are simply taken back into the fish's system. There are other things that can cause this, the most mysterious being fish density. Perfectly healthy bass will not spawn if there are too many fish, of whatever species, in the area. This, I suppose, can be a form of stress, a term we grab when we're a little shaky on what is happening to fish. It may cover a variety of things, but it is very real and affects larger fish more than small ones in most cases. Predation, such as that from panfish that eat bass eggs, is impossible to measure accurately. Of course, once the eggs are hatched, almost anybody in the neighborhood is likely to take a swipe at the fry, including Papa Bass. And now there is a little matter that should be noted by fly fishermen: The female may hang around for some time after spawning.

Smallmouth and largemouth bass prefer somewhat different habitats, although they can be found together in many areas, at least part of the year. I can find no proof that either is the dominant species, but their differences in choice of spawning and living areas in the same lakes have been cited as evidence that one or the other chooses the best spots. Like thousands of other fly fishermen, I have caught largemouths and smallmouths together and behaving much the same *as long as they are living together.* In casting two flies (bug and dropper), I have seen a largemouth on one and a smallmouth on the other on a single cast.

And here comes the temperature business again. Perhaps this is a pretty good summary: Water temperatures above 80 degrees Fahrenheit slow up bass and cause them to seek a cooler place. Water below 55 degrees generally means active feeding slacks off. This does not mean fish cannot be caught in colder water or warmer water—simply that such conditions are not ideal.

For the fly fisherman, temperatures are more important than for other anglers, simply because fly takers are generally active fish. A chilled bass that will suck in a worm from near the bottom is unlikely to squirt to the surface to take a fly or bug. We have mentioned methods that will work on slow-moving bass, but when the chips are down, few fly casters want to bother with those for very long. The thermometer is especially important for the fly fisherman who, after all, is looking for ideal conditions.

In any discussion of bass-fishing conditions, we must face the fact that there is no time when all of the fish are willing to strike a bug, streamer, or nymph. At best, we are skimming only a very small percentage of the fish present—and we might say that the fish that strikes a fly is a nonconformist in most cases. It's different when we cast a fly to a particular fish during some sort of hatch—but it's still only a small number of the fish that will strike on a given lure at any given time. I say this in full knowledge that some bass are caught over and over again in a controlled situation. I am led to believe there are some who can live next to lures all of their lives and never strike one.

I have here a theory that used to bring laughter but now gets respect. Where bass are relatively easy to catch, as when they are "schooling" on top-water baitfish, we find that a certain lure will succeed for a time and then fail to work. We finally settle on something that does better. My rustic analysis is that the fish that struck, for example, a yellow streamer with strips of mylar have all been eaten and the other fish may or may not have different weaknesses.

What does this have to do with management? It simply means that a shock boat may turn up plenty of fish, but the fishermen can't catch them. This is where the thoughty people start making up new lures and methods, and the theory of giving them something different is logical.

We divide bass management into two classifications: controlling the production and controlling the catch. For a long time it was preached that no amount of hook-and-line fishing could damage a bass population, but we didn't have so many fishermen in those days, and they certainly hadn't perfected some of the deadly procedures that work today. There has been a question of closed seasons for a hundred years, and it may continue for another hundred years. A closed bass season in most areas is a waste of law enforcement, but in some cases it is needed protection for overfished populations. The managers should decide, but it is impossible to close a season in one cove where it is needed and leave it open in the next one where nobody seems to catch the fish anyway.

There is the procedure of closing seasons during spawning because the bass are considered most vulnerable then. Here the old story of thousands of eggs being produced anyway generally rings true. Then there is the theory that a shortened season alleviates some fishing pressure, which it does. In most cases, managers feel that sensible catch limits will take care of the overkill problem. But when there are too many fishermen, the limits must be reduced, and we now have some fishing areas with catch-and-release only, which works beautifully on bass, able to survive a lot of rough treatment. One of the most valuable management tools is the slot limit, which means we must release certain sizes.

Both number and size limits take considerable law enforcement. It's relatively easy to simply close a season and arrest anyone who catches a bass, but when a few law-enforcement officers must patrol thousands of square miles of bass water, as in the larger impoundments and in true lake country, the task gets tough.

The slot limit is a marvelous tool but is very hard to enforce. If a certain year class is skimpy for natural reasons or has been pilfered unduly by fishermen who have keyed in on that particular size of fish, a slot limit can save what's left. In other words, if we're getting a shortage of bass from 10 to 14 inches long, we can simply make them illegal to keep. But I am told that many fishermen consider such regulations frivolous, and some who would obey most laws simply overlook these. And in most cases it is pretty easy for bass fishermen to jettison illegal fish when they see an enforcement boat coming around the bend. Since fly fishermen really do have a slightly different ethic from that of most anglers, I doubt if many of them are law violators, but they sure suffer from the depredations of others.

Most bass fishermen keep their fish, although the release ethic is beginning to make itself felt. In fish releasing, the bass angler is far behind the freshwater trout fisherman, and even the saltwater caster. The trout fisherman is more educated along that line, and the saltwater fly fisherman is generally an advanced operator with advanced ideas.

Bass behavior varies so much with water and bottom conditions that even an expert in the field finds it difficult to prophesy just how the fish will perform in a given lake or stream. The very adaptability of the fish can complicate the business of catching them. On numerous occasions I have taken a beating on waters that looked like a sure thing.

In Honduras I went to a lake that certainly hadn't been fly-fished much, if at all. It was weedy, mostly fairly shallow, and known to be full of bass because natives fished it commercially with handlines and plastic worms and did very well on good-size fish. The guide knew the lake well, and I was with a plastic worm expert using spinning tackle. I tried hard with a variety of flies and bugs and caught one undersize bass in two days of perfect weather. The worm fisherman caught plenty of fish. I found no baitcasters who had been doing well on the surface. A perfect top-water lake—but the bass evidently didn't know that.

In western Mexico I went with some plugcasters and worm fishermen to a fairly new impoundment with all of the new-lake characteristics and a reputation for fine bass fishing. Although it was a young lake, there was already some good shoreline weed cover. Before we went out I showed off by hooking a couple of small bass on a bug in the shade of the dock. The native guides and my associates could hardly wait to see me tear up the shoreline fish.

I went along the shoreline with a plugcaster, and every bug and streamer I had was ignored, while he was catching fifteen or twenty nice fish. The only way I scored was with a sinking line and fuzzy streamer, with which I finally caught a couple of good largemouths.

The general appearance and history of a lake give you a good start but are not always reliable. A particular type of food you or I never heard of may be the local staple. And even a favorite bass food may be ignored by fly casters who have been using something else all their lives. When I was very young and chasing smallmouths on Ozark rivers, the natives kept telling me that crayfish were the top natural bait, but I never even associated that with fly fishing. Then an old-timer told me that if I would approach the shallow tails of the pools at dusk and work a brownish non-descript streamer over the rock and gravel bottom, moving it fast, I'd be surprised.

Moving it fast? Like other kids I'd watched frightened crayfish scoot backward at high speed, but I somehow thought of crayfish *baits* as being slow moving. Since then there have been endless carefully tied fly rod crayfish such as Harry Murray's. "Keep the pincers small," fly designers say, "and once they're down near the bottom don't be afraid to yank them around a little."

I have never done enough inquiring about lakes I am fishing for the first time, and sometimes you'll get helpful information from fisheries biologists. "Tact" may not be the right word, but you'll get farther if you show immediately that you have a little background. Fisheries people may not be too anxious to help someone who simply wants to know where the bass are and what to use. Most fishing phenomena have an explanation if you'll dig into the subject.

I used to get up in the middle of the night and drive to a river mouth where it emptied into a bigger stream. At dawn in early spring there would be a riot of striking by black and striped bass on "menhaden" schools. This was roughly a hundred miles from the Atlantic, but any number of anadromous species would use the main river. To accommodate a biologist friend, I sent him a couple of fish from the morning feeding frenzy. He reported that those fish didn't contain menhaden at all but had been feeding on threadfin shad.

Since the baitfish had been called "menhaden" for at least thirty years that I knew of, I thought it was a freak situation, and I talked a good castnetter into picking up some of the bait from several areas in the vicinity while I rowed the boat. They were threadfin shad, all right, and until then I hadn't even examined them. The locals had been wrong for a couple of human generations. I don't think threadfin shad will prosper in freshwater lakes, but I know one introduction produced a single season of "schooling" largemouths.

Most fishermen have one or more lakes or rivers that they feel should provide better fishing, and the usual assessment, not always right, is that there simply aren't enough fish present. Sometimes a body of water contains bass of one kind or another that simply don't go for the angler's method. If a fly fisherman is repeatedly disappointed on what he feels should be productive water, he should check what methods *are* producing catches. If the bait fishermen, the plug throwers, or the worm users aren't doing well, the chances are something is wrong with the water. Maybe it has been checked by the local fisheries people, and too few anglers make intelligent inquiries of state managers.

In one case, all that the anglers were catching were occasional very small bass, and they wondered if stocking was called for. Biologists hesitate to stock fish where there are already bass present, unless there has been some sort of disaster that has destroyed nearly all of the population. A check revealed that in this case there were too many bass and they were stunted. Somewhere above one hundred largemouths per acre, the managers tell me, stunting is likely. Tough problem.

And one of the touchiest setups of all is the small pond where balance would appear to be easily handled. Where largemouth bass and bluegills are concerned, endless experiments are still inconclusive. A hundred bass fingerlings to a thousand bluegill fingerlings, some advise.

In studying scientific and semiscientific works on bass management and natural history, we come up with some incidental facts that at first seem unrelated but can be of considerable help to serious fishermen. Some of them are well worth mentioning.

Relationship of size and age, for example, can be a help in assessing conditions in bass waters. The business of stunting doesn't seem complicated, but it indicates the relation of the fish's environment to its welfare, and some waters simply will not produce record specimens. The large size of southern largemouths, for example, is credited mainly to a long growing season. When fish in certain waters do not grow large, it's only in extreme cases that we use the word "stunted," but some very fine bass fishing is had where fish simply don't get very big because of the conditions under which they live. Perfectly healthy bass can have their growth inhibited by their food supply and water temperatures. Biologists tell us that bass don't really starve to death and that poorly conditioned fish will probably succumb to disease or predation instead. Most of us have caught emaciated bass that had little energy, generally in very poor waters.

I often hear the term "yearling bass," applied to any fish less than

10 inches long. But most bass less than a year old are barely big enough to be caught on a medium-size bass fly, and many "yearlings" have lived for several seasons. Accurately aging bass takes some background in the subject.

There has been some confusion about spawning locations. Rick Hoopes of Pennsylvania, a fisheries biologist widely recognized as an authority on smallmouth bass, says that smallmouths living in moving water will spawn in a current that moves as much as slightly less than 1½ miles per hour or a foot per second. (Incidentally, current speed in miles per hour is routinely overestimated by those who have not actually studied it.)

Hoopes explains that smallmouths will not tolerate silt in bedding areas. Of course, silt is a sign of very sluggish or nonmoving water, and although largemouth bass will fan away some of it for nesting purposes, too much silt will block the operation. At any rate, there isn't much competition between largemouths and smallmouths for spawning areas, the smallmouths preferring gravel and rocks. In lakes, smallmouths usually choose much deeper bedding areas than do largemouths, but in streams, Hoopes says, the smallmouth may spawn in water as shallow as two feet.

Fishing over spawning sites is good for arguments, as I mentioned earlier, and I gathered opinions on the subject from a number of biologists and fishing observers. Recent observations still draw disagreement, but the management people are united in their opinions, having changed them only slightly since I first checked on the subject many years ago. They do not disapprove of fishing over spawning bass.

Although many states have closed seasons on bass fishing during the spawning season, managers generally feel that the closures are not specifically to protect spawners as such. It is simply a good time for bass fishing, and a closed season at that time reduces the harvest as much or more than it would at any other time of the year.

Some fishermen take issue with this conclusion. For one thing, they note that the larger bass are taken very frequently from on or near the beds, and that factor is to be considered if we conclude a large percentage of bass fishermen keep their fish when it's legal. Most fishermen are less likely to release big fish than small ones.

As an experiment, some top-notch largemouth spawning areas have been marked off and closed during the spawning period. Biologists concluded the practice was of no help. When the areas were opened immediately after the major spawning period, some fly fishermen using top-water lures found the fishing exceptionally good in the areas. I took that to indicate a great many good bass had been saved and that the experiment had been a success—but biologists told me it was simply a matter of the areas' being undisturbed for a considerable period and that the fish were unwary. They may be right. Like a lot of other management decisions, it is a gray area. Did the closing of spawning areas actually save any fish? In that particular area, was it helpful to save fish, or was the population capable of standing even more pressure?

In the ongoing curse of pollution, there is one phase that interests the general public: danger to humans through consuming fish containing toxic chemicals. To some extent this may be a blessing. Nonanglers who yawn through reports of dying fish are likely to perk up when there is sign of direct damage to fish *eaters.* It would take a great deal more mercury to harm the fish themselves than it would take to injure humans who ate quantities of them.

The presence of mercury in considerable quantity in black bass (as well as in other edible fish) has kept biologists in trouble for many years. They can measure the amounts and they can announce the logically dangerous level within the fish, but they often cannot find the source. In too many cases, the sources (industrial or agricultural) are suspected, although not proven, and fisheries managers can only say the fish should not be eaten—or that only so much fish should be eaten over a certain period of time.

In at least one case, a fine smallmouth bass fishery was made a catch-and-release area for some years because of the presence of mercury. Eventually the regulations were removed, even though no solution had been found and the source or sources were in doubt. (Incidentally, during the no-consumption period a lot of fly fishermen had a ball. Very little competition.)

In concluding any report on bass management and biology, we must summarize the experts' view on bass stocking. It goes like this:

Bass stocking is not helpful when used simply to increase the population of a body of water that may already have all the bass it can support and that can fill any deficiencies through spawning.

Indiscriminate "layman's" stocking is unlikely to be a help and may actually do harm to a delicate balance. In many cases, the simpler a problem appears, the more complex its true basis.

It is seldom profitable to stock any water with the tiniest of bass fry. Without going into the size designations as set by managers, fish several inches long are most likely to survive.

It is now accepted that stocking is seldom feasible as a "supplemental tool for maintaining population in fished areas." In other words, its place lies in starting a bass population or replacing a population destroyed by some sort of aquatic catastrophe.

Some of the best results in stocking involve simply moving wild fish to the waters where they are needed, but well-run hatcheries do a good job. Most states are not driving for huge hatchery facilities but are now working for efficiency, using the hatchery as a supplement to management rather than as a foundation for the entire program.

We'll always have people who feel fish in the freezer is the ultimate goal, and there are some who feel releasing fish is the height of idiocy. Anglers who tend to associate largely with anglers or with people who accept anglers are sometimes surprised to find well-educated people who feel that catch-and-release isn't real and that it is some sort of joke. These are simply folks who have never read much about fishing, have had no interest in it, and have confined their study largely to cartoons appearing in newspapers at the opening of fishing season. I went for several days on a fishing trip with a fellow who could not believe that any fish should be released—ever. He didn't think it could be part of the game. An illiterate from some backwater of primitive society? No, a university graduate who had chosen the army as a career and was at that time a highly decorated major. Feeling a little silly, I explained the game to him, and he decided it was all a good idea. He began learning to cast better.

It is a surprise to some bystanders to learn that the great majority of sports fishermen are in favor of stricter fishing regulations, generally shorter seasons, and smaller catch limits. This attitude is extremely important to managers of bass waters, as state fisheries people have enough management problems without having to buck the sentiments of the folks they are trying to serve.

In 1991 there were some changes in regulations on smallmouth bass in Pennsylvania. Of course, the conditions could be very different in other states, and my purpose is not to hawk the details of Pennsylvania's highly regarded program. The attitude of the public is of extreme importance in any fish management, however, and the surveys taken by the Pennsylvania managers before setting revised regulations is probably a pretty good reflection of attitudes elsewhere.

Rickalon L. Hoopes produced a summary of the public opinions, and though some of them might be a little different if just fly fishermen had been contacted, these general opinions are valuable to all of us—and surprising for some.

The Pennsylvania anglers felt strongly that the smallmouth bass harvest was too great, and 78 percent said so. Most of them felt there were fewer fish than formerly.

The majority felt that the most important objective was to catch the larger fish. Although fly fishermen like to catch big fish, we must face the fact that fly fishermen are satisfied with smaller ones, and perhaps I can go so far as to admit we simply do not compete much with other anglers as to size. The International Game Fish Association records show that fly fishing is not the best way to catch the biggest bass—even though many fly fishermen for bass have caught saltwater species weighing more than 100 pounds. The same people will go to great effort to catch 10-inch trout.

A Kentucky maker of an unusual design of bass bug issued a promotional challenge to any baitcaster or spin fisherman: If he could not catch more bass on a certain lake with his bug than the other kinds of lures produced, he would pay one hundred dollars to the person using the other method. My point here is that he would deal only with numbers—not weight. He said he frequently caught bigger bass with his bug than were caught with other tackle, but he was not betting on it.

In getting back to the Pennsylvania smallmouth regulations, remember that if you practice catch-and-release, many regulations restricting creel counts may help instead of hinder the fly fisherman. And if, as in Pennsylvania, the size limit on bass is set at 14 inches, there should be better fishing for 12-inchers—a size of smallmouth bass I have never been known to sneer at when it was taken on a Number Six fly rod.

Of the fishermen queried in Pennsylvania, a startling 94 percent wanted more-restrictive regulations. That seems to be a nationwide trend. Without going into figures, though, very few of the anglers who keep their catches collect a limit of fish. That is, a limit of five fish instead of ten fish certainly wouldn't reduce a harvest by 50 percent. And when you get into size limits, Hoopes reports that if a 15-inch minimum size limit were applied in Pennsylvania, the harvest would be reduced by 94 percent. A 15-incher is quite a chunk of bass.

MANY BIOLOGICAL STUDIES attest to the great number of crawfish smallmouth consume. I find crawfish under rocks from tennis ball-size on up, and in a variety of currents from very fast to hardly moving. I do not find many over sand, silt or ledge bottoms unless there are a fair number of freestone rocks present. . . .

The naturals' move across the stream bottom is a slow crawl until the need rises for them to make a fast getaway—such as when being pursued by a bass, when they use their broad muscular tails to swim backwards in a rapid darting motion.

Learn to duplicate both of these motions with flies in both action and appearance. Experience has shown that patterns with exaggerated pincers are not nearly as effective as those with more subdued pincers. The reason for this may be that when a fly is fished deeply the force of the current upon the leader can sometimes cause the crawfish to wobble from side to side in a very unnatural manner. Obviously, the less pronounced the pincers the less apparent this undesirable action will be to the bass.

Harry Murray
Fly Fishing for Smallmouth Bass

ALTERATIONS

Weed Guards

I'm not going into the details of constructing bass bugs or tying streamers, but there are some minor alterations that can be made by anyone on existing lures to make them work better in many places.

Weed guards cause arguments, but there is much bass water where they are almost a necessity. Admittedly, they do not aid in hooking, but with a little care they can become only minor obstructions. There's no way of checking it accurately, but weed guards, especially stiff ones, do fend off some strikes. In most cases, manufacturers make the weed guards stiffer than necessary for 90 percent of bass fishing. A stiff weed guard is needed if you're briskly yanking a streamer through down timber, heavy lily pads, or reeds, but it isn't necessary for the gentle operation of a bug through emergent grass.

Manufacturers use springy wire for some guards and sometimes form a loop with it to protect the hook point better. When using monofilament, they fasten a loop of it in front of the hook, with the other end behind the barb. In other cases it is a loop crosswise of a bug's body just ahead of the barb. Solid-bodied bugs can be bought without guards which can be installed if needed.

With surface bugs made of balsa or cork, it is easy to punch a hole at a backward slant ahead of the hook, insert a single piece of stiff monofilament line (about 60-pound test), secure it with a dab of glue, and cut it so that it extends just a little past the hook barb. This simple rig is remarkably durable, and if there's no longer need for a weed guard it can be snipped off instantly. Long experimentation has shown it is efficient in a variety of surface vegetation and interferes very little with hooking qualities.

Customized Muddler Minnow has a closely cropped head and wire weed guard for use in heavy cover.

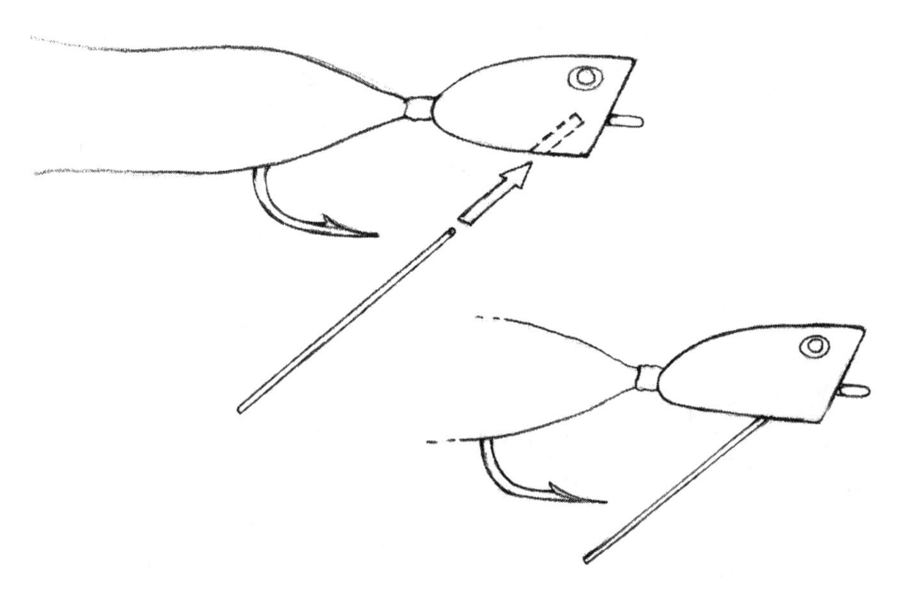

A weed guard is installed on a balsa or cork surface bug by punching a backward-slanting hole ahead of the hook, gluing in a piece of stiff monofilament line, and trimming it so that the guard extends slightly past the hook barb.

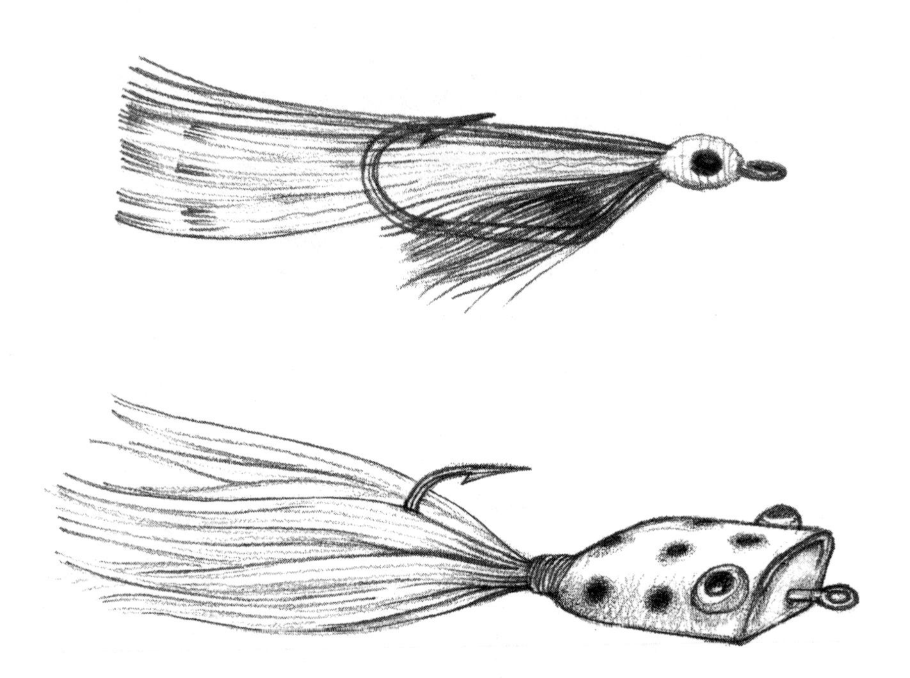

The Keel Hook, as used in the streamer shown, rides with the barb up and is quite weedless. Many users open the hook's bend slightly for better hooking qualities that still retain much of the weedless capability. The imitation frog is retrieved with the hook up and is generally weedless. Some anglers have added a monofilament weed guard to protect the barb when the bug overturns in heavy cover.

Rubber Legs

There is no question about the added attraction of rubber legs in some situations, especially when surface lures are worked slowly. In a few cases they have been the difference between success and failure, especially with panfish. They belong on hard-bodied bugs that are short on hair or on small, waving feathers, and they have greatly improved the performance of some hair bugs with tightly wound bodies. This has been proved when duplicate bugs were fished for largemouth bass from the same boat—except that only one lure would have rubber legs.

Rubber legs are fragile and have disappeared from many commercial bugs that otherwise look like new. Although it's easy to do, few fishermen bother to replace them.

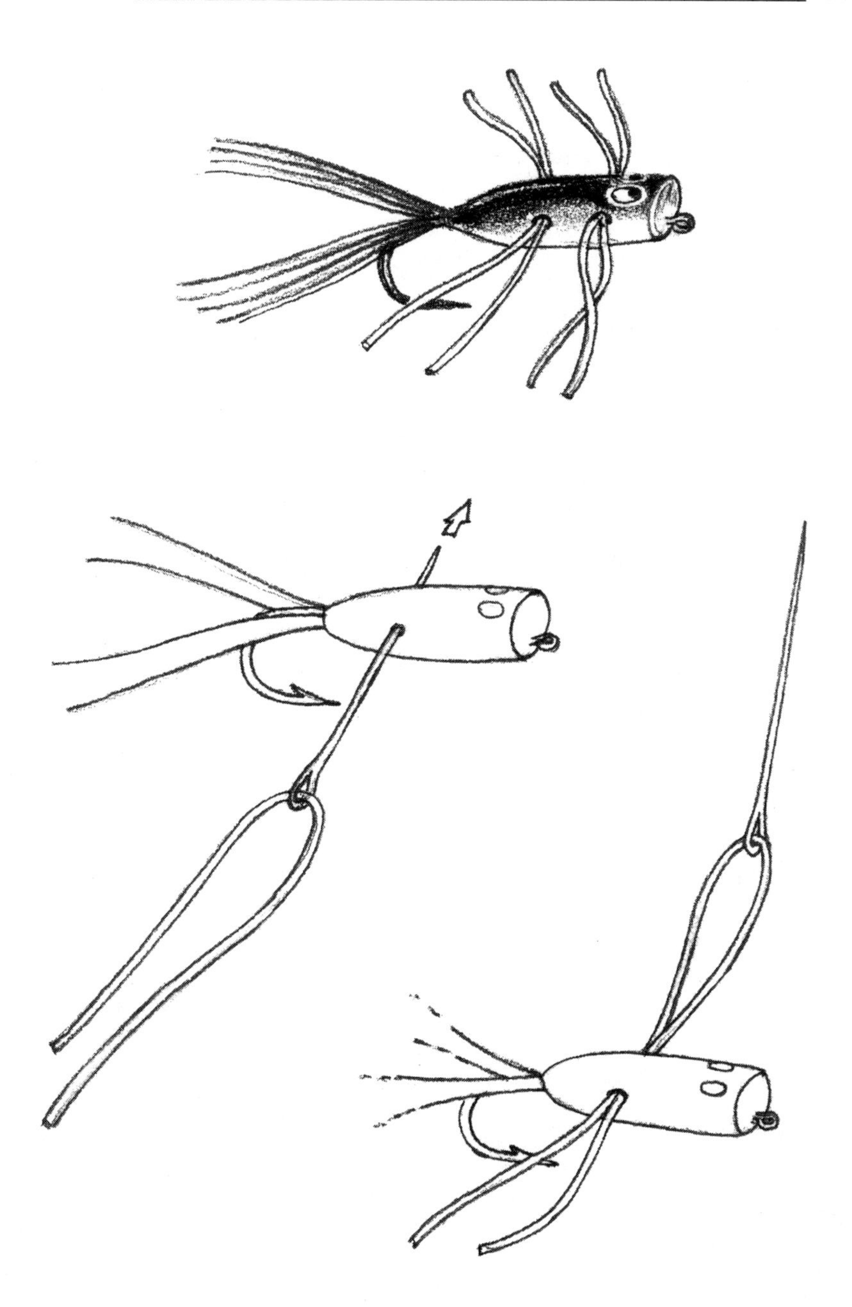

Rubber legs are easily created by threading a large needle with a length of rubber material, pushing it through the body of the bug, and trimming the legs to the desired length.

The little rubber strips can be bought from fly-tying supply houses. The easiest way to install them is to use a large needle, pushing it through the bug's body with a length of rubber leg material, leaving two strands of leg on each side of the bug, which can then be trimmed to the desired length. With the longer bug bodies, two such installations (four legs on

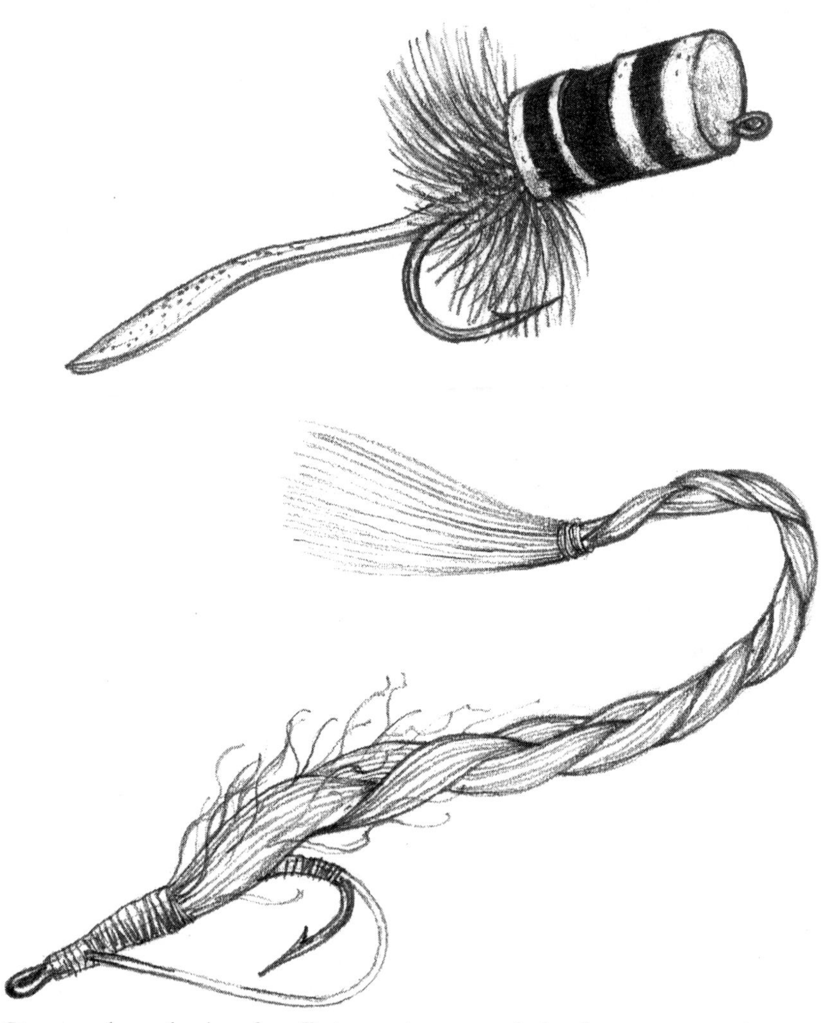

Strange and nameless but often effective creations are worked up by innovative anglers. The striped popping bugs were cut from the laminated soles of shower sandals, and the wormlike streamers were made by braiding Fishair.

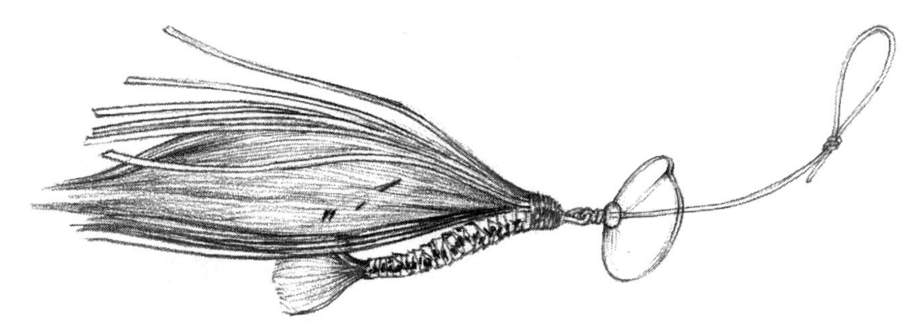

Many attachments have been used to increase action in streamers, but spinners are now seldom used because of casting difficulty. The Fludder, a commercial product shown here ahead of a streamer (Gold Lizzie pattern), is a simple plastic disk with a groove on the leading side. Installed with a bead on the leader, it causes a lure to vibrate when being retrieved. The streamer shown is on a "bend-back" hook, which retrieves with the barb up and is fairly weedless.

each side) is about right. Many rather expensive bugs have gone through two or three sets of legs.

When added to a tightly wrapped hair bug, the legs are generally fastened to the hook shank behind the bug proper, but with a little effort they can be placed farther up in the bug's body. Admittedly, they disfigure the creation a little, but fish accept them despite the aesthetic loss. It's easy to dismiss rubber legs as window dressing, but they have sometimes made a big difference in careful tests.

FLY FISHING FOR bass is perhaps the most exciting and rewarding phase of the sport. Historically, it represents the first method of presenting an artificial lure to largemouths and smallmouths, tracing the origins before the advent of the revolving spool reel and plug casting. The enjoyment of dropping a hunk of hair or cork on target as a tight loop of fly line shoots through the air is reward enough for many fishermen, and the explosive strike of a bass merely adds frosting to the cake. . . .

Some of the limestone rivers have a hatch of mayflies every evening, and most of these insects are white or yellow (light). Number 10 dry flies will take plenty of smallmouths in this situation, but you must fish them like trout with drag-free floats.

Mark Sosin and Bill Dance
Practical Black Bass Fishing

APPENDIX II

KNOTS ENOUGH

FLY FISHING FOR bass requires very few knots, generally only four connections—line-to-leader, leader-to-leader (in tapering), backing-to-line, and lure-to-leader.

As shown here, the improved clinch knot is good as a solid, strong and compact attachment for the leader to the fly.

With some lures, especially the diving and wiggling bugs, and some streamers, a loop connection will give more action. The one shown here has had other names, but the "nonslip mono knot" is as good as any, as attested to in *Practical Fishing Knots II* by Mark Sosin and Lefty Kreh. Its loop holds and it's stronger than most others.

The blood knot is smooth and strong for connecting sections of leader used in tapering. The surgeon's knot does the job quickly but is a little bulky and tends to collect trash particles found in much bass water.

The nail knot is ideal for connecting the leader butt to the line and the line to the backing, which is usually 20- or 30-pound test Dacron. The standard nail knot is shown here. The tube nail knot is the same except that a small tube replaces the nail and the small leader or line end can be pushed back through it rather than alongside the nail. (Less chance of a rough connection.) Nail knots can be rounded off with small quantities of epoxy to allow them to slip through guides easier.

In using monofilament it is essential that knots involving large sizes be left simple and pulled tightly, preferably while wet. In the aforementioned nonslip loop knot, Kreh and Sosin give different numbers of turns around the standing line. That's seven turns for leader of less than 6-pound test, five turns for 8- to 12-pound test, four turns for 15- to 40-pound test, three turns for 50- or 60-pound line, and two turns for anything heavier than that. Of course, these size recommendations are

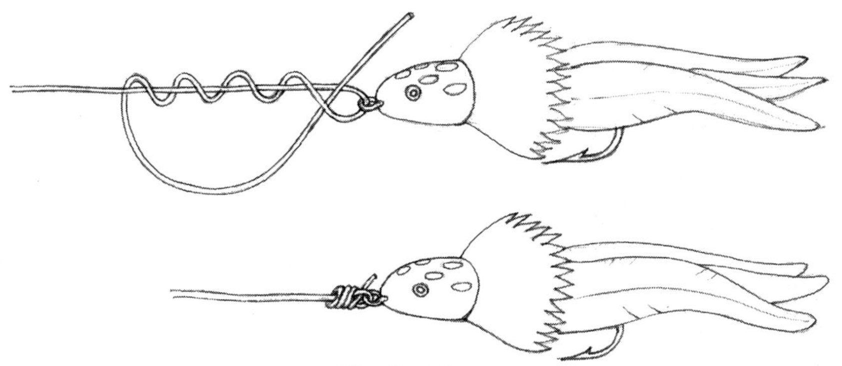

The clinch knot.

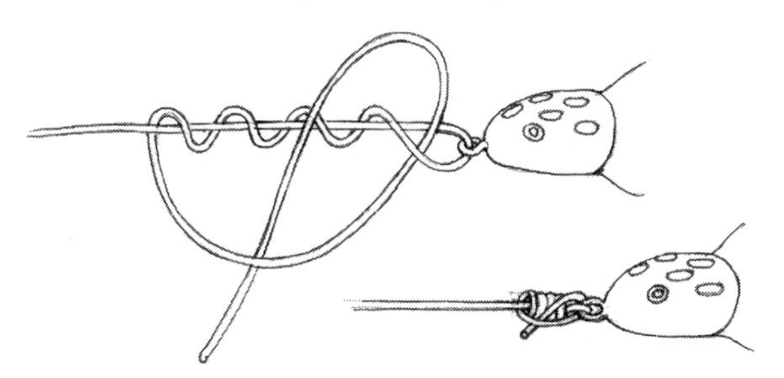

The improved clinch knot.

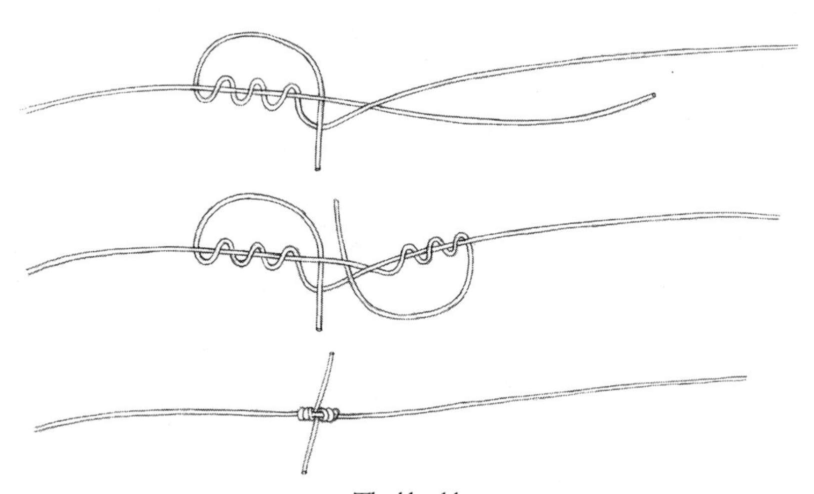

The blood knot.

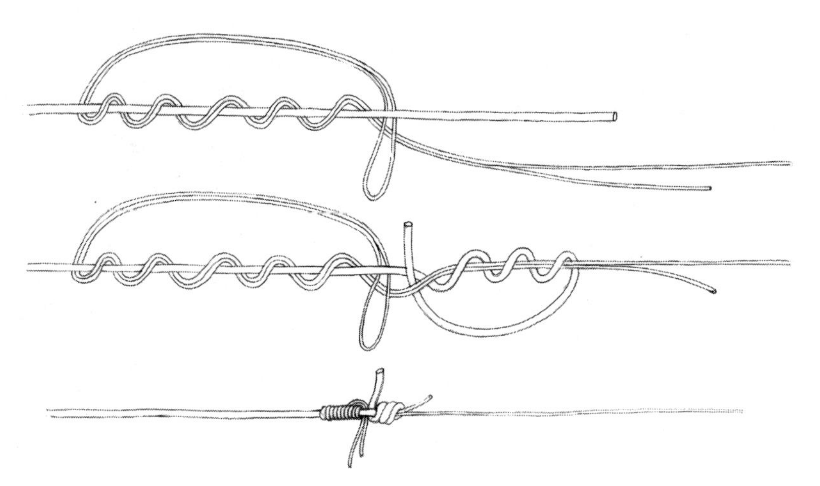

The improved blood knot.

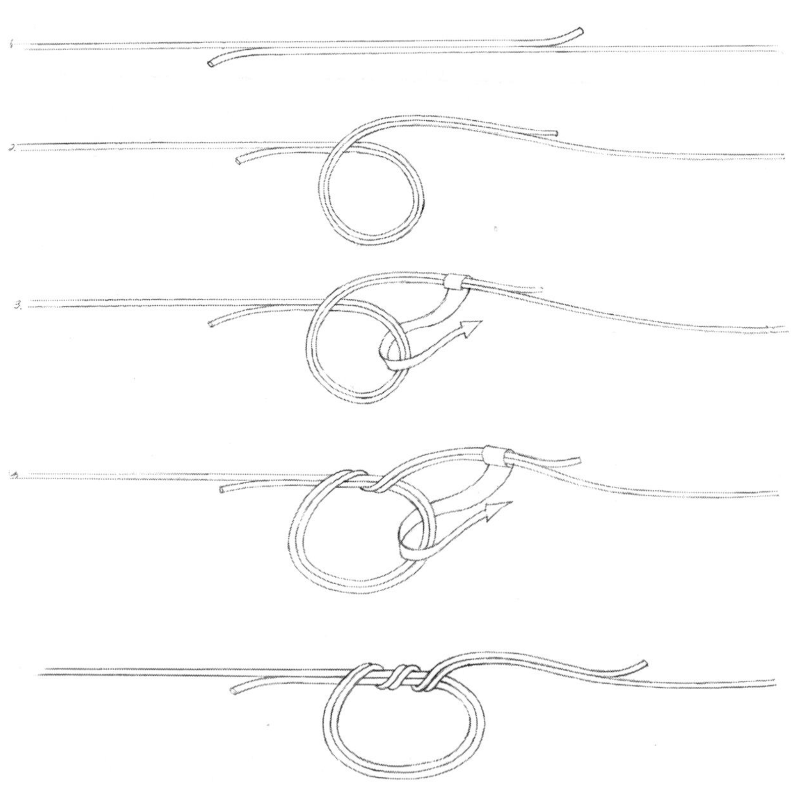

The surgeon's knot.

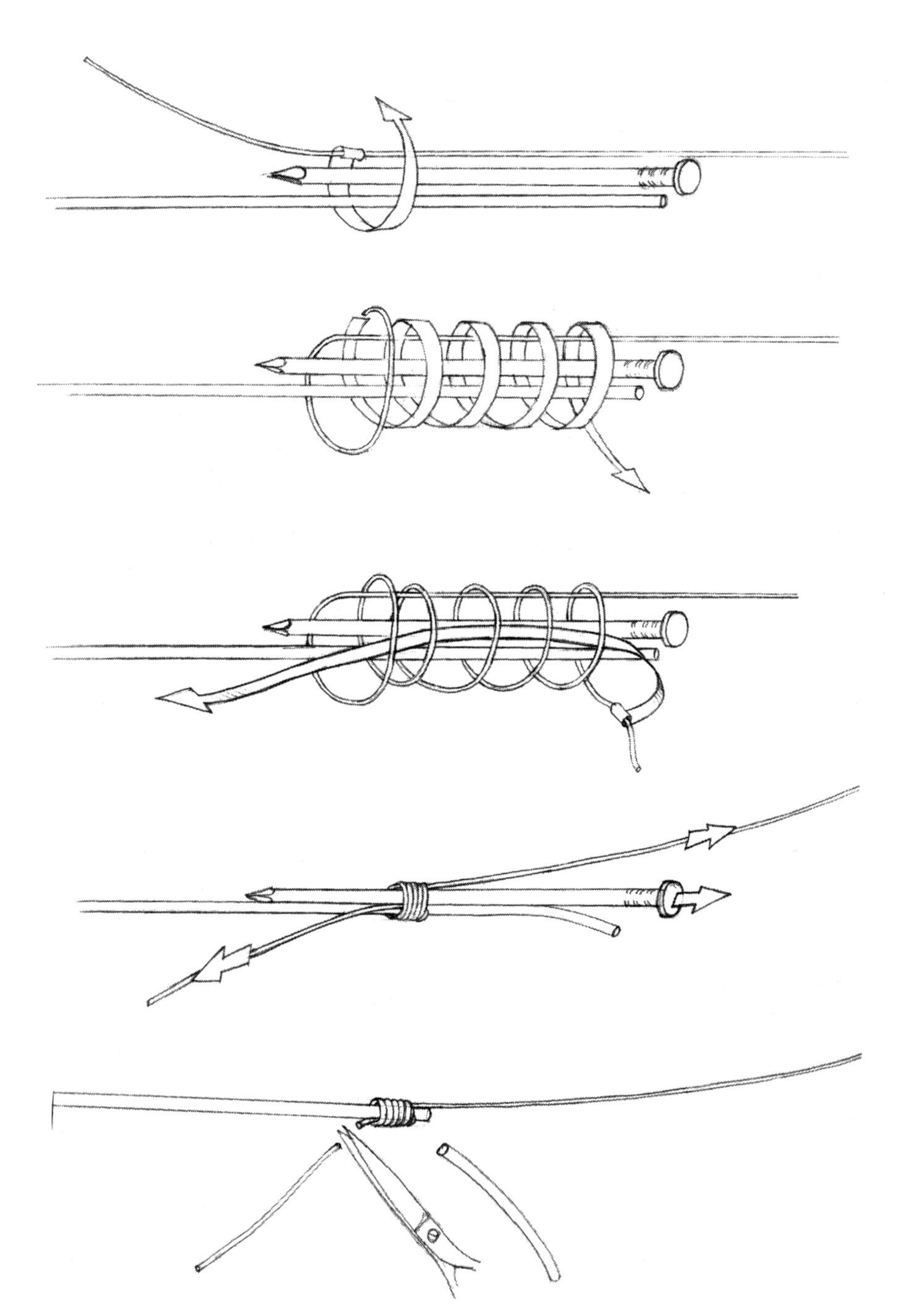

The nail knot.

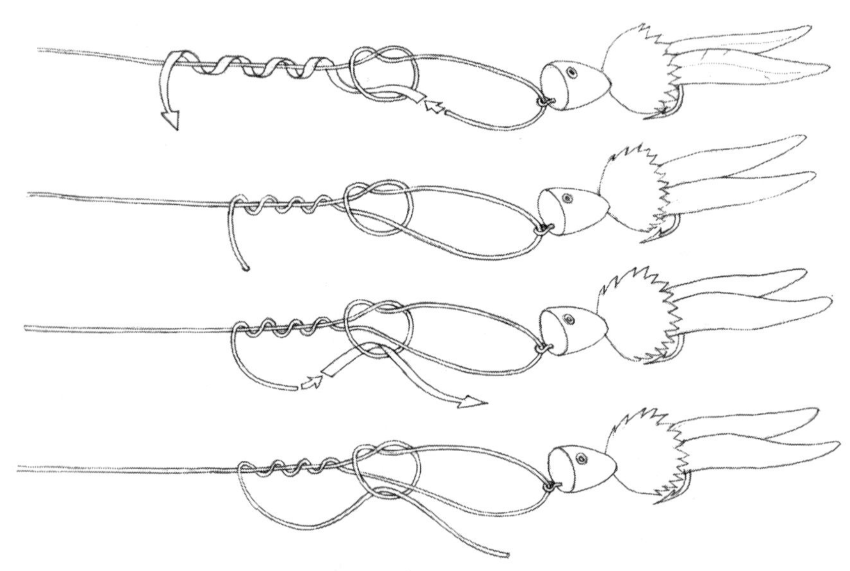

The nonslip mono knot.

not cut in stone, and some mono is harder than other material—the very hard finish being more difficult for solid connections and harder to use in complex knots.

The vast majority of knots that fail are not drawn up tightly enough in the first place, and many have not been tested after long use.

If I were asked to make one overall statement about localized weather trends, it would have to be this: bass become most active at the *start* of changes in conditions. They can be nervous, fast-moving, cautious, but so are other species then. And this behavior may only be because there is a sense of urgency—such as land animals often display before a cold front or storm—to feed and then seek shelter. Because fish are in an agitated state, it is better to work them from a greater distance, not right on top of them as you must when they are hidden in supercover. But the start of a stormy trend is a good time to be fishing. It's a time when predators are feeding. . . .

Hot weather can be tricky, but it's not impossible. Most anglers know that a bass's metabolism increases during the warm weather. So the fish must eat more. Many anglers say that you can't prove it by them. Well, it's true. Largemouths do consume more, but they do it in fast, gluttonous spurts. There's another thing: In summer, it's quite possible that the bass in your lake are confined to very limited areas because of reduced oxygen content in much of the water.

Jerry Gibbs
Bass Myths Exploded

Index